Reminiscences

of

Vice Admiral John L. (Jack) CHEW
U. S. Navy (Retired)

Oral History Office
U. S. Naval Institute
Annapolis, Maryland

Preface

This volume contains the transcript of ten interviews with Vice Admiral John L. (Jack) Chew, USN (Ret.) covering his eventful naval career. They are a part of the Oral History program of the U. S. Naval Institute and were taped during a period extending from September, 1972 to December, 1973 at the Admiral's home in Annapolis, Maryland. He read the transcript later and made various corrections. The MS was then re-typed and indexed.

There are many high points to the career of Admiral Chew. There are certainly some dramatic ones. His experiences during the final battle in which the USS HELENA participated (July, 1943) and during the horrendous weeks that followed on Vella Lavella are a part of the unforgettable saga of World War II. Other noteworthy events came when the Admiral commanded Destroyer Florilla Four in the Atlantic (1961-2) and conducted the recovery operations for the Project Mercury manned space flights; when he served (1962) with the Joint Chiefs of Staff during the Cuban Missile Crisis; and later when he injected some of his characteristic drive and imagination into the Navy's program for Anti-Submarine Warfare in the Pacific.

John T. Mason, Jr.
Director of Oral History

February 1979

VICE ADMIRAL JOHN LOUIS CHEW, UNITED STATES NAVY, RETIRED

Born in Annapolis, Maryland, on September 22, 1909, Vice Admiral Chew attended High School there, and Junior College of Augusta, in Augusta, Georgia, prior to his appointment to the Naval Academy, which he entered as a Midshipman on June 29, 1927. He was graduated and commissioned Ensign on June 4, 1931, and reached the rank of Vice Admiral, to date from November 25, 1965.

His early service included gunnery duties as a junior officer on board the battleship MARYLAND, duty as Gunnery Officer of the destroyer OVERTON and the minesweeper NECHES, and as First Lieutenant of the destroyer MONAGHAN. In June 1938 he returned to Annapolis for instruction in General Line at the Naval Postgraduate School, and in July of the next year joined the USS HELENA (CL-50) as Air Defense Officer, Gunnery Officer and CIC Officer. He remained on board that new cruiser from her commissioning date throughout the early period of World War II until she was sunk at Kula Gulf in August 1943.

The senior survivor of the HELENA, he was in the water for two and one-half days, then was sheltered by natives on Vella Lavella. He is entitled to the Ribbon for, and a facsimile of the Navy Unit Commendation awarded the USS HELENA, the first ship to be awarded that citation (which was established on December 20, 1944) as follows:

"For outstanding heroism in action against enemy Japanese forces afloat in the Solomon Islands-New Georgia Areas. Gallantly carrying the fight to the enemy the USS HELENA opened the night Battle of Cape Esperance on October 11-12, 1942, boldly sending her fire into the force of enemy warships, sinking a hostile destroyer and holding to a minimum the damage to our destroyers in the rear of the Task Force. She engaged at close quarters a superior force of hostile combatant ships in the Battle of Guadalcanal (Third Savo) on the night of November 12-13, 1942, rallying our own forces after the Flagship had been disabled and contributing to the enemy's defeat. In her final engagement in the predawn battle of July 5, 1943, the HELENA valiantly sailed down the restricted and submarine-infested waters of Kula Gulf under the terrific torpedo and gun fire of the enemy to bombard Kolombangara and New Georgia while covering the landing of our troops at Rice Anchorage, and twenty-four hours later her blazing guns aided in the destruction of a vastly superior enemy naval force before she was fatally struck by a Japanese torpedo. Her brave record of combat achievement is evidence of the HELENA's intrepidity and the heroic fighting spirit of her officers and men."

For meritorious service while attached to the HELENA he was awarded the Navy Commendation Medal with Gold Star and Combat "V."

During the period September 1943 until May 1945, he was Ordnance Instructor at the Naval Academy, and at the commissioning of the USS HELENA (CA-75) in September 1945, became her Executive Officer. He was detached in June 1947, after the HELENA engaged in occupation duty in both the European and Asian Areas, and from July of that year until June of the next he was Commanding Officer of the USS STICKELL (DD 888), operating in the China area.

Another tour of duty at the Naval Academy, this time as an instructor and later assigned to the Executive Department and as Executive Officer of Bancroft Hall, preceded his assignment from April 1951 until June 1953 as Joint Plans Officer on the Staff of the Commander in Chief, Naval Forces, Eastern Atlantic and Mediterranean. In July 1953 he reported to the Navy Department, Washington, DC, for duty in the Strategic Plans Division of the Office of the Chief of Naval Operations. He served there until July 1956, and in August assumed command of the USS PAWCATUCK (AO-108).

On December 8, 1956, he was detached from command of the PAWCATUCK with orders to command the USS ROANOKE (CL-145), and in March 1958 returned to the Office of the Chief of Naval Operations, Navy Department. There he served in the Fleet Development and Maintenance Division as Director, Staff Ship Characteristics Board. On September 25, 1958, he reported as Director Shore Establishments and Maintenance Division (his title was changed on December 5, 1959 to Director of the Shore Station Construction and Maintenance Division). On April 18, 1960 he assumed duty as Deputy Commander of the Military Sea Transportation Service, with headquarters in Washington, DC.

In June 1961 he became Commander Destroyer Flotilla FOUR which was re-designated on July 1, 1962 Cruiser-Destroyer Flotilla FOUR. "For exceptionally meritorious conduct...from June 10, 1961 to May 24, 1962 as Commander Task Force 140 (Commander Project Mercury Recovery Force)..." he was awarded the Legion of Merit. The citation further states: "Skillfully directing the recovery operations for Project Mercury manned space flights during this period, Read Admiral Chew....made an invaluable contribution to the successful completion of these sub-orbital and orbital flights and to the prestige earned for the United States thereby. In addition to directing the Recovery Force from the Control Center at Cape Canaveral, he also coordinated Contingency Recovery planting and information dissemination, keeping far-flung units around the world alerted as to the flight status..."

On October 24, 1962 he reported as Deputy Director (Operations) J-3, the Joint Staff Office, Joint Chiefs of Staff, Washington, DC, and for "exceptionally meritorious performance of duty..." in that assignment from October 4, 1963 to July 1, 1964, he was awarded the Joint Service Commendation Medal. On August 11, 1964, he assumed command of U. S. Naval Forces, Japan. In August 1965 he was assigned as Assistant Chief of Naval Operations (Plans and Policy)' Navy Department, and on January 12, 1966 became Commander Anti-Submarine Warfare Force, Pacific Fleet. "For exceptionally meritorious service...from January 1966 through June 1967..." he was awarded the Distinguished Service Medal. The citation further states in part:

"During this period, Vice Admiral Chew demonstrated an extraordinary ability in combining outstanding leadership and keen insight to produce unprecedented advances in antisubmarine readiness in the Pacific. Under his professional guidance, the accomplishments in command and control which envelop the many facets of research, theory, and development of tactics and operational applications, have undergone extensive and far-reaching changes, resulting in the highest level of ASW readiness in the Pacific since the inception of Anti-submarine Warfare Force, Pacific. Keenly aware of his responsibilities toward the overall effectiveness of our ASW force, (he) guided the ASW force to overall knowledge of ASW problems and accelerated the pace toward the solving of these problems. Under his expert direction, many new ASW concepts have emerged and many new procedures were implemented to meet one of the greatest challenges of our Navy today--the submarine threat..."

In July 1967 he became Commander of the U. S. Taiwan Defense Command and in September 1970 was assigned briefly to the Office of the Chief of Naval Operations, Navy Department. On October 1, 1970, he was transferred to the Retired List of the U. S. Navy.

"For exceptionally meritorious service...from July 1967 to July 1970 ..." he was awarded a Gold Star in lieu of the Second Distinguished Service Medal. The citation continues in part: "As the principal United States Military Representative to the Government of the Republic of China, Vice Admiral Chew was responsible for providing guidance to the military leaders and to the President of the Republic of China with respect to U. S. military policy and to present and project Republic of China and United States military operations in the Taiwan area. His professional skill and diplomacy were major factors in achieving an improved readiness and defense posture in Taiwan. Through his outstanding performance, Vice Admiral Chew has furthered the continuing rapport existing between United States Forces and the military units of the Republic of China. The security of the United States and Free-World interests in Asia has been richly enhanced by his many contributions while assigned to this position of trust and great responsibility..."

In addition to the Distinguished Service Medal with Gold Star, the Legion of Merit; Navy Commendation Medal with Gold Star and Combat "V"; and the Navy Unit Commendation Ribbon, Vice Admiral Chew has the Joint Service Commendation Medal; American Defense Service Medal; the American Campaign Medal; Asiatic-Pacific Campaign Medal with six operation stars; World War II Victory Medal; Navy Occupation Service Medal, Europe and Asia Clasps; China Service Medal, extended; and the National Defense Service Medal with bronze star.

His "Home town" address is his official address also: 15 Southgate Avenue, Annapolis, Maryland. In 1938 he married Helen K. Loughan of Los Angeles, California, and after her death married Mrs. Julia Pierson Wilcox at Annapolis in 1960. He has two children, Margaret A. (now Mrs. Hawes Campbell) and John L. Chew, Jr., and three step-children, Virginia E. Chew, Thomas Wharton Chew and Stanley Carter Chew.

Navy Office of Information
Internal Relations Division (OI-430)
19 March 1971

DECLARATION OF TRUST

The undersigned does hereby appoint and designate as his (her) Trustee herein, the Secretary-Treasurer and Publisher of the United States Naval Institute to perform and discharge the following duties, powers, and privileges in connection with the possession and use of a certain taped interview between the undersigned and the Oral History Department of the United States Naval Institute.

1. Classification of Transcript.

(✓)a. If classified OPEN, the transcript(s) may be read or the recording(s) audited by the qualified personnel upon presentation of proper credentials, as determined by the Secretary-Treasurer of the U.S. Naval Institute.

( )b. If classified PERMISSION REQUIRED TO CITE OR QUOTE, the user will be required to obtain permission in writing from the interviewee prior to quoting or citing from either the transcript(s) or the recording(s).

( )c. If classified PERMISSION REQUIRED, permission must be obtained in writing from the interviewee before the transcribed interview(s) can be examined or the tape recording(s) audited.

( )d. If classified CLOSED, the transcribed interview(s) and the tape recording(s) will be sealed until a time specified by the interviewee. This may be until the death of the interviewee or for any specified number of years.

2. It is expressly understood that in giving this authorization, I am in no way precluded from placing such restrictions as I may desire upon use of the interview at any time during my lifetime, nor does this authorization in any way affect my rights to the copyright of my literary expressions that may be contained in the interview.

Witness my hand and seal this 6th day of March 1979.

[signature: John L. Chew]

I hereby accept and consent to the foregoing Declaration of Trust and the powers therein conferred upon me as Trustee:

[signature: R T E Bowler J]

Interview No. 1 with Vice Admiral John L. Chew, U.S. Navy (Retired)

Place: His residence in Providence, Annapolis, Maryland

Date: Thursday morning, 28 September 1972

Subject: Biography

By: John T. Mason, Jr.

Q: Well, we're delighted that you're going to do this series with us on your biography. You've had a rather exciting naval career and I'm sure that, in transcript form, it will eventually prove of great interest and value to historical writers and researchers.

Would you begin in the proper way, Sir, by giving me the date and place of your birth? I know that. I visited your birthplace this morning. But begin in that way and tell me something about your family background and your education prior to the Naval Academy.

Adm. C.: Thank you very much, Mr. Mason. I might question the statement that it's of immense interest to anyone in the future but, as you say, I have had a fascinating life in the Navy.

To begin at the beginning, I was born where you erroneously went this morning, literally in 15 Southgate Avenue. I guess in

Chew #1 - 2

those days you weren't born in a hospital -

Q: And this being in Annapolis, Maryland.

Adm. C.: Yes - and I attended the local grammar school. Before that, I was taught by a very good friend up the street so that when I entered school I entered the fourth grade and continued through the Annapolis Grammar School and the Annapolis High School.

During my senior year in high school I took the substantiating examinations for the Naval Academy. In those days they had regular examinations and substantiating examinations to substantiate your high-school diploma. A regular exam was not necessary.

Q: This was verification of the credits from high school?

Adm. C.: Verification of the credits and you took the exam in math and English only.

Q: I think at this point you'd better lap back and tell me something about your father. Was he a naval officer? What was his background?

Adm. C.: No, my father was a college professor at St. John's College. He taught math and was head of department. He also had a very well-known prep school for the Naval Academy, Wilmer and Chew, and there are many many old-time naval officers who remember my father with great admiration and affection.

Q: Well you actually had it made, hadn't you, in preparation for the examinations?

Adm. C.: Strangely enough, my father actually was not concerned or didn't urge me to go to the Naval Academy. He died when I was a sophomore in high school, so the effect of his counseling was certainly confined to the earlier years, and during those years he made no effort to influence me to go to the Naval Academy.

Q: What was your mother's attitude? Was she of the academic background too?

Adm. C.: No, my mother was from Augusta, Georgia, and thereby hangs a little tale as to how I was appointed to the Naval Academy. She was interested really only in my becoming self-sufficient. She was a very practical woman, a very interesting woman, but as far as urging me in any academic pursuits she kept strictly out of it, thinking, I believe, of the practical aspects of how I was to make a living.

Q: Were you an only son?

Chew #1 - 4

Adm. C.: I'd had a brother who died years before I was born, so to all intents and purposes, I was an only son. I believe my mother was in her early forties when I was born.

During my early years I had a rowboat and I might say that my rowboat and its very primitive sail and lee board probably gave me the training that eventually saved my life. I used to take that little boat all over the Bay. I had turned over in the middle of the Bay and been picked up by a Navy ship at anchor. I'd been picked up by fishermen. I'd been able to swim to shore on several occasions, and I went through really what amounted to survival training at the tender age of fourteen.

I think I started to say something about how I was appointed to the Naval Academy.

At the age of 16 Mr. Gambrill, who was then the representative from this district, gave me a third alternate appointment and, as was to be expected, the principal got in. So in those days, once you had qualified mentally you were then forever qualified. So here I was, qualified mentally and, so far as I knew also qualified physically, with a third alternate and no way of getting into the Naval Academy.

I went to Washington and, if I remember correctly, through the clerk in the then Bureau of Navigation, now the Bureau of Naval Personnel, I received a list of every congressman and senator who had an appointment to the Naval Academy.

Q: You showed real initiative in taking this step!

Adm. C.: Well, by that time I was thoroughly convinced that this was what I wanted in life. I wanted to go to the Naval Academy and I had planned, as best I could, to enter the Naval Academy willy-nilly.

So, armed with my list, I went to Washington for as many days as it took me to see every congressman and every senator who had a vacancy.

Q: You were, in effect, a lobbyist!

Adm. C.: I was a lobbyist. It was interesting because some of the congressmen were most receptive, some, of course, wouldn't see me, but many were interested from the point of view that I was willing to come and see them and said, "Well, if you were in my district there would be no question I would give you my principal, but from a political point of view I really can't."

So after seeing them all, my mother who, as I said, was from Georgia, wrote her brother and suggested that whatever influence he had in Augusta be exerted to possibly get an appointment from Representative Carl Vinson.

Carl Vinson suggested, since I was qualified and since he did not have a qualified appointee at this particular time, that I come and live in Augusta (my mother's home town) for a year, become a resident of Georgia, and I could have his appointment to the Naval Academy.

Q: How far is Millidgeville from Augusta?

Adm. C.: I don't know whether they've redistricted Georgia or not now. Millidgeville and Augusta are not far apart. I think about sixty miles, if I remember correctly. Anyhow, it was all within the same congressional district of Georgia. So, old man Carl appointed me to the Naval Academy, and it's interesting to note that many, many years later, when I was appearing before the House Armed Services Committee, he looked over his glasses and said:

"If this young man doesn't do very well, I'll bust him back. After all, I appointed him to the Naval Academy some thirty years ago."

I have a great deal of affection for Carl Vinson, not only because of his ability, the way he ran the committee, but because it was through him that I was appointed to the Naval Academy.

Q: That's a very interesting point.

Adm. C.: My life at the Naval Academy was a fairly routine one. I participated in the usual things. I was a member of the boxing squad. I earned my "N" in tennis, played three years on the tennis team, I had minimum success in those days. I was a two-striper and, from my point of view, that was all that was necessary because if you had any stripes at all you got liberty

Chew #1 - 7

every afternoon while the rest of the midshipmen did not!

Q: And the regimen was pretty strict, wasn't it?

Adm. C.: The regimen was pretty strict.

The regiment of midshipmen, as it was then called, was about 2,100. In our plebe year, for example, it was even less because the classes of 1929 and 1928 were quite small, and 1930 and 1931 were fairly large, about 600. So you had about 600 and then about 200 and then 300. So it was only about 1,800 when I was a plebe.

Q: You must have been quite popular in the class because you had a home base?

Adm. C.: Well, in some ways that really didn't effect status in the class, except as a plebe you were a crab and subject to a certain amount of suspicion!

Q: That's an expression I haven't heard.

Adm. C.: Specifically, it was normally applied to girls. Any girl who lived in Annapolis was known as a crab. In the broader sense, anyone who was born in Annapolis or lived in Annapolis was a crab, from the locality of Crabtown, which the city of Annapolis was practically universally know as. Instead of going out into town or into Annapolis, you went out into Crabtown, rather than the name with which it was christened.

But, as I say, my life at the Naval Academy was fairly normal. I think the significant thing about the Naval Academy to me is that when I was commissioned my doubles partner, who now lives in St. Thomas, by the way, Ed Robertson, and I, having taken the oath of office in Memorial Hall turned to each other and in one voice said, "Zilch (we called each other that), we're ensigns." Unlike most college graduates, who seem to wish for the good old college days, I never had any desire to return to the Naval Academy as a midshipman.

I later returned twice, once in 1943 as an instructor and in 1948 in the executive department.

Q: But it was only a springboard for you for what you wanted to achieve?

Adm. C.: To return to the old college days, I never had that desire. In fact, and whether this was a psychological thing or not, throughout my naval career which spanned nearly forty years of commissioned service, I would have a periodic dream which, I might add, was updated. It started, I think, when I was about a lieutenant commander during the war, of going back to the Naval Academy as a midshipman, but I was really a lieutenant commander, and my purpose was to find out how the Naval Academy was progressing. I'd been sent there by the CNO or somebody, or the Secretary of the Navy, or maybe Carl

Vinson, I'm not sure, and I was to go back in the guise of a midshipman and spend about a week. The amusing thing to me, and at least it showed I was reasonably logical, was that when I was a lieutenant commander I did fairly well. I could run to formation and so on. But my last dream was about four or five years ago. I was a vice admiral and I had a hell of a time. I couldn't run to formation, I really wasn't interested, and I had a great deal of difficulty with my gray hair in disguising myself as a midshipman!

Q: I think it's very interesting that you never wanted to play the role of Joe College and go back again. It probably indicates early maturity, you know.

Adm. C.: I'm not so sure it indicated an early maturity, but it certainly was uppermost in my mind and I never had the desire. You remember in the thirties, in the Depression, everybody thought, "Oh, boy, if I could only be back in college again. We had such a great time." I didn't feel that way at all.

Q: And the psycholgist would say, go back to the womb!

Adm. C.: Go back to the womb.

Q: For protection and security! You said that it was hard work.

Chew #1 - 10

How did you do scholastically?

Adm. C.: I did fairly well scholastically. It seems to me I graduated around 65th in my class of 441.

Q: As you look back on the period there and the course given, what did you deem most valuable to you in your naval career?

Adm. C.: Well, contrary to the proponents of education now, I thought that the Naval Academy provided a pretty well-rounded career. Of course, it was math-oriented, engineering, which led to navigation, which led to ordnance and gunnery, which, incidentally, I taught when I came back the first time. But I thought that the humanities were adequately covered, perhaps not in the sense that we cover them today, but I didn't feel that when I graduated - and it used to make me very mad to be accused of it - that I had a "military mind." I felt that my education had been sufficient to give me enough curiosity to explore further and to prevent me from becoming a stereotyped military mind, whatever that is.

Q: Tommy Hart once told me that his purpose when he was there was to see that the midshipmen developed a sense of leadership and that they also became gentlemen. These were the two objectives of education. How does that tie in with your own experience?

Adm. C.: I think from a practical point of view we have a tendency to overplay the gentlemanly part, because I think after all our purpose is to be able to protect the country in time of war, and I'm not so sure you have to be a gentleman to do that.

As far as the leadership is concerned, I fully concur, and to reinforce that, I might add that in 1949 I was one of the first heads of the leadership department at the Naval Academy. I thoroughly enjoyed it. I was then a captain. Harry Hill was superintendent. I was directed to explain our leadership program to a group of visiting military. When I asked to whom I was to give this little talk the Superintendent replied, General Eisenhower, Admiral King, General Arnold, and I believe he also said Admiral Halsey.

There I was talking to those eminent leaders on leadership!

After it was all over we went over to the Superintendent's house for a cocktail, and General Eisenhower turned to me and said:

"That was a pretty good show. I know exactly how you felt. I've felt that way before myself."

So I always had a very warm spot in my heart for General Eisenhower because never in my life had I felt more inadequate speaking on leadership to that particular group.

Q: To the top leaders in the military!

Chew #1 - 12

Adm. C.: The top leaders in the military in our era.

Q: How did you enjoy the summer cruises, and what did they contribute to your education?

Adm. C.: Very much. The summer cruises were really sort of the indoctrination to seagoing life, plus the fact that they always afforded me a good time. Being a tennis player, when we were in Europe, we were usually invited to some very nice places to play, and as a result met people, some of whom I kept track of throughout the years.

I enjoyed the shipboard life. I was glad to get away from the academic routine. I enjoyed the relative freedom of liberty in foreign ports where nobody could look over the wall and see whether you were doing the right thing or the wrong thing.

Our three cruises really were not three cruises. Our youngster cruise, of course, was in 1928 and, for some reason or other, the European cruises had been called off. I've forgotten the exact reason. But our cruise was to the east coast and to Guantanamo, which wasn't as exciting perhaps as it could have been. Our second-class cruise was not a cruise at all because it was the first year that they decided to indoctrinate the midshipmen in aviation as an integral part of the Naval Academy curriculum, and we had what was called aviation summer.

Q: Here, on campus?

Adm. C.: All of the second class stayed at the Naval Academy

Chew #1 - 13

and we had indoctrination flights in, I think they were, Martin seaplanes and the old F-5Ls. I've forgotten the exact designation of the planes, but we flew as students in the aircraft and we studied aviation. We had a very relaxed summer, I might add. Since it was the first aviation summer the work load was light and I remember well the initials CFA on every afternoon schedule (at least the only printable one.) This meant "continue forenoon assignment." Usually by then people were tired of the forenoon assignment, so we had ample opportunity to play tennis, to relax, to sail. And, all in all it was a very pleasant summer.

Q: Were you intrigued with the idea of aviation?

Adm. C.: No. Strangely enough, I never have been. All during my naval career I watched people who were aviators, but for some strange reason, possibly connected with my rowboat activity in the Chesapeake Bay, I always wanted to be a sailor and not a flying sailor. I had no desire to go to Pensacola and never once thought of it. In fact, I was asked once why I didn't go and I said because I really wanted to be - I suppose the common term is - a black-shoe naval officer. But I did enjoy the aviation summer.

I suppose, honestly, I don't like to fly and as many hours as I've spent in airplanes, it's only been recently that I feel completely at home. Being basically an engineer at heart, I know that there are certain mechanical things in that they are aircraft, and sometimes they break, and when they break up there you don't have any place to go. Consequently, I suppose I'm a congenital coward so far as air travel is concerned.

I really never wanted to be an aviator although I've flown many times, and actually once, coming across the Pacific, flew the Mars. I was sitting up in the co-pilot's seat and the Pilot said, "Hey, I want to go back to the head. You take it." So I flew this lumbering truck for about five or ten minutes, I guess, with nobody in the seat beside me, and kept her on an even keel. It seemed fairly simple, and I just hoped all those "things" out there would continue to operate while I was in the driver's seat!

Q: What about your senior-year cruise?

Adm. C.: My first-class cruise was a very interesting cruise. We went to Norway, to England, to Germany, and I might add that that was, of course, the year 1930-

Q: That was the Depression?

Adm. C.: It was the Depression year but it was also the rise of Hitler.

There again, speaking of the people that you meet on those cruises, during the time we were in Kiel I met a young cadet - I think he was a cadet or a sublieutenant - named Carl Adolph Zenker. We had a great time and I corresponded with Zenker up to the time of the war, and then, strangely enough, when I was ComCruDesFlt Four in Norfolk my wife had dinner one night with the Dennisons and their guest of honor was Admiral Carl Adolph Zenker, who was the CNO of the postwar German Navy. I was in Cape Canaveral as the Recovery Commander for Mercury and unfortunately did not see him.

He was a very efficient CNO, but gather he had changed a great deal from the days when I know him as a youngster.

Q: These cruises you took were in the post coaling era, so they were much more pleasant actually, weren't they?

Adm. C.: Oh, yes. As a matter of fact, I had seen, when I was a young boy coaling exercises - at least had been told vividly of them, because the first class at the Naval Academy, I think the class of 1928, was the last class that actually coaled ship.

When I was a young boy here in Annapolis, and here again, you might say that this had an effect on my desire to go to the Naval Academy and become a naval officer, there lived across the street - this is 15 Southgate, now, the one that you went to - a lieutenant commander by the name of Millington Barnett McComb, who taught me as a young kid how to sail, took me on cruises up and down the Bay. In those days the Naval Academy had only two yachts, the _Argo_ and the _Robert Center_. The _Argo_ was a big yawl and the _Robert Center_ a big sloop, both oceangoing yachts.

Commander McComb used to take the _Argo_ and we sailed up and down the Bay on numerous occasions and, as a kid, I was the crew or one of the crew. I think my thorough enjoyment of this type of relaxation, if you want to call it that, possibly had some effect on my desire to go into the Naval Academy. In fact, I sailed competitively at the Naval Academy for a while in the company competition and then later on, when I went to my first assignment at sea, the _Maryland_, I was the sailing officer. I had the dubious honor of sailing those weird concoctions that the battleships generated to compete for the coveted Iron Man, which was the symbol of athletic supremacy in the Pacific Fleet. With all that sailing, my boyhood sailing, my Naval Academy sailing, and my _Maryland_ sailing - my _Maryland_ days' sailing - gave me enough of that particular sport to last me the rest of my life, and I am now of the view that a sailboat is a large, plastic hole in the water filled with money. I don't need one.

Q: Well, financially I guess you're better off!

Adm. C.: I would think so. Jimmy James asked me the other day if I wanted to buy a boat and, in keeping with what you were saying, he said I'm too Scotch and too Welsh to have to invest all that money in a boat and never use it. Do you want to buy it? I said no. I told him of my boating days, and he said, "I think you've got a point."

Well, getting back to the cruises, as I said, our first-

Chew #1 - 17

class cruise was, I thought, fascinating and interesting. I still have some pictures of the midshipmen days. Our first-class year was uneventful.

Q: On a cruise like that there's a certain amount of application of the technical knowledge you've acquired, isn't there?

Adm. C.: Yes. Of course, we were given assignments as assistant navigators and, not positions of great importance in the gunnery and in the firings, but those that would normally be filled by junior officers. We stood junior officer deck watches. I think that every effort was made to give you an indoctrination of how you would be expected to behave once you became an ensign and took up your duties officially.

Q: On a cruise like that, was there any textbook learning?

Adm. C.: Yes. Well, we had I believed they called it a journal, which was probably a hangover from the old days of an ensign's journal. It seems to me we had to keep a notebook that was in some respects equivalent to a journal. I think we kept a navigation and engineering notebook. They rotated us through the various departments during the three months of the cruise. It seems to me we had to keep some sort of a journal, and if I remember correctly I think we were even marked on it. There is a strong possibility that the marks on those journals that were made during the summer cruise might have had some effect on what your assignment would be your first-class year, whether in fact you'd get any stripes or whether you'd be a 2PO. It was an indication of how hard you'd worked and how interested you were. So in that respect, you could call it a slight academic exposure, but not very much.

I've digressed a lot, so I'm sort of -

Q: Well, we've come to the end of the Academy period, and you graduated and got an assignment. Was it the one you asked for?

Adm. C.: Yes. I felt very fortunate. It was either my first or second choice and I was very happy with it because I had friends who were going to the same ship, and in those days I think we had about eighteen or twenty going to each battleship, and I had specifically asked for the Maryland and some of my friends were in the Maryland so I was indeed very pleased with the thought of going to that particular ship.

Q: Was it not true that in that year some of the men were not commissioned?

Adm. C.: No. 1933 was the class that was not all commissioned. Due, I guess, to lack of funds or the needs of the Navy. As a result when the men came back in preparation for WWII, they came back as 1933 B&C depending upon their marital status. 1931 was the last class that could marry on graduation, after that 1932 had to wait two years as did '33.

As a matter of fact, our class was interviewed by industry and very few people got out on graduation. There were a few, but times were pretty tight and you were assured of at least $125 a month and a place to put your head. Quite a few were married.

Q: Were you one of those?

Adm. C.: No, I was a bachelor for seven years, and I'm sure you've heard the arguments of bachelor ensigns against the married ensigns.

Chew #1 - 19

It appeared to me always a trifle to my disadvantage, that I might go ashore in Los Angeles and come from liberty at two o'clock in the morning, and then because I was there, at five o'clock I was rudely awakened and told to get my little behind up and be a boat officer in the fog. I would go back and forth picking up liberty parties and at seven o'clock I would see the married ensigns coming happily back to the ship. I've always remembered that! I wonder how it fits into womens' lib nowadays?

Q: Who was skipper of the Maryland at that point?

Adm. C.: I was in the Maryland three years and we had three skippers. In those days it was about a year that everybody commanded a battleship because it was in preparation for his ultimate appearance before the selection board as to whether he would make admiral or not.

I remember Captain Bingham was the last. I'd have to look up the other two.

Q: I merely asked that to determine whether you had a really good set of commanding officers on board. This is always important to a young lad.

Adm. C.: Well, you know, strangely enough, at that particular time the captain was on such a high plane that if the ship were well run, you were really more influenced by the division officers, by the lieutenants, by the lieutenant commanders. For example, one that I remember quite well on the Maryland was Lieutenant Brumbaugh, who later was the guy who went in the Enola Gay and armed the first atomic bomb. He was an ordnance PG and I think the anti-aircraft officer at the time or assistant gunnery officer, I've forgotten which.

The first division officer, for example, was Stu Reynolds, who now lives in Coronado. That level, I felt, had a great deal more influence on us that the captain, provided, of course, the ship was a happy one and the Maryland was a happy ship. I think she won the engineering "E" one year. She never won the battle efficiency "E" but she won the Iron Man one of the years that I was aboard her. She was a good athletic ship and she was generally known as a happy ship.

The only time you ever saw the captain, really, was during Saturday inspection when you got yourself all decked out in your fore-and-aft hat and frock coat and he looked you over. I didn't see a great deal of the captain, as I say. I was influenced more probably by the younger officers than I was by the more senior.

I might also add that I think that you were influenced a great deal by the senior petty officers. I remember the names of a great many of the senior petty officers in the Maryland. One of them had a very, very funny piece of advice that I've never forgotten. His name was Madden. He was the first class fire controlman, and when I reported aboard I was put in the F Division, which was the fire-control division. Madden was the typical old-time sailor. I think he eventually made chief, but he was then first class. He took me aside, this brand-new ensign, and he said:

"Mr. Chew, I want to tell you how to be a success in the Navy. There are three things you've got to do. The first is always make quarters in the morning - that makes a very fine impression. No matter how hard a night you've had before, get there. The second thing is always take off your hat when you walk through the crew's mess. It makes the crew respect you. The third thing is never lose an opportunity to say something good about yourself because they'll remember what was said but they'll forget who said it."

That was the secret of success, according to Madden.

I thought it was a fairly philosophical approach to life from an old salt.

I remember the bo'sun's mate who was also the quarterback on the football team, a chief by the name of Frenchie Dagle. I remember these names, as you are certainly impressionable when you go aboard your first ship, a little bit in fear and trembling, I might add, but since I had friends who were a class ahead of me there, I remember my welcome aboard. The ship was in dry dock at Bremerton, and I had read all the books about how you reported aboard your first ship. You were supposed to stay aboard two weeks and you're supposed to sit down and learn the names of everybody. I walked across the gangplank which, technically, is a gangplank because it spans the chasm between the dock and the deck of the ship, and I was met by a classmate and he said:

"Go down and get your golf togs on and let's go play golf."

I'd been aboard twenty minutes and I said: "Look I'm supposed to do all this. I'm supposed to stay aboard three days and learn this, that, and the other."

"Oh," he said, "the hell with that. Let's go and play golf. Nobody's aboard anyhow. That's a bunch of baloney."

That was my introduction to the Maryland. I had a happy three years on that ship, going through, as all ensigns did, assignments in gunnery, engineering, and communications.

Q: What appealed to you most?

Adm. C.: I've always liked gunnery and deck. I preferred that. Engineering, although I enjoyed it, I couldn't see myself standing in an engineroom for the rest of my life. I liked to be up in the sunlight, and if you remember, in those days, they called engineers snipes because they were always pale in comparison with the deck force.

She was a fine ship and she acquitted herself very well during World War II.

Q: Yes, indeed. She was in the Pacific largely during these three years?

Adm. C.: Yes, she was in the Pacific all the time. The only time she came round to the Atlantic, which was fun, was at the very end of my cruise. The whole Pacific Fleet, if you remember, came round to New York. That was in 1934.

Q: Was this to be reviewed by the President?

Adm. C.: To be reviewed by the President, yes, President Roosevelt. We steamed up the Hudson River and anchored in the river, staying there about two weeks. I was detached from the Maryland in New York and went to my first destroyer.

Q: That was quite a gala occasion, wasn't it, when the fleet came to New York?

Adm. C.: The fleet review, yes. It was quite a sight. In fact, it was the first time, I think, that the so-called battle fleet, which was the Pacific Fleet, and the scouting fleet, which was the Atlantic Fleet, got together. In those days, they called them the battle force and the scouting force. Together it was the U. S. Fleet, and that was really the first time they'd gotten together for a grand review since the days of the Great White Fleet of Spanish American War era.

Q: Was that meant to have international impact?

Adm. C.: At that time, I'm not sure. My memory of the international situation, other than the rise of Hitler, is not too clear. I really don't know whether that had implications that I didn't recognize at the time or not.

Q: You say you were detached immediately after that review.

Adm. C.: I was detached during our stay in New York. I've forgotten how long we stayed. About two weeks. It seems to me I'd been there about two weeks, and I was ordered to a destroyer, the *Overton*, and we called it the 239 Maru. She was a four-piper and she was a member of Destroyer Squadron Ten, which we called Straggling DesRon 10, because we were straggled all up and down the east coast and our mission was to train Reserve crews of the active Reserve.

The *Overton* actually was stationed in New York, and we alternated between Brooklyn and 96th Street. They used to have an old pier there, and there was an armory at 96th Street. We would take out a Reserve crew from New York, Brooklyn, or possibly from New Haven. We'd go up and down the coast during the summer and pick up our Reserve crews, Reserve units, who were members of the active Reserve, and take them on their two weeks' training cruise. Our nucleus crew was very small. We had on our particular ship the Squadron Commodore and his staff, i.e., one officer, and the ship's company consisted of a captain, the exec, the chief engineer, and Chew. That was all. Four officers and sixty-four men for a four-piper.

Q: Those were the poverty days!

Adm. C.: Poverty days, and of course during our cruises we would be augmented by these Reserve units who would fill the necessary gaps to provide us with an adequate crew. When we would discharge one crew and go back to our dock at 96th Street, we would go back usually with four officers and sixty-four men.

I thought back to the days of World War II when we had 200 and 300 on a destroyer. I often thought that sometimes we were a little bit plush.

The <u>Overton</u> stayed in commission as a four-piper during the war. I've forgotten exactly what happened to her. She may have been traded to England as lend-lease. She was a fine little ship.

I stayed only about - less that a year - and was then ordered to new construction in Boston. Really, this is sort of an interesting story concerning my arrival in Boston.

I was a bachelor still, and I got on the train and arrived in Boston, went over to the Navy Yard, and there was one of the ships of our Straggling DesRon 10 we had operated with during the preceding summer. She was commanded by Lieutenant Commander Ted Gibb. It was the <u>Manley</u> (DD-74). She was an old broken-decker of World War I vintage. When the first squadron of broken-deckers arrived in Queenstown during World War I it was Admiral

Chew #1 - 26

Taussig, then Commander Taussig, who made the now famous answer to the then British query of "how soon can you be ready?" "We are ready now."

Q: Yes.

Ad. C.: I went to the Navy Yard and said:

"Captain, can you give me a place to stay for a while until I can find an apartment in Boston or Cambridge or wherever I can find a place to live that's within my means?"

He said, "Sure, Jack. Let me give you a little advice. You can stay aboard the <u>Manley</u> as long as you want, until you get yourself settled, but don't go out and get some sleazy apartment. Go out on Beacon Street, get yourself a good-looking dolly and give the Navy a good name."

That was my advice from Captain Gibb. As a matter of fact, during one of the America Cup races he was the - I've forgotten what they call it - the control ship that tried to keep the yachts and everything out of the way of the racing boats. I believe President Roosevelt was there at that particular race and sent him a message saying: "Are you in the race, Captain Gibb?" He was that kind of guy!

So I finally got an apartment in Cambridge, right off Harvard Square. I think the ship was two or three months, maybe a little more -

Chew #1 - 27

Q: She was the what?

Adm. C.: She was the Monaghan, No. 354. She was the first of the gold-platers, and I stayed on her about two and a half years.

Q: That must have been a good bit of training for you.

Adm. C.: That was a good bit of training. I had a great deal of shiphandling. I had a great deal of shiphandling on the Overton, strangely enough, because there were only four of us. Of course, the exec did take a lot, but when we were running without Reserves or really when we were running with Reserves, if the Reserve officers did not meet the qualifications set by the captain, and they were pretty strict, it put us on a one-in-three basis. So we got a great deal of shiphandling and a great deal of watch standing.

Q: I was referring specifically to before the commissioning of the Monaghan, being there, and the construction, and so forth.

Adm. C.: Yes. Well, I thought that was a great help in learning the ship, plus the fact that the nucleus crew was, of course, also there. It was particularly beneficial for the engineers because they saw their equipment going in. I was the first lieutenant and torpedo officer, so I could see the installation of the tubes and I could see the installation of the fire-control gear. You remember, in those days, the first of the gold-platers was the Farragut, and she went out without any director at all. The fire-control gear was late in coming. I think actually we got ours before we left. But those early ships went out without any guns on them. But I know the Farragut went out without a director.

Q: Did you go down to Newport to the Torpedo School?

Adm. C.: Before I went to the Monaghan - I'm trying to remember. I had two schools, and I'm trying to remember whether they were before going to the Monaghan or before going to the Helena. Both of them were in New York. I went for about three weeks to the Arma Engineering Company in Brooklyn, where I learned about the Arma fire-control system and the gyroscopes associated with it. Then I went to the Ford Instrument Company in Long Island City, and during that time I lived in Sutton Place with a couple of other guys who were going to similar schools.

Q: You'd taken the captain's advice, apparently, living on Sutton Place!

Adm. C.: Well, as I say, I'm not sure whether the schools were before the Monaghan or before the Helena. I think they were before the Helena.

Q: That sounds more likely, I imagine.

Adm. C.: In fact, I'm sure they were because I'll tell you the story of how I was assigned to the Helena after I've finished the Monaghan.

Q: I just wondered as torpedo officer on the Monaghan if you had gone down to learn a little more about torpedoes.

Adm. C.: I was the only torpedo officer, I think, in the fleet who hadn't gone to school, and talking to my classmates I really was not too dismayed at not having gone because they had to go back to their Naval Academy days and learn how to sketch a torpedo and I sort of remembered that a little bit, anyhow. These were a little bit better torpedoes and a little bit newer.

Q: They were still steam?

Adm. C.: They were steam, yes. This was before the electric and before we had any acoustics. They were simple contact warheads, but they were good torpedoes. But as far as I can remember I didn't go to school. I did go, as I say, to the Arma School for fire control and to Ford, where I learned about the intricacies of a Ford rangekeeper.

So I spent two and half year on the Monaghan. We had very interesting cruises. We went from the east coast to the west coast, where we were eventually home-ported in San Diego. Our shake-down cruise was to northern Europe. We went back to Ireland, both to Belfast and to the Republic of Ireland. We went in to Cork, Portsmouth, then went back up to the Firth of Forth, the anchorage for Edinburgh, and also Amsterdam.

My skipper was a very interesting man; R.R. Thompson. He was later skipper of one of the heavy cruisers during the war. He was a commander. We had the roughest crossing of the Atlantic Ocean I have ever witnessed in my life. As a matter of fact, it was so rough that the ships, though new and with aluminum superstructures, ruptured both the longitudinals at the break of the deck, and also the aluminum columns that held the superstructure. So, of course, we had considerable repairs to be made after our return to the yard.

I remember Captain Thompson well. As we were just about to get in to Belfast, we'd gone through a terrific storm, he said:

"I'm glad to get even into this section of merrie old England. That old business about Britannia ruling the waves, as far as I'm concerned, they can have it."

A sentimental and rather unusual thing happened to me on our shake down cruise aboard the Monaghan.

In my earlier days, I had a slight tendency to be seasick. Gradually, as I became more experienced I got over it. I'd been subjected during the Overton days to some heavy weather, but I would occasionally feel very queasy, and this particular night it was as rough as anything I've ever known. I was standing my watch on the bridge with a bucket! And I can assure you it was quite necessary!

After my watch I came down to the ward room flopped on the transom too tired to go to bed, and also thinking it the best place to stay as the ship was pitching and rolling like a wild horse. Lowell Thomas was coming over the radio. If you remember, at the end of his program he always had some little homily, and this particular night it was about college football stars.

"Tonight, I'd like to talk about the little college football stars of all time. Of course, you hear of the Red Granges, you hear of all the well-known big college stars, but you often lose sight of the little colleges that have football teams that produce men that, had they played for bigger institutions, might have been better known than the well-known stars of their time." He then mentioned some linemen and some backs. "but the greatest quarterback of all time, for little colleges, was a guy by the name of Johnny Chew who played at St. John's College."

Not that it cured my seasickness. It didn't. But it was a very pleasant and heartwarming thing to be in the middle of the Atlantic Ocean and hear such accolades about your father years after his death from Lowell Thomas.

Q: I didn't know that you were a friend of his!

Adm. C.: I've never met him but have always had a very soft

spot in my heart for him.

Q: On this shake-down cruise, did you have an Alcoa man on board, since you had aluminum -?

Adm. C.: No, we didn't. As I remember we had no technical representatives at all. Actually the longitudinal stiffeners were not aluminum. They were steel, and the working of the ship had been such that they had cracked, and then the corner posts of that aluminum superstructure also cracked. This was remedied in the ships that came along afterwards.

Q: But it must have caused some concern to them, did it not, when it was reported?

Adm. C.: Yes, I think it did. As I say, it was remedied. Of course, you know the Monaghan was lost in that typhoon during World War II. She was one of those ships that was with Halsey in that tremendous typhoon in the Pacific, off the Philippines. She was lost and I've forgotten what others. But she was a good ship.

As a matter of fact, one of the little stories of - do you want sea stories like this? Isn't it sort of tiresome?

Q: Sure.

Adm. C.: I remember our second exec was a guy named Pete Hale. Pete was a fine officer and one of his many distinctions was that he was an aerologist and a weatherman par excellence, having been to school in Norway - where they sent them for their last part of their PG. Pete was an expert on weather, and he used to come back in the morning and look at the log. The quartermaster always had to write down the cloud cover, you know, the percentage and what kind of clouds they were. Finally, in exasperation one day, he turned to the quartermaster when we were in San Diego and said:

"Smith (or Jones, or whatever his name was), look stop trying to look up at those clouds in San Diego and determine what they are. Just put down STCU - stratocumulus - and you'll be right 98 percent of the time. Damn it, do it the way I tell you."

Q: Good advice from a weatherman!

Adm. C.: Yes.

With the Monaghan we made, in addition to our shake-down cruise, a cruise to South America, down the west coast to Callao, which is the port for Lima, across the line, did all that. I'm trying to remember where else we went. We went somewhere else, because I made two shake-down cruises to South America - or two cruises.

Chew #1 - 34

Q: The fact that on your shake-down you went to Europe and then went to Latin America, does this reflect pride on the Navy's part in this new gold-plater?

Adm. C.: Yes, I think so. I think also that it was very much in keeping with our policy of showing the flag at that time. Of course, this was 1935 or 1936.

Q: Reflecting a certain attitude in the White House itself?

Adm. C.: Yes, I would think so, very strongly. I'm trying to think where else we went in South America. For some reason or other my mind's a complete blank, but I do remember Lima and Callao, and going up from the port city to the capital.

Interview No. 2 with Vice Admiral John L. Chew
Place: His residence in Providence, Annapolis, Maryland
Date: 15 November 1972
Subject: Biography
By: John T. Mason, Jr.

Q: Admiral, last time you gave me a very interesting account of your assignment on the destroyer Monaghan, fitting-out and commissioning her, and some of your travels afterwards. Do you want to resume the story at this point, Sir?

Adm. C.: After leaving the Monaghan, I was assigned to the Neches, one of the older oilers. She was home-ported at San Diego, and during the year that I served in her we did a sort of a ferry hop, fueling in Long Beach at either the Union Oil or whatever company had the contract, filling, and making a trip either to Panama, Honolulu, or Bremerton. After each trip we would come back and sit in San Diego and refuel destroyers for about two weeks before proceeding on another trip.

Q: There was no high-seas refueling?

Adm. C.: There was no high-seas refueling in those days, no.

Q: Was it dreamed of, as a technique?

Adm. C.: Yes, I think it was dreamed of and I think it had been seriously thought about, particularly the fueling astern, which is what I believe the Russians use right now. Actually, we were more of a transport tanker, filling the tanks in Panama for their ultimate use, the same in Bremerton, and the same in Honolulu. I might add that it was a very pleasant run for a bachelor because we had two weeks in San Diego with very little to do, and then a fairly long sea cruise. I think it took about fourteen days to Panama, eight days to Honolulu, and four days to Bremerton. At each place we would stay two days. In the case of Panama, we would normally go through the canal to the east coast to discharge our cargo, and then come back to the Balboa side, so that we had normally a couple of days' liberty on each side of the canal.

It was a very uneventful type of life.

Q: Was the cargo purchased from oil companies or was it Navy oil, or what?

Adm. C.: The cargo was purchased from oil companies. As I remember, one of the most frequently visited docks was the Union Oil Company, and I remember it vividly - I was the division officer. There were two division officers. One was the gunnery officer and one was the communication officer. I was the division officer of the after end of the ship and it was my responsibility to handle the after lines. I remember getting an 8-inch hawser tangled around one of the screws. I felt that I should be the one to go in the murky waters of San Pedro Bay to clear the propeller since it had been my responsibility. I got over with a saw and we pumped the oil forward, lifted her stern out a little bit, and I was able to saw the hawser off the screw. As you well know, with a reciprocating engine, if you get an 8-inch hawser around the screw it just stops the engine.

Q: Indeed it does!

Adm. C.: It can't carry away an 8-inch hawser. But, I enjoyed the tour on the Neches.

Q: In retrospect, what did this tour of duty contribute to your career, to your greater knowledge?

Adm. C.: I think it gave me a better appreciation of the logistics problems the Navy faces. For example, here we were a full-fledged ship doing nothing but delivering oil to the places that it was needed.

I also had a very fine course in navigation. I think at that time I was going up for lieutenant, and consequently

Chew #2 - 38

I was at times assigned as assistant navigator. I was able to navigate and when the time came for my examinations I was sort of a professional expert, having navigated a great deal. It also gave me an appreciation of shiphandling in a low-powered ship, and it stood me in good stead in later years when I commanded an oiler.

In those days, they were called tankers. The Neches was a tanker and it was only after the development of the fueling-at-sea techniques that they were called oilers, instead of tankers.

Q: What was her speed?

Adm. C.: It seems to me we cruised at 11 knots, wide open 11.5. I remember the engineer officer said, "Our normal cruising speed is top speed. If I burned the wardroom furniture in the boilers, I could probably get another two-tenths of a knot out of her."

At that time, having been stationed in San Diego - I was married during my tour in the Neches and, upon completion of that tour, came back to the postgraduate school at the Naval Academy as a student. It was my first tour of shore duty and one of the few in my first fourteen years of naval service.

Q: Is this what you asked for?

Adm. C.: I asked for postgraduate training. In those days, and I think this is of a certain amount of significance, the most desirable course from a general line officer's point of view was an ordnance PG, because I think in those days the ordnance PG had a certain amount of prestige that the general line or even engineering PG, or possibly even communications PG did not have. I had applied for postgraduate training when I was in the Monaghan, and I remember Captain Thompson's endorsement on it, which rather disappointed me but frankly proved to be basically correct, if you look at history. He wrote on my request for ordnance PG that Mr. Chew was a good basic naval officer and it would be a great pity to have him specialize, and therefore he recommended only a general-line course. I was, of course, disappointed because several of my close friends did get the ordnance PG and I didn't.

I came back as a general-line PG, which was a one-year course, and like all PG students we studied hard during the week, played hard during the weekend, and I thoroughly enjoyed postgraduate school. I found it not too difficult as I had enough experience professionally so that the academics didn't stump me. It was a good refresher course in engineering, ordnance and navigation.

Q: Well, indeed, that's the very purpose of the PG school!

Adm. C.: That's exactly the purpose of the general-line

school and, as I remember, Captain Thompson was essentially correct if he could predict what, to me, has been a reasonably successful career.

Of course, at the time of postgraduate school, war clouds were beginning to gather, and I could see that my next sea cruise no doubt would be very full and very interesting. I'm not a seer and I didn't anticipate the war and couldn't predict it.

Q: It was pretty clear, wasn't it?

Adm. C.: It was pretty clear, I thought, and inevitable within a given time frame. The precise time frame, as I said, I was not able to gestimate.

At the end of postgraduate school I had applied for new construction, specifically for a cruiser. The gunnery officer of the cruiser, who has become a lifelong friend, was then Lieutenant Commander Irving T. Duke, who later became a vice admiral, and Uncle Irv, as I affectionately knew him, interviewed me for a possible job as assistant gunnery officer of the Helena. In his typical way, he turned to me and said, "Well, Chew, I really asked for somebody else, but the Bureau of Navigation told me that I couldn't have him. So I guess I'll have to take you."

Those were his exact words, and it's interesting to note that the person for whom he asked was later right out here at the Severn School, a classmate of mine, who long since has retired.

So I was assigned to the Helena.

Q: Are you referring to Corky Ward?

Adm. C.: No, I'm referring to Don Wilbur, who is the comptroller at Severn. He retired as a captain and was a classmate of mine.

In preparation for my tour as assistant gunnery officer, I was assigned temporary duty in the Bureau of Navigation and then at the Gun Factory in Washington while the ship was being readied for commissioning. Then, of course, I went as a pre-commission detail and lived in Brooklyn. I thought it was a very elegant address. It was the Clark Lane, and if you really slurred over it it sounded more like Park Lane! It was right across the street from the old St. George Hotel.

We worked hard in the pre-commissioning detail. I think by that time, which was 1939, the war coulds were definitely forming and, if I remember correctly, it was 1940 that the Neutrality Patrol was started. So you could see the handwriting on the wall. Everybody, I think, had a purpose in life, and I remember well, vividly, saying as we were working on the alignment of the battery or checking the installation even during the pre-commissioning detail, saying in essence, "God damn it, we're not going to make any mistakes because you and I may have to fight this ship and the chances are we will. So let's make it the very best that we can possibly make it."

Chew #2 - 42

Q: Does that imply that there were changes made in some of the engineering installations?

Adm. C.: No. I think the ship was built pretty much according to plan. She was one of two cruisers, the St. Louis and the Helena - the only two of the 6-inch-gun cruisers that had 5"/38 twin mounts. Later they became standard on all of the cruisers and the battleships. That was their primary anti-aircraft battery.

Q: Was that an Oerlikon?

Adm. C.: No, that was the 5"/38. In addition, she had the 40 mm. and also 20 mm. The 20 mm. was the Oerlikon. The 40 mm. was the Bofors. We had 40 mm. quadruple mounts, 4 5"/38 twins located sort of on the corners, and 40 mm. quadruple mounts in between, and then 20 mm. sprinkled liberally throughout the ship.

Q: She had a formidable armament then?

Adm. C.: She had formidable armament. And, of course, she had the five turrets of the 6"/47 caliber, which was her main battery.

The gunnery officer was a perfectionist and I think of all the people under whom I served in the Navy I could say that I learned more from him than I did from anyone. Of course, it was at a very learnable age. I was younger, terribly enthusiastic, and used to get pretty upset with my boss at times, but in later years the things that he taught me stood me in very good stead.

Q: His high standards are what made an impression?

Adm. C.: Incidentally, he was an ordnance PG and I sort of eyed him with envy in this particular aspect, and I was coming along as assistant gunnery officer without the benefit of his educational advantages. So I realized that I had to work harder possibly than I would have normally had to.

Q: It was kind of a PG course in ordnance that you got from him, wasn't it?

Adm. C.: It was a PG course in ordnance under him, I assure you, and it was a great privilege to work under Irving Duke.

Our progression in the Helena was very pleasant, even with the war clouds over us, we had a very interesting shake-down cruise to South America, stopping in Rio - no, excuse me, stopping first in Buenos Aires, then going over to Montevideo and going aboard the hulk of the Graf Spee. I think somewhere in the basement in all the junk that I have in the house there is an optical prism that was sort of burned and melted that I removed from one of the bridge telescopes or bridge optical instruments from the Graf Spee. Most of us went aboard.

Of course, by this time having seen the effects of war, it brought home very closely and very vividly the fact that it was inevitable, and of course at that time the Neutrality Patrol had been in effect.

We had, as I say, a very pleasant shake-down cruise to South America, came back to, I think, the east coast after our shake-down to complete our work-up. At that time they didn't have the very extensive courses that they developed at Guantanamo, where a ship went down and went through a full course of sprouts and became "proficient" or ready for active duty. We did it sort of by miss and by God, but we worked diligently, and then finally went around through the canal and were stationed in Honolulu.

Q: You became a unit of the Pacific Fleet?

Adm. C.: Became a unit of the Pacific Fleet. I'm ashamed to say I can't remember the number of the cruiser division and it really doesn't make much difference. But we worked with the Boise, the Brooklyn, and ships of that class that were stationed in Pearl Harbor at the time.

Our time in Honolulu prior to the outbreak of war was very busy. We trained extensively, we shot a lot, we were out a great deal, and we tried to keep certain ships in and certain ships out at all times.

Q: This was under Admiral Richardson, was it?

Adm. C.: Yes. Then of course, it was also the policy continued under Admiral Kimmel, and, at the time of Pearl Harbor the carriers happened to be out. I think the policy had been in effect even then.

As I said, by this time, we well recognized, it was as plain as the nose on your face - and here again I reiterated during training that we can't afford to make mistakes now, you're going to fight this ship, it's self-evident, and we want nothing short of perfection. Of course, I was adequately supported in that by my boss. I remember working long hours, day and night, aligning batteries, making sure that everything was as perfect as our equipment would allow it to be, and we did have good equipment. When the war broke out the Helena had one of the first SG radars. She also had a good air-search radar and fire-control radars. This was not the case in certain ships that were at Pearl Harbor and members of the Pacific Fleet at the time.

Q: What special measures of alertness did you take when you were in Pearl Harbor? Or were there any special ones?

Adm. C.: I'm trying to remember whether we had any particular measures of alert. We had practice alerts, of course, air alerts, but to be precise the night of December the 6th I was at the - I've forgotten the name of the club, whether it was called the Honolulu Club, it was a downtown club and I was there with a number of friends and my wife. Admiral Theobald, who was then one of the cruiser division commanders - and incidentally whose son is a classmate of mine and is retired and lives here in Annapolis - Admiral Theobald and I were talking at the bar, and I remember his words. He said, "History will record the maldeploymant of the United States naval forces."

Admiral Theobald was quite a scholar. He was head of the postgraduate school at the Naval Academy before it moved to Monterey, and a bit of a martinet, at that.

That was Sunday night, December 6th - I mean Saturday night, December the 6th. We went home, and I was, of course, awakened by the sounds of gunfire and you could see the bursting of anti-aircraft shells. I immediately got dressed. We had a very elegant car which I think I paid $46 for. It was laughingly called the gnu gnoiseless gnash. I jumped in the car and made it back to Pearl Harbor, slightly under fire, between really what amounted to the second and third attacks. Of course, by that time the harbor was a shambles.

Q: Where was the Helena berthed?

Adm. C.: The Helena was berthed just outboard of the dry dock where the Pennsylvania was, and outboard of us was the old minelayer the *Oglala*. The *Oglala* had taken a torpedo and capsized and sank alongside us. Prior to my getting there, we had taken one torpedo which unfortunately had exploded in the forward engineroom.

In answer to your earlier question, of course the ship was wide open. All of the hatches were open and, as general quarters were sounded, people were running to and from their berthing spots - this was late Sunday morning - to their battle stations, and most of our casualties, aside from those who were actually in the engineroom, were from flash burns because, as the torpedo exploded in the forward engineroom, the flash came up the open hatches from the engineroom and went all along the third deck where people were running to their battle stations. We lost, I think, 42 men that morning. There were no other losses from other hits because that was our only one.

As you remember, again in keeping with the question of what security measures were instituted, in order to have the crew reasonably comfortable, the uniform of the day was shorts. Consequently a great many of the casualties could have been attributed to the uniform which was nothing but shorts and a skivvy shirt.

The pendulum, of course, immediately swung the other way, and after the results of the attack had been assessed we all went to flashproof clothing and antiflash ointment on our faces and all sorts of things. But I think the lesson was well learned.

There was another lesson that we learned the hard way and I can't help but be interested in some of the articles that are appearing in the paper now about the plushness of the admirals' cabins. The results of the later actions in the war clearly demonstrated the hazard of fire, and on the <u>Helena</u>, even though we had metal paneling in the wardroom we immediately went through, ripped out all the paneling, ripped out all of the decorations; took out everything so that our wardroom throughout the war was bare steel bulkheads. Of course, in the intervening years an effort to make living a little more comfortable and a little more competitive, I suppose, with civilian life, the pendulum has swung back now to the point where apparently there's a great deal of criticism of the decor of the flag cabin in some of the carriers, resulting in that rather disastrous fire so recently in the news. Believe me, ours was spartan, spartan, spartan. There was nothing. We took down what few curtains we had and we ripped out even the sheet metal paneling. We ripped up the linoleum on the decks. We had bare steel decks. Of course, the wood decks were not taken up and I think properly so because they were topside, but there was a tremendous effort made to reduce fire hazards.

A: Admiral, when she was being commissioned, what sort of a course of sprouts did you have in damage control?

Adm. C.: I think our damage control was really pretty good. That the hatches were open on Sunday morning, December the 7th, was normal because we were in port and presumably a secure harbor. I think that it would have been an unnecessary annoyance to have the ship in battle condition when no one at all, including everyone in the United States, ever expected such an attack. At sea we didn't have these problems. We normally cruised in Condition Y, which was sort of a semi-battle cruising condition, but in port with everything open, let's face it, we weren't ready.

I think it's interesting to note that that morning the first person in my battle station, and I was not there, as I said, during the initial two attacks, was the talker and he picked up the phones and the first word he said was, "Mr. Chew ain't here. Commence firing." I might add he'd been pretty well trained, too.

Well, to get on a little bit more with the chronology, of course, as everyone knows, after the initial attack we were very jittery. I remember one night we fired at our own planes coming in from the Saratoga. We also took a few pot shots at Venus! I'm sure you've heard of that?

Q: Yes.

Adm. C.: Everybody was a little bit trigger happy. Having been severely damaged in our forward engineroom, we still had the after engineroom we had mobility, but because of all the water in the forward engineroom and the size of the hold we'd increased our draft considerably, and the question came up during the day as to whether to try to exit, for example, like the Nevada did and ended up aground. The captain very wisely said, "We'll stay here."

They had a brand-new dry dock in Pearl Harbor, and we were the first ship that was put into it. We had a temporary patch put over the torpedo hole in the side.

Q: It must have been difficult to assign priorities at that point!

Adm. C.: Well, we had been relatively undamaged, except for that forward engineroom. The other ships, as we all know, the Oklahoma was capsized, the Arizona was a shambles, the Maryland was on the bottom, the California was on the bottom in pretty sad shape. Of course, the Arizona was never raised. The Oklahoma was brought back upright and eventually salvaged. The Maryland and the California were restored to active duty, as was the Nevada.

Since we had been only moderately damaged, it seemed, I think, prudent and I think a wise decision, to put us into the dock and patch the side and get us back to Mare Island as soon as possible to be made ready for further action. That turned out to be the case and actually we were in good enough condition, except for our limited speed and only two screws out of our four to act as a convoy ship for one of the first convoys that took dependents back to the United States. In fact, my wife was in one of those ships that we were convoying. We made it back to San Francisco rather uneventfully. Everybody, of course, was extremely concerned with the devastation that had been wrought. There would surely be a follow-up attack. I was convinced of it, as I think most people were. In retrospect, it was a great surprise that the Japanese didn't follow up. It seemed almost inevitable, and of course that contributed to a certain degree to the nervousness of the people who were there in Pearl Harbor and, as I said, took pot shots at Venus.

So we made it back to San Francisco, and the ship went in to Mare Island where she was completely repaired. I've forgotten whether we got additional radar equipment then or not. We were probably the most up to date in terms of radar of any ship in the Navy. We had the surface-search, the SG, the air-search, the SC, we had fire control radars on both of our antiaircraft directors, and we had fire control radars on both of our main-battery directors. Of course, our 40 mms. were line-of-sight guns, but we had lead sights for those. When we came out of the yard we were a pretty up-to-date fighting unit with, by that time, a reasonably experienced crew. Of course, the experience had been all bad but at the same time once you've been subjected to fire you have a hearty respect for it, and people now realized that they had the war to fight, or at least as long as they were going to survive probably in this ship.

I've forgotten precisely how long it took us to be made ready. Of course they worked as rapidly as they could, and we finally, if my memory serves me correctly, took about two or three months, so it must have been March or April - perhaps you could tell me that because it was the first Battle of Savo Island at which we lost the Quincy, Astoria, and the Vincennes that took place on our trip out to the Pacific.

We were ordered out and had a merchant convoy which we stayed with all the way, and our destination was Espiritu Santo which was to remain our base until we were sunk over a year later. We arrived in Espiritu Santo and began really the defense of Guadalcanal. I don't think you could call it the Battle of Guadalcanal because there were so many naval engagements around Guadalcanal that the campaign itself really didn't end until the island had been completely secured, and that was a little while after I left. But our basic mission was to protect the Marine garrison on Guadalcanal.

Before our first surface engagement we were subjected to air attacks. I remember an ensign reporting to the ship and saying, "I'm an identification expert. We've got to have all the lookouts properly trained so they can identify an SBO, TBF, Zero, a Betty, etc." I said, "Son, pardon me if I sound a little pontifical, but we don't have any identification problem around here. Everything we see is enemy and you just shoot. We haven't seen a friendly plane for so long that we don't know what one looks like."

It was at that time our Air Force were flying B-17s and they never came close enough, so we really didn't see them. We saw very few fighters, and one of the first carriers that was out there was the Wasp, which later was sunk. So our problems of identification were not immediate.

Our first surface action was called by two names - the Second Battle of Savo or the Battle of Cape Esperance, and our mission was very simple. It was to intercept and destroy the "Tokyo Express" that used to come down and reinforce the Japanese troops on Guadalcanal.

Our first task force commander was Admiral Scott, and I remember Uncle Irv coming back to the ship prior to our departure from Espiritu and he said:

"Our orders are pretty simple. Our orders are to intercept and destroy the Japanese forces. The amplifying orders go something like this: when I say shoot, shoot, and God damn it, when I say don't shoot, don't shoot."

This, I think, reflected the thinking of the previous engagement in which I believe there had been incidents of firing on our own forces. In the night actions everybody was a little bit concerned, and his chief concern was really to prevent firing on our own forces.

The destroyers with us that night were the Farenholt, Duncan, Laffey, Buchanan and McCalla. I'm trying to think which ships were with us at the first Battle of Cape Esperance, but the significant part of the action was the fact that the Boise was a part of our task force. The Salt Lake City, the Boise, the San Francisco, and the Helena, and several destroyers. The destroyers that worked very closely with us, most of which were commanded by my classmates, were the O'Bannon, the Nicholas, deHaven, and Radford, and that outfit. I'm wrong. They were with us in our later actions.

Q: The Benham was one, wasn't it?

Adm. C.: The Benham was not one of them.

The Boise was hit badly and I remember steaming right past her when her forward part was blazing. Of course, the crew got that under control and saved the ship. We sailed right between the Boise and the line of fire. The Helena had a good picture of what was going on. We were in column, and of course the column was designed to avoid having ships fire at their own forces. I think the old classical deployment of ships in a screen, then a line, and then other ships closer, going forward to make a torpedo attack, was overshadowed by the fear of firing on our own forces. So the destroyers led the cruisers, and then maybe a destroyer or two would tail along behind.

As I remember, I think the Furotaka or the Kinugasa was sunk that night. Our basic cruiser damage was to the Boise. The destroyers that were hit were the Farenholt and Duncan. As you know, the Duncan sank.

We made the run up through the Slot, met the Japanese force, and they turned back. So they never reinforced the garrison, and actually we accomplished our mission.

Q: How useful was your radar at that point?

Adm. C.: Well, as I said, we had a very fine picture and we were feeding information to the flagship as accurately as we could and I think that the information was very useful. It was surprising to us that we were not at least temporarily designated as the flagship because we had better equipment, there was no question about it, and we had a better picture of what was going on in night action than most of the other ships. The Salt Lake City, for example, didn't have SG radar. The Boise did, but she was hit rather quickly and her effectiveness, of course, was seriously reduced. But the Helena gained a reputation that night and ensuing nights because we had developed a continuous-fire doctrine from our 6-inch guns. Once the order was given to commence firing with our radar solutions in continuous fire, we could put out about 90 6-inch shells a minute. Almost like a 6" machine gun. The effect is tremendous. Each of our fifteen guns was firing at the rate of about six rounds per minute, some a little higher, so that you could go even as high as 110 rounds per minute, which again gave you almost the effect of an automatic 6-inch machinegun. We were very successful in standing off the Tokyo Express.

Q: How much practice had you had prior to that in night battle?

Adm. C.: Well, during our period in Honolulu we had trained rather diligently, but actually battle is a little different from target practice.

Q: But the mere act of practising -?

Adm. C.: Well, the development of our doctrines had been accomplished during our training period, and I think very soundly so. I might add - and I'm sure that anyone who was ever in combat would agree - I was afraid, you can call it scared, I was plain afraid. Anybody that isn't is an idiot, particularly when you can't see. The only things you can see really are the flashes and you know they're shooting at you, and you know if you take a 6-inch shell right beside you, you're not long for this world.

Actually, that night we were not hit at all. There were a few shrapnel scratches here and there, but we had no injuries, no casualties. We went back to Espiritu. I think it's interesting here to note that by that time - I'm going back to my logistics statement that I made in the Neches - we were actually running low on everything.

Q: Shells, I would think!

Adm. C.: Shells, our expenditures were very high. We were running low in food. Later on, we really ran out of clothing. The reason being quite different, because during one of our sweeps we were a part of the task force with the Wasp - I'm getting ahead of myself a little bit here. But as I said, the first battle that we participated in was the Battle of Cape Esperance or the Second Battle of Savo.

Maybe, chronologically, I think the next one was the famous Battle of Guadalcanal, November the 13th, in which we had thirteen ships. I've never forgotten this. We had thirteen ships, November the 13th, and the last ship was the Fletcher, and she was the 445, which added up to thirteen! I've always felt, as a result of that battle, that thirteen was my lucky number because, the thirteen ships - let me see, there were eight destroyers, five cruisers, the cruisers were the Atlanta and Juneau which were light antiaircraft cruisers and the San Francisco, Portland, and Helena in the cruiser column. It was a hodge podge of cruisers and destroyers and showed how desperate we really were.

Q: It reflects the state of the fleet?

Adm. C.: It completely reflects the state of the units available. There was the Portland, an 8-inch-gun cruiser, there there were the Atlanta and Juneau, really 5-inch-antiaircraft gun cruisers - that was three, the San Francisco was an 8-inch gun cruiser, and the Helena a 6-inch-gun cruiser. So we had two 5's, a 6, and two 8's.

That was the famous night that we steamed up the Slot and went right between the two Japanese columns, and the order to fire was, "even ships fire to port, odd-number ships fire to starboard." We were an even numbered ship, so when the order came to commence firing, we were to fire to port. Because of our radar equipment we could see the picture develop. I was next to the captain in antiaircraft defense, which was the open bridge. Helena had a small conning tower, or armored bridge, and above that was an open bridge which in those days was what was really required for basic antiaircraft defense.

The plotting room officer, Washburn, who was later lost, called me on the phone and said, "For Christ's sake, Jack, what are we going to do? Throw potatoes at them? We're so close."

We steamed between the two columns, firing. That night we lost the Atlanta, and Portland was disabled and remained. The San Francisco was cut to ribbons. She was flooded - I've forgotten how many holes she had. I went aboard her when we got back to Espiritu. Most of her topside people were casualties. Bruce McCandless took over in the conning tower. The captain was killed, the admiral was killed. Of course, Admiral Scott was killed in the Atlanta, and Captain Hoover -

Q: John Hoover?

Adm. C.: No, it wasn't John Hoover, it was Gilbert Hoover, who in my opinion was one of the finest naval officers that ever drew the breath of life. I feel so strongly about him that it almost brings tears to my eyes.

We steamed out the next morning and we had San Francisco, Helena, Juneau, O'Bannon, Fletcher and Sterret I think. I can't quite remember. We lost Barton, Monssen, Cushing and Laffey. The Portland remained off Guadalcanal. So we had really five ships of the thirteen - maybe we had six, I've forgotten precisely. We were steaming south at the maximum speed that the San Francisco could make, and her speed was limited not by her engineering plant at all, but by the fact that if she increased her speed she took in so much water through the holes in her skin that she was unable to control the flooding. Her armored box was reasonably intact, but her topside was just cut to ribbons.

Juneau had only one screw. Her one engineroom had been flooded, I think from a torpedo hit, so she had been put on our starboard quarter of the three cruisers that remained of the five. One of the destroyers had been sent to the south to send a radio message to tell of the situation that existed at the time, because again we had heard that there would be air attacks.

Incidentally, I forgot one very important thing. That afternoon before the so-called Battle of Guadalcanal, we had steamed into Iron Bottom Bay and we had received word of an air attack. I might add that the coast watchers and our intelligence were so good that the air attack, which was predominantly Bettys, arrived more precisely than did our usual target planes for antiaircraft practice off Pearl Harbor. I think they were predicted to come sometime around 3:30 or 4:00 in the afternoon and at the predicted time the first of them appeared. We were proud of our antiaircraft batteries and we had a field day.

<u>San Francisco</u> was hit in her after control station that afternoon, but I think she was the only casualty. If I remember, the exec was seriously wounded in the after control station.

The attack was completely beaten off and no planes returned to base. I think there was a wave of eighteen and we got them all. So that was the prelude to the Battle of Guadalcanal, which occurred that night.

We were, of course, reinforcing the Marines, and the transports had been sent to whatever a safe area is. I don't think there were any, but at least they'd been separated from the combat forces to unload their supplies.

As we came out the next morning, the three ships and the remaining destroyers limping back to Espiritu, it was a bright, sunny day and the sea was like oil. Actually, there was no oil on it, but it was that glassy. I was on the open bridge with the Captain. We were zig-zagging as best we could because

Juneau had trouble turning to port - her starboard engine was out. I remember seeing the torpedo headed towards what I thought was our stern. Juneau was on our starboard quarter, 700 yards away. San Francisco was leading the column - no, she was astern. The torpedo passed astern of us, hit Juneau, there was this tremendous explosion of such force that a part of one of her 5-inch mounts, a rather significant part, went flying over us, 700 yards away! You could see a pall of smoke and then, unbelievably, nothing, absolutely nothing.

Captain Hoover was standing beside me, or perhaps more properly, I was standing beside him, and he said:

"My God, I can't believe it."

We had no antisubmarine protection. It was obviously a submarine that hit. The one destroyer that we had leading us had been hit on the fantail and it looked like a bunch of mosquitoes had gotten in there and chewed it all to pieces. She had no depth charges, no nothing. And, of course, the only sensible thing to do was to get the hell out of there as fast as we could.

Prior to that time - prior to the torpedo attack, we had stopped for a short time to have Juneau transfer her doctor and we transferred our doctor over to San Francisco to take care of the wounded. Again, miraculously, Helena had only minor damage in the stack. She'd been hit amidships a little bit, but her armament hadn't been impaired at all. One 6-inch gun I think was out of commission, but there had been reasonably light damage. As I said, San Francisco was a shambles. Juneau had but one engine, and, of course, that transfer saved that doctor's life.

There's quite a command story involved in this because Captain Hoover was then, as he had been, the senior officer of the task force, and he rightfully, in my view, saw no chances of survivors. We had no effective ASW protection of any sort. To have even stopped and looked would, in my view, have been the utmost folly.

Q: You'd have been the next one!

Adm. C.: Of course! We made the best possible speed San Francisco could safely make, steaming toward Espiritu.

Perhaps you are familiar with the fact that he was severely criticized for his failure to pick up survivors. How anyone could have criticized his decision is unbelievable. It turned out that either seven or eleven, I've forgotten the precise figure, were picked up many days later in pretty sad shape. But how any survivors could have ever gone through that explosion I'll never know. Of course, as I said, Captain Hoover was severely criticized and later relieved of his command.

Q: For that so-called failure?

Adm. C.: Yes. Again, in my view, he was one of the most bril-

Chew #2 - 63

liant naval officers we had. He was a fine leader, the crew was devoted to him, he had earned two Navy Crosses as a squadron commander prior to taking command of Helena, and I think - well, I know I, a grown man, cried when he left the ship.

Q: Was anything ever learned about the Japanese submarine that launched that torpedo?

Adm. C.: We never saw it. But, oh, one other thing too that again made me feel that the decision to relieve him was completely erroneous was that about an hour after that, after the Juneau had been sunk, a B-17 passed overhead laboriously - and I mean it was laboriously, we sent a message by flashing light to the B-17 to tell of the tragedy, and ask him to report it to the Fleet Commander. It reminded me of the Battle of Jutland and the Queen Mary - wasn't it the Queen Mary that blew up and the Queen Elizabeth went right over the spot? Well, that could have happened. I wouldn't have believed it but, by God, it did happen.

We sent this message via the B-17 to tell of the fate of Juneau and our predicament, which was pretty sad by then with the San Francisco limping along her decks practically awash, and our destroyers down to nothing. The message was never received!

I think it's of interest to note that later on - and how many months later on I don't know - Gilbert Hoover's actions were completely vindicated by Admiral Nimitz. But the damage had been done.

Q: Nimitz, you mean, in reviewing the whole - ?

Adm. C.: In reviewing the whole thing, but the damage had been done, he'd been relieved by Halsey, who was at that time the fleet commander. Just incidentally - should I name names now?

Q: Oh, surely.

Adm. C.: Allright, The chief of staff was Miles Browning. I think it was at his instigation that the recommendation was made to relieve him. We were sick about the whole thing. It's one of those cases in the Navy that prevented a brilliant man from becoming a flag officer. He had the capabilities. I think he was of the vintage that produced so many. I don't know whether he was a classmate of Bill Kitt's, but a great many of them made flag rank along in there, and he was one of the most competent. But as a result of the Juneau affair he was prevented from making it. And even though, as I said, he was later vindicated by Admiral Nimitz, it was too late. It was very sad.

Q: One of the fallacies of the system?

Adm. C.: Yes, but understandable, completely understandable, and possibly due to personalities. You can't tell, but it's been ever thus.

One thing that I mentioned earlier and, in terms of chronology, I can't quite remember whether it was after November but it had its humerous aspects, although the net result of the action was sad. We were in a task force with Wasp when she was torpedoed. I was on the open bridge at the time. It obviously was after the Battle of Guadalcanal because the captain was Captain Reed. I remember his coming to the open bridge. I'd been on watch at the time since we were in an antiaircraft alert condition and there was the Wasp belching black smoke, and he said: "Where are the airplanes?" And I said," "Captain, there aren't any airplanes. That's from a submarine."

So he said: "Get the antiaircraft batteries ready," and I said, "They're ready, but that's a submarine and I suggest we get the hell out of here or at least do whatever you think best, but I wouldn't stick around and get one in us, too."

Well, it so happened we all stuck around and, since we did have destroyers with us, we were able to "contain" the submarine. However, we lost Wasp. If you remember, we had to put torpedoes in her ourselves to get rid of her.

Q: Yes.

Adm. C.: After taking off survivors. That was related to my previous comment about running out of clothes. We took aboard, I've forgotten whether it was 400 or 600 survivors of Wasp in <u>Helena</u>. We took them to Espiritu and, of course, some of them were in pretty sad shape as regards their wardrobe, so most of our crew gave up suits of whites or dungarees, or whatever was necessary to clothe them. So, in addition to not having ammunition by that time and not too much food, we didn't have many clothes either.

In fact, prior to that time, Gilbert Hoover had said: "Look we've got to make a stronger pitch for this because obviously we can't fight either on an empty stomach or with empty guns."

Q: What was the state of the base at Espiritu?

Adm. C.: Well, it lives rather vividly in my memory because when we first got there it was nothing. Its chief inhabitants, aside from the ships that were there, which were not too many either, were the tremendous bats that used to fly from the main island of Espiritu over to a smaller island. They'd do it at night and they were a marvelous sight to see, but it was eerie. They must have had $2\frac{1}{2}$ feet or 3 feet wing spreads, and every night they'd fly from one island to the other. It was not comforting but I suppose if you don't have a thing about bats, why, you can live with it.

Q: Most people do!

Adm. C.: I do. Well, in answer to your question as to the state of the base, it was built rather rapidly from nothing by the Seabees. They put down pierced-steel planking for the runway, and the storage facilities were open spaces under the palm trees or Quonset huts. They eventually had a sick bay and even Navy nurses. We had a marvelous surgeon on board, who became a captain and was later head of the hospital in Sasebo when I commanded <u>Roanoke</u> out in WestPac. I said to him one day "Hey Doc, we've got dollies on Espiritu Santo, what do you think of that? Navy nurses." He said, "I don't think very much of it. You watch! They're going to be nothing but trouble." I don't think he was completely accurate, but I think he had a thing about Navy nurses in forward areas and he probably made a pretty good analysis of the situation. But it was always amusing to me that he thought that they could have gotten along without them and it would have been better to have some good corpsmen. That's an aside of no significance whatsoever, and probably in today's era of women's lib, unprintable!

But the base itself was a sprawling base, as in most places in the South Pacific. In Vietnam now you see piles of ammunition under the palm trees as we did in Noumea and in Espiritu. You'd see supplies of 5-inch shells stacked up under a palm tree, and I thought after the war, it's going to take a long time to get rid of them if they don't shoot them up. In that particular area I think they were successful in shooting them up. In other areas I'm sure they had the problem that I anticipated. Again, back to my logistics. Although I'm not a logistician, Mr. Mason, believe me, I'm acutely aware of the problems.

Q: I was thinking in terms of repair facilities there, too?

Adm. C.: Oh, the repair facilities consisted of a tender. I've forgotten which one was there. They varied. After the Battle of Guadalcanal we were fortunate enough to be ordered to Sydney - well, this rather answers part of your repair question. We couldn't have our termite job and our superstructure sewed up adequately at Espiritu. There were no other places available, so we were sent to Sydney. Plus the fact that our bottom was pretty foul by then. We'd been running for quite some time. We went into Cockatoo Dock in Sydney and had a week of typical leave liberty and recreation. It was a great rest for the crew. Everybody enjoyed it, as everybody enjoys Sydney that I've ever heard of in the U. S. Navy. Maybe there are some misfits, but very few that I know of.

After Sydney we went back up on the line. Still I would say our mission was the protection of the troops on Guadalcanal. We saw the Marines leave but they were relieved by the Army. We were part of that operation. We were a part of numerous air attacks, as we steamed up and down the Slot, and one I think of historic significance in terms of equipment. As I said earlier, we had good fire-control radars, a fine battery, a well-trained crew, and we were chosen - I say with pardonable pride and I think justifiably - to make the first combat tests on the then very hush-hush and now very common VT fuses.

The officer who was sent out to witness the combat test was none other than the famous Deke Parsons, who was the rider, I guess, of the Enola Gay when she dropped her first atomic bomb. He came aboard with our first load of VTs and we were up in the Slot. I've forgotten just the reason why - oh, in addition to our night actions, we had periodic shell bombardments of the Japanese positions, but that was so routine that I even forgot to mention it. It was a little harrowing because you never knew what was going to happen - whether there would be a submarine in the place -

Q: How far did you stand off?

Adm. C.: We stood off about 6,000 yards, and we had a very fine and very easily defined demarcation line that we'd shoot to the north of this area or to the south of that area, and we normally shot a barrage coverage type action, tearing up the trees and hoping that there were Japs there. Our fire was controlled pretty much by a forward observer on the beach. As I say, we participated in a number of these, so many that I've sort of forgotten. As the positions became more secure on Guadalcanal, we started to go and bombard further up, but I digressed a minute from the story about the VT fuses.

We had Leander as a part of our task force.

Q: That's the New Zealander?

Adm. C.: The New Zealander, and I've forgotten what other ships. Suddenly out of the sky, bang, came a dive bomber and he hit the Leander right on the after turret and blew it all to hell. But as he pulled out of the dive - I can remember that guy, seeing him so well, we were ready and we started in with a VT fuse and we got him on the first three shots: Deke Parsons said, "Boy, this beats target practice all to hell." We downed, I think, three planes that day with the VT. Of course, this was a great boon to our antiaircraft defenses, tremendous, and we were, of course, very proud of ourselves. We thought that we were the greatest thing since canned beer.

I was proud of our battery. I was, of course, the assistant gunnery officer with the antiaircraft officer, and this was truly an innovation in antiaircraft fire. But as I started to say, our bombardments shifted from Guadalcanal as the positions there became more secure, and really I would say that the back was broken of any serious attempts to reinforce the Japanese after the Battle of Guadalcanal on November 13th. There were a few sporadic efforts, but none the magnitude of the reinforcement after that night. And, of course, they had one or two battleships at the time and that's what did all the damage to the <u>San Francisco</u>.

We fortunately - well, we obviously were noticed because one of the more humorous aspects of just after we opened fire, a searchlight, fortunately on our port side, opened right up on us and one of the clowns on the bridge doffed his hat as if he were a performer on a stage. And I said:

"For Christ's sake, get on that and shoot it out." And the next salvo, out went the light, there was a hell of a big explosion and a lot went with it. So we were very fortunate there.

Getting back to the bombardments. I didn't mind the ones at Guadalcanal because we probably had our friends around if anything did happen, but we started going up into Kula Gulf, and Kula Gulf was like a wash basin. There was Kolombangara on one side - well Kolombangara was the big one with the mountains, and I'd have to look at the map to think of the other one. We'd go in a circular course around the gulf, bombarding the air strips. We'd do it one way one time and then do it counter-clockwise the next time. Just as an aside, Admiral Taussig's daughter's husband was killed on one of those forays in Kula Gulf, on <u>De Haven</u>, I believe, when she was hit by submarine torpedoes. We made a fairly straight run, particularly during our bombardment periods and were sitting ducks for submarines. We were easily discernible, although we had good Black Cat - you remember, those were the PBYs that were painted all black and were our night scouting planes - we had good Black Cat coverage as we would go up and down the Slot. We were never quite sure what we would meet and we were also getting a little bit further away from any friends because there were none there at all.

The destroyers, some of them, used to come in on the other side of the bases, bombard through the channel entrance on the other side - I'll have to look at the map. I should have done that first so that I'd know the names - but, of course that's really where we met our end, going up again on what could have been a bombardment mission but also to intercept some destroyers that were coming down. Admiral Ainsworth was then the task force commander, and I think in the ensuing months we'd learned a lot - the commanders had learned a lot. We relied more on our radar, we trusted it more, and we were better able to interpret it. We were better able to discern false echoes - in fact, we were just more competent primarily because we were more battle-experienced. I doubt if there has been any other ship - maybe I'm bragging a bit - that had the combat experience at that particular time that Helena had - numerous antiaircraft attacks, many shore bombardments, and two major night actions. We all felt more confident.

Q: Well, you'd had a baptism of fire!

Adm. C.: We'd had a tremendous baptism of fire and been fairly lucky, and although I felt after our return from Sydney, we couldn't keep this up forever without getting hit. I hoped that it might be minor in nature and not of such significance that it would send us to the bottom. But we had gone up again and this time, I think, our adversaries were only destroyers. I don't think at that time we really had appreciated the tremendous significance or tremendous power of those Japanese torpedoes, one of which sits outside the armory at the Academy. We were thinking in terms of our old 21-inch torpedoes that could run 6,000 or 8,000 yards at slower speeds than the Japanese. We didn't anticipate nor did we expect the violence of the explosions. We detected them on our radar. By this time, we had Honolulu and St. Louis with us as well as Nicholas, O'Bannon, Radford and Jenkins, and, I thought we were well in command of the situation. I think it had been Admiral Ainsworth's plan to turn prior to reaching the critical torpedo range, but he did it too slowly, and didn't turn in time.

Wait a minute, Jack, when I came back to the Naval Academy after the sinking of Helena, I gave a talk to the first classmen. It was published in the Institute Proceedings in August 1945 and is more accurate than my memory is 30 years later. Let's use that for this part of my story.

* At that time, for security reasons, there were a few things I couldn't mention such as the coast watchers, but we can discuss that later on.

Note: The quote from the article in PROCEEDINGS - pages 73-107.

We steamed to the south of the New Georgia Islands all day on July 6, 1943, and had some much needed rest after recent engagements with the Japs. In fact, I went so far as to shave. This I feel I never should have done, for in so doing I broke one of the rules of my superstitious ritual on board ship, which was never to shave before going into battle. I believe the average sailor is superstitious. I know that I am. I had a set routine which I went through every day. I wore a pair of old brown shoes to which I had become particularly attached. I always wore a flash-proof jumper which I had had on at Pearl Harbor. I thought it would bring me good luck and would not consent to its being washed in spite of the unpleasant odor which it had developed. I was never without the ordinary hunting knife which my wife had sent me. I carried my wallet which contained the usual odds and ends together with my wife's picture and the picture of my daughter. It also contained a four-leaf clover, which my wife's mother had sent me from California. Before going into battle, I always gave my wife's picture a husbandly peck.

Late in the afternoon word came that the "Tokyo Express," a variable force ranging from two or three destroyers to several destroyers and one or more cruisers, was on its way again down the "Slot." This was the V-shaped landlocked body of water extending from Bougainville to Guadalcanal and Tulagi. We were ordered forthwith to turn around and go up to meet the Japs. We had not had enough rest, for it was difficult to sleep in the daytime because of the heat. It cooled off very little on shipboard until three o'clock in the morning. The steel plates retained the tropical heat of the day that long, and made it almost unbearably hot below decks 24 hours a day.

To return a moment to the subject of superstition, I was for once in my life not completely afraid this time on the eve of battle. To say that I was not without fear would be a gross exaggeration, but comparatively speaking, this time I was going into action with little apprehension. Previously we had always been pessimistic as to the outcome of our bouts with the Japs. This time I thought we had everything to our advantage. We had an experienced strong task force, and we were just going to lick hell out of them. We had also come to regard the <u>Helena</u> as a lucky ship. The number thirteen had appeared with an amazing frequency in the affairs of this ship and her task force. Our ship's doctor, Commander Ivan King, (M.C.), U. S. Navy, an amateur numerologist, worked out a long list of examples of this, most of which I have forgotten. In the battle of November 13, the previous year, we had in our force thirteen ships, and the last destroyer had the number 445, the sum of which amounts to thirteen. Besides she was named after a man whose middle name was Friday, Frank Friday Fletcher, and she had thirteen officers on board. We opened fire in that battle at 0148, also making the sum of thirteen. Up to our last battle, we had had a total of two surface engagements, four air attacks, and six bombardments. One more would be, we thought, the lucky thirteenth. So we confidently steamed into the night ready to meet the enemy.

We picked up the Japs about 0157, making the sum of our lucky thirteen again. But this number was soon to cease being our ship's talisman, though the luck of some of us was to continue after the Helena was hit by three torpedoes from Jap destroyers. The first torpedo took the bow off, complete with number one turret. The second and third struck us amidships. The noise of the battle was deafening enough, but the shock from the explosions of the torpedoes was terrific. As assistant Gunnery Officer, I was in charge of the anti-aircraft batteries. I was at my station, and was thrown against the overhead, but was not injured because of my steel helmet. There were numerous instances of men having their teeth knocked out and of broken bones and bruises and cuts. A column of water, possibly 150 feet high, went up over the bridge. One of the men thought we were sinking, because the water came into the top hatch. I was stationed just behind the bridge about amidships. After the noise of battle and the subsequent explosions of the torpedoes subsided, the silence which followed was something I shall never forget.

Most of us immediately realized that the ship was done for. I was ordered to get the life rafts off the forecastle. Fortunately there was no fire, and as far as I know there were no explosions of any sort following the torpedo hits. With the power gone, it became pitch black. Most of us carried little emergency flashlights with us, but we did not want to make too caused this sickness. I had a beautiful handle-bar moustache, which turned out to be a great handicap. It became completely saturated with oil after I got into the water. Every time I breathed I got the smell of that oil. I will never wear another moustache! Several of our officers had them. Lieutenant Richard Lull Cochrane had a fiery red one, which he always claimed was longer than mine, but I was sure that mine was at least more bushy. Very few had full beards. They were too uncomfortable in the heat of the tropics.

There were no rafts in our group, and very little wreckage floating around that the men could take hold of. Besides it was very dark; this made it difficult to see anything on the water. Strangely, the next day I saw a letter floating on the water, which had been written to the Gunnery Officer. I remember having seen only one piece of wood. We had removed all wooden articles on board the ship before the battle. There was practically nothing left on the Helena that would float except the rafts. If we had had a line, it would have been of great aid to use in keeping our group together. As it turned out, men were continually drifting away from the group, and Lieutenant Commander Warren Boles repeatedly swam out to find them and bring them back. We doubtless lost several men that way during the first night. Of course, some of them had been injured and others were suffering from shock, but on the whole most of us were in fairly good shape. We sang some songs, such as "Hail! Hail! the Gang's All Here," to keep up our spirits. There was also a lot of yelling and shouting to attract the notice of rescuers. I tried to signal one of the destroyers with my emergency flashlight, which continued to work for several hours after the sinking of our ship. Some destroyers came by us, but, after we had signaled and been discovered, the destroyer would be a mile or so beyond us. There being men scattered all about, they simply picked up those nearest to them. In fact, one destroyer nearly ran us down in the darkness. Rescuing survivors in enemy waters is a particularly hazardous undertaking, and our destroyers did a magnificent job in picking up as many as they did. As always, there was danger of enemy submarines, and in addition there were still enemy surface vessels in that area. Indeed, during the rescue operations it was necessary to delay picking up survivors in order to engage additional enemy ships.

Early the next morning, I found it difficult to see because of the oil that had gotten into my eyes. It was similar to the sensation of having soap in one's eyes-soap which one was unable to remove. About dawn we sighted a ship. She was an injured Japanese destroyer which had hidden in the lee of an island and was attempting to make a get-away. Our destroyers discovered her, and we soon found ourselves in the middle of a battle with the projectiles flying over us. We did what we had been instructed to do when underwater explosions occurred; we lay on our backs and crossed our legs to keep from being injured internally. One of our destroyers went past us at high speed, but could not pick us up. Finally the Japanese destroyer was hit and began to smoke furiously. We could not see very well from the surface of the water because of the oil in our eyes and the continuous bobbing of the waves.

Then in the early morning light, to our astonishment, we discovered that the bow of the <u>Helena</u> was still floating. I left my group and swam over to it. There were a few men hanging on to it, and some were even on top of it. This floating remnant of the ship was about 50 feet long, and its deck stood about 20 feet above the water. I was too nearly exhausted to pull myself upon it. There were some chains attached to it, and I was able to hang on to one of these and get some much needed rest. I concluded that, if we were sighted at all from the air, the floating bow would be the first object to be seen. And so it happened. About ten o'clock a Liberator flew over us and dropped three rubber boats. One sank, but we recovered the other two. There were no supplies nor medicines with the boats, but fortunately all our officers, medical corpsmen, and pharmacist mates always carried with them morphine surrettes or hypodermic needles for emergency relief in case of injury. These were to be of use to us. The rubber boats unfortunately were large enough to hold only about four men comfortably. By that time all the members of our group had swum to the vicinity of the floating bow. They had been reduced to about 50 in number. We had one man with a broken leg, and another with two broken arms and two broken legs. Chaplain H.J.R. Wheaton was suffering severely from shock. He had been in the lower part of the ship when she was hit and had managed to get out through an escape hatch. Another man was suffering severely from cramps, possibly caused by shock. We placed our sick and injured men in the rubber boats.

I began to realize that the floating bow, instead of being a place of refuge for us, might turn out to be the opposite. Jap planes were likely to come along soon, and either bomb or strafe us. In fact, a few came over us later, and one actually fired a burst in the water. Why they did not fire into us I shall never know. Perhaps they could not tell us from Japanese survivors because we were black with oil which completely covered us. I decided to get away as soon as possible, and try to reach the island of Kolumbangara, which was only about 8 or 9 miles distant, I thought. I had previously studied the charts of that area, and knew that the island was occupied by the Japanese; but I hoped that we might land at night and then eventually make our way to our forces on New Georgia.

The two rubber boats were tied together with a line. With our sick and wounded placed in them, we pushed off from the floating bow about eleven o'clock in the morning. I understand that it sank later that afternoon. All that day we slowly made our way toward Kolumbangara. We had had no food nor water to drink since we left our ship. The ship's rafts had food, water, and medical supplies; but the rubber boats had none of these. We developed a system, according to which each man had his turn at resting on one of the boats. With the number of men we had, this amounted to only about ten minutes of rest to about two hours in the water. As one of our men who had been taking his turn on a boat slid over the side to begin swimming again, his knife caught on the boat and cut a hole in the rubber. We all thought this was indeed the end. But providentially there was a pump and a patching outfit in the boat; so with these we proceeded to try to stop the leak. This repairing outfit was practically the same as that used in mending an autbmobile inner tube. It included a patch and a tube of cement. We took turns with our knives, our teeth, and our fingernails at trying to get the cover off the patch, but it would not budge. In the meantime the air was leaking out; the boat had partially sunk and was rapidly filling with water. In our desperation we placed the patch over the hole with the cover still on, plastered the cut with cement, and pumped up the boat. Lo and behold, the raft held! We all heaved a sigh of relief. Sudenly one of the men cried, "There goes the patch!" It just floated away. I think some of us offered a few prayers then. To our amazement, the boat did not sink. What must have happened was that the hole in the inner tube and the hole in the casing became displaced in such a way as to seal up the cut and prevent the boat from leaking. After that, we did not have any more trouble with it. Incidentally, that night we said the Lord's Prayer as best we could all together.

During the second night we tried to make Kolumbangara. We could see the outline of the island in the dark, and the next morning it was quite clear to us. It is almost circular and has a mountain rising from its center, about 6,500 feet high. Its great height no doubt led us to misjudge our distance from it the previous day. Not only was the island held by the Japanese, but we learned later that it was their main base in the New Georgia group. Since we had a good breeze blowing up the "Slot" that morning, I decided to try to reach Vella Lavella. I knew this island was also occupied by the Japs, but I thought there might be fewer of them there and our chances of survival better than on Kolumbangara.

With each boat was a couple of poles intended to be used as paddles. We lashed two of them together in the form of a crosstree, and improvised sails by taking off our shirts and tying them by the sleeves to the poles. By that time the men had become greatly discouraged because they had been in the water more than 24 hours without any food or drink. The Helena sank about 0230 on Tuesday morning and it was then daylight on Wednesday. Our number had been further reduced. The man with the two broken arms and two broken legs had died the preceding day, and several more had drifted away and been lost during the night. One man died of shock or cramps, quite unexpectedly to me, just after he had been given a rest in one of the boats and was getting into the water again.

When we got under way on the new course toward Vella Lavella under a good breeze, the spirits of the men rose and they seemed more hopeful. The boats were no longer tied together. One seemed to make a little better time than the other, and I told Lieutenant (j.g.) J. B. Anderson, who was in charge of that boat, to go ahead and try to make the island. That morning a crate of potatoes floated near us. We opened it and ate the potatoes raw, after considerable discussion as to their probable effects on us. Some of the men were refreshed by the water they contained. But the only effect on me was that they made me sick. Strangely enough, on the second day I was not thirsty, and I did not hear any of the men speak of wanting water. Possibly, as a doctor suggested later to me, some water had been absorbed into our systems, particularly through the wrists. Few of us had been out of the water for more than very short periods.

For some time Vella Lavella had been clearly visible in the far distance; but we found it impossible to reach the island on Wednesday evening and were forced to spend another night in the water. By Thursday morning, most of us were getting near the point of exhaustion. I thought the island was then only 2 miles distant from us. That was a mistake, for it turned out to be 6 or 7 miles away. To us in the water it looked like a very desirable place to reach. Beyond its beaches could be seen the green jungles reaching to mountains about 2,500 feet in height. The island, I afterwards estimated, was approximately 25 miles from the place where we last saw the floating bow of the Helena. I decided early Thursday morning that I wought to try to swim to the island where I might possibly get aid from the natives in rescuing my men. I asked if anyone would like to try to make the attempt with me. Lieutenant Commander Boles and T. E. Blahnik, Boatswain's Mate Second Class, agreed to join me. Boles was a typical New Englander, who took things in stride; he was a very strong man and an excellent swimmer.

We still had on most of our clothing, though by that time it was completely oil-soaked. The water near the floating bow had been free of oil, but we repeatedly were running into large quantities of it. I remember swimming through one patch, late Thursday afternoon, 200 or 300 yards wide. It was this oil and not the sharks that caused most of our trouble. But probably it protected us from the sharks. It is possible they do not like their food served with a heavy oil dressing. I saw some of them, and our marine officer, Major B. F. Kelly, had a shark take a nibble at his foot. Somehow, after we had been in the water for many hours, we did not seem to give much thought to the sharks. I think our uppermost thought was how to get our boats to land. Of course, we thought of food too; and we worried about our families and what they would think if we were reported missing.

Lieutenant Commander Boles, Blahnik, and I started swimming toward Vella Lavella about six or seven o'clock that Thursday morning. I had by that time discarded my life jacket. It was very heavy with oil and water, and had but little buoyancy left. By adjusting my life belt around my chest I could rest much more comfortably and swim more easily. I swam breast stroke, as did the other men. The men around the boats just paddled along, though some of them varied their swimming by using the side stroke, or an occasional dog paddle. It turned out to be a long, long swim for the three of us. Sometimes I must have been only half awake, as I found myself more than once swimming in the wrong direction. I began to have hallucinations, or perhaps I was dreaming. Repeatedly I thought I was to meet a man who was to take me to a cocktail party at the Residency.

I had heard that name applied to a British Government House somewhere. I even found myself diving and swimming under water to meet this man. Blahnik, later, told me that he had a similar experience. He said that he was swimming under water to meet a man who, he thought, was going to rent him a bunk for two bits. A part of the time during this long swim I must have been completely out of my mind. We swam on and on and on until about four in the afternoon-approximately ten hours. And we had thought we were practically exhausted when we started!

As we approached the island in the later afternoon, I saw a canoe coming out from the beach with two natives in it. They took one look at me when they came alongside, examined my identification tag, and asked, "You Melican?"

I replied, "You betcha!" And the next thing I remember I was on the beach, where I found that a few of our men had arrived already on some of the Helena's rafts. The next thing I recall, a native was giving me a drink of coconut milk from a shell. It tasted like the nectar of the Gods; it was wonderful. I had had no food nor drink since the sinking of our ship very early on Tuesday morning; it was then late Thursday afternoon about 62 hours later.

Meanwhile the natives in their canoes picked up our rubber boats and brought them with the other survivors to the beach. Boles and Blahnik had reached the island just ahead of me. After my drink of coconut milk, I found a pool of fresh water and went into it with my clothes on to try to wash off the oil.

Providentially we had landed on the beach opposite the side of the island where the Japanese garrison headquarters was located. Fortunately there were none of their patrols out at that time on the side of the island where we landed. It is remarkable that the Japs did not discover us as we swam toward the island that afternoon, but we were very small objects out at sea. Apparently the natives did not see us either until we were quite close to the beach.

When we were finally ready to leave the shore for a hide-away in the hills, a native asked me if I thought I could walk. I said, "Sure!," got to my feet, and immediately fell flat on my face. Then I was placed in one of the litters of copra bags and poles which had been made for those too weak to walk, and was carried up into the hills.

The natives took us about $2\frac{1}{2}$ miles from the beach. It was a pleasant excursion for those of us in the litters who were merely too weak to walk, but tough going for the others. First it was necessary to cross a thick swampy jungle, into which one sank up to the knees. Then we followed a very rough winding trail along the mountain side. The island had been occupied by the Japs for about a year and a half. When they first came, they killed 25 or 30 of the natives for no apparent reason. This wanton murder fostered a deep hatred of the Japs, and the natives abandoned their villages along the beach and sought relative safety in the hills. Before Vella Lavella was invaded, the natives supported themselves largely by raising coconuts and selling them to island traders. They are also fishermen, and most villagers had small garden plots. All these had to be abandoned when they retreated into the bush.

Fortunately for us these natives were not cannibals. They had been converted to Christianity by Protestant missionaries, Baptists from New Zealand, I believe. Their headquarters had been at Munda. They had translated the Bible into the native dialect, called Roviana. The language was not unpleasant to the ear, though it was somewhat gutteral and the sound "mb" was frequently repeated. With us the natives talked Pidgin English, the general language of the South Seas. This is a mixture of English and the native tongue, or a very simplified native adaptation of English. Our friendly islanders were reasonably well civilized. They were having considerable trouble because of the Japanese invasion, for they had been dependent upon the inter-island steamers for salt and their supply had become exhausted. They had, in other respects also, been reduced to the barest essentials of primitive life.

The natives had a hard time moving our 104 exhausted men into the hills. They took us up to Tom's house, around which we established our camp. Tom was a Chinese, who became our strong defender. We found that there were about 35 Chinese on the island, who had been traders before the Japs came. They had fled to the hills along with the natives, probably in advance of them. Tom's cottage, which he placed at our disposal, looked like a typical summer vacation shack on Chesapeake Bay. It had a porch and a galvanized tin roof. There was only one room, in which was one large bed and another smaller one. On the porch was a cot. There were, of course, no modern conveniences, such as a kitchen and bathroom. But Tom had a table, a couple of chairs, one or two spoons, and, believe it or not, a clock, which had been made in Hongkong, according to an inscription on its face. As far as I remember, we had only one watch among the survivors which was still running after being so long in the water. It was a self-winding wrist watch, and kept perfect time. We placed our three wounded and ill men on the beds. Nine or ten more men slept on the floor in the house and on the porch.

Adjacent to Tom's shack was a small native hut of a rather strange construction. It looked like a chicken house. The front was open, and it stood above the ground about 2 feet. One side was raised another foot or so. It had grass or rattan walls except in the front which was entirely open. There was also a sort of a little porch, directly behind which was a room completely closed off except for a door. Maybe this was for the women, who we learned were kept quite secluded by the men of the island. Strangely enough, we never saw one woman the entire time we were there on Vella Lavella. The native house, though it looked like an open front hen house, was very comfortable with floors of split bamboo or of similar material. In this house about 30 of our men slept on the floor. The natives have no chimneys for their houses, but build a fire inside the main room. The smoke goes out the door or through the cracks. We did not need any fire, even at night. It was just cool enough to make the cover of a burlap copra bag seem comfortable.

The natives came the next morning after our arrival, and hacked off some palm leaves with their knives, cut down some poles, lashed all these together with vines, and put up one half of a lean-to. Then they quietly went away. It looked as though they were members of some labor union with extremely limited hours for working. But the next day they returned and finished the job. Under this grass or thatched roof the rest of our men slept. These three strangely assorted buildings constituted our quarters while we remained on the island.

The only natives whom I learned by sight were the chief and two others, who were very helpful to us. I had no fear of the islanders, except a slight uneasy feeling when some of the older people were around, who I imagined eyed us as if they were wondering how well we might taste in a stew. Previous to 1912 when the missions were first established on the island, cannibalism had been practiced by the natives. Although very black, our islanders were the counterparts of some white people that I had seen. Of course, their noses were flat and their hair was bushy, and one's imagination had to be stretched a bit to discover any likenesses, still as our saviors they looked mighty good to us. We estimated that there were about 3,000 natives on the island. Vella Lavella is one of the Solomons which belong to the great mass of islands known as Melanesia. The Gilberts, the Marshalls, and the Carolines belong to the basic Micronesian group of islands. The Samoans belong to another large and more highly civilized group known as Polynesians. The latter are very hospitable, and as a mark of their hospitality turn over to a visiting dignitary a number of their women. But that was not the custom of our islanders. Besides, we were not exactly what might be called "visiting dignitaries."

Our food problem was one of our major difficulties. As the natives had given up their farming plots and their coconut groves along the beach, they were short of food themselves; but they managed somehow to bring us potatoes, taro root, and tapioca from their meager supplies. The taro root looks like a big potato, but it has an indescribable taste unlike that of any other vegetable I have eaten. There are two varieties, one red and one white. We did not have a chance to taste individual vegetables much, for we collected all these strange foods and threw them into a big pot. This native pot, incidentally, looked just like the ones I had often seen in cartoons in which cannibals were roasting missionaries. Possibly it had served that purpose in years gone by; but when we fell heir to it, I think it had recently been used for boiling clothes. Our men who had escaped to the island on rafts brought some of our emergency rations. These included canned meat, somewhat like spam. One can of this was supposed to be enough for four men per day. But we had so little food that we issued only four cans a day for 104 men. This meat we threw into the pot with the other stuff, and made a kind of weak stew. For flavoring we had one small piece of rock salt which we found in

Tom's cottage; but this did not last long. We found two or three kinds of aromatic leaves which we thought improved the stew a little. The natives also brought us papayas and bananas. This fruit, if ripe, we gave to our invalids. The green fruit we found we could eat when it was cooked; so this also went into the stew. With such limited food supplies, we could have but two meals a day, and only stew for each meal. The men used coconut shells as dishes, but we did not have enough of these to go around; so we ate in relays, but did not bother to wash the shells until after each meal. Most of the men still had their knives with which they made themselves wooden spoons.

We had one real feast while on the island. There were some cattle in the hills, we were told; but they were wild and could not be secured without being shot. We were not strong enough to go cattle hunting, and besides, the Jap patrols were between us and the cattle. But some of the natives managed to kill a cow. They had difficulty in getting the meat to us because of the Japanese, but at last two groups of our friends got over the hills, each carrying a joint of beef in a sling made of palm leaves. We had no way of preserving this meat; so it all went into our pot, and we had a grand one-course banquet. There was one joint of meat that was exceptionally high. I inquired of J. L. Johnson, S1/c, our head cook, "What do you think about it?"

He replied, "I don't think we had better take a chance on it." So we gave it a decent burial. But that night, B.G.

Atkinson, MM2/c, a pleasant sort of fellow who had lived a very rough life as a miner in the Yukon, asked me what we had done with the piece of meat.

After I told him, he said, "Give it to me and I'll fix it." I consented, and we disinterred the meat. He washed it off and cooked it for about two days, making the most delicious broth you ever put in your mouth. At least, that is how it tasted to half-starved men. After having this one good meal of beef, we all felt that life was really worth living.

Our water problem was quite simple. Tom had put galvanized iron gutters on his cottage, which conducted the rain water into a barrel. As it rained about three times a day, the barrel was always practically full. There was a stream at the foot of the hill below our encampment. As mayor of our town, I had made a law that only those who could carry a breaker filled with water back up the hill to camp would be permitted to go to the stream. Every one wanted to go down there to bathe, but I was somewhat afraid they might be discovered by the Jap patrols. These water breakers were wooden barrels with a tap on one end for drawing water. They had been brought to the island on the ship's rafts. When full of water, each weighed about 50 pounds. Very few of our men at that time were strong enough to carry that much weight up the hill, although the distance was but a mile and a half. I succeeded in doing it, but it took me fully a day and half to recover from the effort.

Very fortunately for us, five 25-pound cans of coffee washed up on the beach below our camp. This was a luxury which helped greatly to sustain the morale of our men, as we had no cigarettes nor chewing tobacco - a great deprivation. Tom had a book of Chinese cigarette papers in his cottage, and one day one of the men came up to me and said,"How about a cigarette paper, sir?"

I replied, "Fine, but what for?"

"Well," he said, "I am going to make a cigarette out of coffee. Would you like to try one?"

I excused myself by saying,"I have given up smoking for a while." So he made coffee cigarettes for himself. Later one of the natives brought us a twist of tobacco, which had been grown on the island. It was the strongest I had ever tasted and hardly suitable for cigarettes. The men, after trying it, decided to mix the tobacco half and half with the coffee. This was an entirely new blend, I assure you. They would smoke these cigarettes down to the point where they had to get a piece of straw with which to extract the last puff of smoke.

When we first arrived on the island, we were all suffering from an ailment known as "immersion ankles." These sores, which made walking very painful, were caused by our being so long in the water. After cleansing the open sores, the medical corpsmen treated them as well as they could with sulfa powder. We had some medical supplies which had been brought to the island on the rafts from the Helena. The corpsmen rendered invaluable aid to us. They made a syringe with which they washed out the men's ears and removed the accumulated oil. They treated the sick and the wounded man, whose broken leg they kept packed with sulfa. His wound was wide open with the bone showing, when he reached the island. They drained about a cup and a half of water from the hole. Very likely the salt water prevented gangrene from developing. Although he suffered terribly, he survived this ordeal without losing his leg. The chaplain only partially recovered from shock before we were rescued. There was another group of survivors from the <u>Helena</u> who had landed around a small point of land from us. There were 61 of them. We never saw them, but carried on communications with them through notes carried by natives. One day, the man with the stomach ailment became quite ill, and we asked a native to inquire if they had any medicine which might help him. He returned with a bottle of Scotch. It was never opened, and we left it on the island when we departed - Mr. Ripley will kindly take note. In spite of poor food, we had no dysentery or other disease of any sort. But later, after we had left the island, several of the men came down with dengue fever and malaria. The mosquitoes were very obliging. Around sunset they would come out in swarms. Once I counted about 15 on my wrist at one time. They were very active from about sunset until dark; then they would go away and did not bother us any more during the night. They never disturbed our sleep.

As mayor, I depended a great deal on Major Kelly of the

marines, whom I appointed my chief of police. He saw to it that my rules and regulations were carried out. He was also in charge of the sanitary arrangements for our encampment. These were in accordance with Marine Regulations, but he forgot that some of our men were too weak to walk 40 yards. So it became necessary to set up an emergency can in the middle of the camp. It was a large 5-gallon job lined with leaves. Then I made a regulation that any one caught defiling the camp would be punished by being forced to carry the emergency can every morning out of the camp and empty it. One poor devil about six feet two was caught by our efficient police force violating the regulation. Though very tall, he then weighed only 110 pounds and looked like a thin man in a circus. It certainly was a sight to see him with that large can on his shoulder, taking his punishment. There were no other violators of our sanitary regulations. Our laws were simple and few in number - just those necessary for safety's sake.

Major Kelly and his police force, which consisted of marines, gunner's mates, and experienced deck ratings, were in charge of the defenses of the camp. Kelly carefully placed his fire points and cover points, and kept a regular watch. No city ever boasted a more efficient police force. But our armament approached the ridiculous. We had one Jap rifle with three rounds of ammunition, and Tom had a shotgun with one shell in it. We also had a 44-caliber carbine, a Remington, a Springfield, and an English rifle with a curious assortment of ammunition varying from one round up to 30 rounds per gun. There was one 38 revolver and a 45 automatic. The 45 had its clip, and the 38 its magazine. The marine corporal, M. F. Frisbee, took charge of all these assorted firearms for "Kelly's Irregulars," as we called them.

By this time we must have looked very much like Falstaff's famous company of thieves, cutthroats, and jailbirds. My oil-soaked clothing had been discarded. Tom gave me a pair of Japanese shorts, and that was my sole article of apparel. Like most of the other men, I had made a pair of wooden go-aheads or clogs, which gave some small protection to the soles of my feet. We had very soon run out of soap. Some of the men tried to wash the oil out of their clothes by rubbing them on the rocks, but they gave this up as a hopeless job and made themselves new clothing out of burlap copra bags, furnished by the natives. A hole was cut at the top for the head and two holes on either side for the arms. A piece of vine was used to tie them around the middle. Frankly, they looked like hell.

The jungle noises at night were terrifying at first, but themen soon got used to them. I do not know what varieties of animals made those strange noises, as the only wild life we ever saw was an occasional bird. But, of course, we did not move far from our hideout, and didnot see much of the island. Our greatest fear was that of being discovered by the Japanese and of being surprised and overpowered by them. Though Major Kelly was a typical fighting Marine, and there was plenty of fight left in our men, yet in our weakened physical condition and with practically no arms, we could have put up but little resistance. We had planned, in case we were attacked, to retreat farther into the hills. We were not to attempt to fight it out, but to hold and then retreat, hold and retreat again and again until the Japs, we hoped, would give up the pursuit in fear of being ambushed. They could not afford to extend their lines of communication too far as there were only 300 to 400 of them on the island, we were told. After retreating, we planned to establish another hidden camp with the aid of the friendly natives. These islanders continually assisted us in numerous ways. There was a Jap landing boat or barge about 6 miles up the beach from us, which gave us a great deal of concern. Just what it was doing there we did not know, nor did we know if it had armed men in it. We began to imagine that the enemy knew that we were on the island and were only waiting for a favorable opportunity to pounce upon us. So we prepared for the worst.

Usually we were not much concerned about a Japanese attack at night. We did not believe that they would go into the jungles then in search of us, as they were probably afraid to go out among the natives in the darkness. They had reason to fear them, for the standard native weapon was a long sharp knife, similar to a machete. Each native always carried one of these knives with him, and held it suspended from the little finger of the right hand. I have heard that the little fingers of many of the islanders were permanently curved from this odd custom.

We established a daily routine. I tried to keep the men occupied as much of the time as possible. We got up with the sun, about six o'clock. After a prolonged period of stretching to get the kinks out after a night on the ground or on the equally hard and uncomfortable floor, we washed ourselves as well as we could without any soap. The problem of cleaning our teeth became very annoying, until we found that an excellent cleanser was a piece of lime peel. Fortunately the natives brought us a lime occasionally. Then we began to wonder when breakfast would be ready. This was one of the main events of the day. Of course, breakfast and dinner were exactly the same, but the morning meal came first and we were somewhat hungrier at that time. Breakfast was usually not ready until about ten o'clock, when Chief Cook Johnson would announce ceremoniously, "Chow is ready!" After this meal, we had to clean our wooden spoons and the coconut shell dishes. Everyone was then required to walk around the camp at least two times for exercise. After that, we proceeded to sweep the camp and put everything in shipshape order. By that time we would have the first of what we called "air raids."

Almost every day planes would pass overhead, and we would duck under cover for we did not want to be seen by either friend or foe. Our own aviators might have mistaken us for Japs and bombed us. The "air raid" would usually last about 5 or 10 minutes. There were five or six of them a day, and we became so experienced that after awhile we could tell from the sound of the motors whether the planes were Japanese or American. Occasionally we were given a special treat of an air battle, either over the island or the near-by waters. We would stand around and watch, and every time a plane was shot down we would cheer, although we could not be sure that the victor was one of our planes. Of course, we restrained our cheering when the Jap patrols were reported to be in our vicinity. By the time we had had two or three "air raids" and had gotten our camp cleaned up, it was time to begin to worry about our afternoon meal, which was usually not ready until after two o'clock.

Throughout the day there was a lot of talk about food. The men abandoned entirely the standard topic of conversation almost universally heard on shipboard-women. Instead of hearing somebody ask, "Do you remember that little blonde you saw me with at the movies in Norfolk?" all you could hear was something like this: "Do you remember that little place in San Francisco? They sure served swell steaks all smothered in onions. God! what I wouldn't give for one of those right now." The men also talked about their families, and worried about them being notified that they were missing. They had a very deep and genuine concern for their loved ones. There was not much talk about the chances of our being rescued. They did not seem to be particularly concerned. I suppose they felt, as I did, that we could stay there indefinitely. If we could have continued to get anough food, we could have survived until the island was captured by our forces about a month later.

In our camp we had a cross section of the crew of the Helena. Besides the Marines, we had pharmacist mates who were busy all day long. We had several cooks, who were not kept so busy unfortunately, and a metal smith who repaired our large copper kettle. We had a barber, seamen, fire control men, firemen, machinist mates, a turret captain, storekeepers and two yeomen. We did not have much paper work for the yeomen, I assure you. There was a chaplain too, but he remained too ill to be of much aid. Most of our men were fully and heartily co-operative, and did everything in their power to make our camp as pleasant as possible. Of course, some were more helpful than others, and some naturally were more ingenious than others. I suppose the one who contributed most to keeping our spirits up was Atkinson, the oldest man among us. He had many stories to relate. He had been a miner, and said that, as far as he was concerned, being a castaway on a Japanese-occupied island was much more pleasant than mining for gold in the Yukon.

To demonstrate how efficient our Marines were, here is a little story about Major Kelly. One day he came to me and said, "Mr. Chew, are you not in command here?"

I replied, "I suppose I am."

Then he continued, "Someone has stolen a can of our emergency meat. If I find out who it is, will you sentence him to death? If you do, I'll kill him myself."

I had made no law covering such a crime, and refused to commit myself as to the punishment. Fortunately we never discovered who stole that can of meat. But I believe my conversation with the Major got around. No more meat was stolen. Probably the guilty man had no evil design. He was doubtless so hungry that he just took it without thinking of how he was wronging the rest of the men.

Our camp was pleasantly located on the slope of a hill which was heavily wooded. The trees were large and tall, most of them rising to a height of 125 feet. I did not know their names, as I am acquainted with only common trees; such as, oak, pine, elm, cedar, and birch. They were different from all of these. Their leaves were very large, and they afforded good shade and excellent cover from the planes and the enemy patrols. Though we were not in the jungle, there was a thick undergrowth with many long tough vines, which the natives used in building their houses. The sun did not penetrate much through the trees and vines. From our camp we had only two small restricted views of the beach and the sea beyond, one to the east and another to the southeast. We were on that side of the island. The other group of survivors were to the north of us, on the opposite side of a small point from where we landed.

It was very dark in those woods after nightfall, and as we had no light we lay down to sleep early. Each day, about 5:30 in the afternoon, we held an evening prayer service. Every man in camp was always there. They needed no urging. Some of the natives whose names I knew were usually there as well as others whose names I never knew. The Chinese did not join us in these services as they usually kept pretty well to themselves. Various people led our prayers. We did not have a single English Bible among us, but the natives read from their Bibles at the services. We always sang a hymn, usually "Rock of Ages," which the natives knew. They sang in their native language and we in ours. It made an unforgettable scene in the midst of the dark green forest. I shall never forget the earnest faces of the natives as they sang. Equally serious and sincere were our men as they joined in the prayers and the singing. Shipwreck and danger, hunger and loneliness had brought most of them nearer to God than they had ever been before. Some were so overcome that they broke down and wept like little children.

On the seventh day after we reached the island, word was brought to us that we were going to be rescued. The instructions were that our group as well as the one across the point from us was to be picked up early the following Friday morning. We were to be on the beach where we had landed at four o'clock in the morning. We were ordered also to take all the Chinese on the island with us when we were evacuated.

We had a hard time getting down to the rendezvous on the beach. We started from the hills around three o'clock in the afternoon so that we might reach the beach by dark. We were afraid that, even with the native guides, we would get lost at night. It was all that we could do in the daytime to get through that jungle, which was between the hills and the beach.

It would have been impossible for us to pass through it at night. We arranged for the strongest of the able-bodied men to be stretcher-bearers for the sick and wounded. Unfortunately all the Chinese could not arrive at the meeting place at the appointed hour, but we took eleven or twelve with us. Major Kelly's "Irregulars" brought up the rear as our covering force. We did not want to get down to the beach too early, because once we arrived we could not get back into the hills again until the next day, if we were discovered by the patrols of the enemy.

Finally we got under way. Major Kelly's force marched between us and the known position of the barge and the Jap patrol. Incidentally, that barge had caused us constant anxiety while we were in camp. We had even been tempted to go down one night and try to push it off into the sea. Then one day an American plane riddled it so that it could not have been gotten off the shore.

As we were going down the hill, I lost my entire group of about one hundred people. Taking a native for a guide, I thought I would go down by a little shorter route and get to the beach somewhat ahead of the rest. When I got there and rested for awhile, I began to worry about the nonappearance of my party. I could not see them, though I knew exactly where they should be. They had seen me but thought that I was a Jap and had turned back into the jungle again. This is an excellent example of how thick that jungle was. Eventually we all got together again on the beach about an hour later just as darkness set in.

Lieutenant Commander Boles had been sent down ahead to act as a pilot for the rescue ships. He had an unusual experience He was a very large man and suffered greatly from lack of food. I gave him eight malted milk tablets, which had been among our emergency rations, to last him from three in the afternoon until four the following morning. When he arrived at the deserted village on the beach, he generously gave the tablets to some natives who happened to be there, and then lay down to get some sleep on the porch of a native hut. After a while he was awakened, and looking us, he saw eight or nine islanders. Each carried some article of food carefully wrapped in leaf slings as a token of appreciation of his generosity. For a moment he thought he was still asleep and dreaming, for there before him were baked sweet potatoes, papayas, bananas, etc. Warren told me that he had the greatest feast he ever had in his life, better even than the cow we ate in our encampment. When he had finished, he mistook the approach of our party for a large Jap patrol. He hastily scrambled into a native's canoe, and hurried away up a creek to hide in the jungle. After a while he discovered that it was a false alarm.

The plan to rescue us was a bold one. We heard later that Rear Admiral Richmond Kelly Turner initiated the plan. It was a difficult scheme, for aside from the fact that the enemy was in control of the waters around Vella Lavella and Kolumbangara the available charts of the narrow channel into the former island were unreliable. The rescue too had to be made at night because daylight would have exposed the ships to air attacks.

Captain Francis McInerney, U. S. Navy, a former neighbor of mine in Annapolis, was then commander of a destroyer squadron. He was placed in charge of the expedition. He arranged for two destroyer-transports to handle the actual rescue work and four destroyers to screen them. The transports were the *Dent*, commanded by Lieutenant Commander Ralph Wilhelm, U. S. Naval Reserve, and the *Waters*, under command of Lieutenant Commander Charles J. McWhinnie, U. S. Naval Reserve. Captain Thomas J. Ryan, U. S. Navy, commanded the destroyer screen, and Commander John D. Sweeny, U. S. Navy, the destroyer transports.

At the appointed time, Lieutenant Commander Boles went out to guide the boats to the beach. The transports moved in as far as they dared in the shallow coral-studded waters, and then Higgins boats were lowered. I assure you it was the most wonderful feeling in the world to see those boats coming in to our beach. They came rushing in with all their guns ready for a fight. Our hearts filled with pride when the full realization of what was being done dawned upon us, as we had considered ourselves as expendable. The fact that our Navy could and would attempt such a daring and hazardous undertaking under such conditions was beyond our wildest dreams.

Without any confusion, we were all quickly embarked, and

away we went from Vella Lavella. The group north of us had been picked up previously about midnight. With them was one of our Army aviators who had been shot down over the island. When I got on board a destroyer, my first thought was of food. The crew of the ship had prepared big pots of soup for us. I consumed five big bowls full, and drank I do not know, how many cups of coffee. My second desire was for a bath. I wanted to get under a real shower again with plenty of soap to wash away the oil and grime. After these primary needs had been satisfied the doctor attended to the sores which still afflicted my ankles.

Although I had not had any sleep for more than 24 hours, the excitement of being rescued drove all thought of sleep out of my head. We just sat around in the wardroom talking. We had been completely cut off from the world. We knew nothing about the invasion of Sicily. We did not know what naval actions had taken place in the South Pacific while we were on the island. We did not know how our force had made out the night the Helena was sunk. So we got all the news then and there, and of course had a lot to tell our friends about our recent adventures. We spend the remainder of the night talking.

We were rescued early on Friday morning, and arrived at Tulagi the following night. Upon arrival, we had a great celebration on board. There were several war correspondents there. They said we could send a Red Cross cable to our families if we wanted to, but that our individual stories would be published in our home-town newspapers. So all the survivors were listed by name and address. The Helena had been announced as sunk on Tuesday morning. That was Monday in the States, and the story had appeared in all the Wednesday papers. One of our chief worries on the island was whether or not the Helena had been reported as sunk. I had assured the men that she would not be so reported for at least a week or perhaps longer.

The next morning the task force commander called up and congratulated us on our escape. At Tulagi there was a regular survivor's camp, where we were provided with food and clothing. Each man was given a clean suit of dungarees and some skivvies. The American Red Cross supplied an excellent kit of toilet articles, which included tooth paste, toilet soap, laundry soap, and shaving gear. We were well taken care of.

After the war is over, I should like to return to Vella Lavella, and see the natives again who befriended us in our time of great need. In their treatment of us they exemplified all the Christian virtues. We shall never forget how they aided us and how they generously shared their own meager supplies of food with us. Before we left the island, we gave them all the money we had, some of us having as much as $15 or $20. I hope they made good use of it when our forces took over the island a month later. My feeling for the kinky-haired, dark-skinned islanders is like that expressed by Kipling for Gunga Din: "An' for all 'is dirty 'ide, 'E was white, clear white, inside."

(The preceeding account of the sinking of the Helena was an article published in Proceedings, August 1945)

Interview No. 3 with Vice Admiral John L. Chew, U. S. Navy (Ret.)
Place: His residence in Providence, Annapolis, Maryland
Date: Wednesday morning, 29 November 1972
Subject: Biography
By: John T. Mason, Jr.

Q: It's good to see you again this morning, Admiral. Last time, you concluded by reading your talk to the 1st classman made in 1945.

Adm. C.: Yes Dr. Mason, and I did leave out as I told you, a few things I'd like to tell you now since I'm not inhibited in any way, either by security regulations or audience.

In the talk there was no mention of coast watchers or "Bish", the Reverand Sylvester. During the war their identity, and even the knowledge of the existance of coast watchers was held very closely. And for good reason, since the information they furnished was invaluable to us and their safety in enemy held territory was, to say the least, precarious. I thought Bish, whom I knew was a missionary, was the coast watcher also, but found out just recently from talks with Walter Lord who is now writing a book about them, that he was not, but just a dedicated missionary who had elected to stay to be of assistance to the natives and to the coast watchers. As senior survivor on the island, I was never told by Bish of the existance of the coast watcher nor did I ever see him, so tight was the security! He, Bish, acted as a relay and, of course, was of tremendous help to us both in dealing with the natives, and advising us on every day life in that isolated part of the world.

The other significant incident that was omitted in the talk was that concerning the Japanese patrols that made routine sweeps along our beach. One night one of them strayed too close to camp and with the help of the natives was captured. After a hurried meeting of the Major Council I asked for recommendations. They said "We don't take prisoners! We can't! We haven't even enough food for ourselves". My answer was "That seems sensible. Make it merciful, but he must be killed."

Q: You couldn't let him go!

Adm. C.: Couldn't let him go because there was a Japanese garrison on the other side of the island. We couldn't take him with us. We couldn't even feed ourselves. I suppose, in after thought, we could have, but at the time it seemed the only sensible decision to me, just as I'm sure it seemed the only sensible decision to Captain Hoover to leave the scene of the Juneau. And if you think back afterwards

Chew #3 - 110

and say, well, maybe it might have been this way, it could have been that way, all you do is confuse yourself.

So, he was killed. I have his sword right now. I don't know where it is, but somewhere or other. He was carrying an old beaten-up Japanese sword, with all the wrappings off the hilt but the wooden scabbard was still there and the blade was intact. Whether he was an officer or not I don't know. In any event, without the help of our native friends, he would not have been captured and who knows, he might have disclosed our camp location, and I might not be here today.

I also forgot to mention that when we landed at Tulagi there on the packing case that served as our dresser, or whatever it was, in the quarters, was a bottle of whisky from Admiral Halsey.

We spent a day or so on Tulagi and then went over to Guadalcanal, where they dutifully had an air raid the night we were there. I thought, gee, it will be bitter irony after having gone through all this, for somebody to drop a bomb into the middle of Guadalcanal and end it all. Fortunately, they didn't hit anything, and, boy, when that air raid warning went I dove for those trenches like nobody human.

Within a day or so we were back in Noumea which, at that time, was Admiral Halsey's headquarters. We had an exciting trip in an old DC-3 going to Noumea. The plane inadvertently strayed over one of our own carrier task forces, and was intercepted by our own fighters. Fortunately they recognized us in time and held their fire. The crew had neglected to turn on their IFF! It was scarey!

I believe I mentioned that after staying the night on Tulagi we were immediately taken to Guadalcanal for air evacuation, and subsequently evacuated to Noumea. At that time, there was really no hospitalization involved. As I mentioned before, I had rather severe immersion sores, and I think I told you that the corpsman said, "You'd better get your Purple Heart," and I said, "What for?" He said, "Well, you've got immersion sores." I said, "Look, I'm so happy to be here. Just give me an aspirin and forget it!"

Q: No, you didn't relate that. I'm glad you have done so.

Adm. C.: Well, it was true, and he said, "Here's your form." I said, "I don't want any form. I'm delighted to be here and I appreciate Admiral Halsey's bottle of whisky far more than your offer of a Purple Heart."

This, I might add, was not heroics but just happened to be the truth because when you've survived a period in your life including many hours in the water and days on a hostile island, when you return to your own service and your own people, you're so happy that you're alive, these little amenities, I think, are suddenly put aside in the larger context of just being there.

Q: A senseof gratitude overwhelms you!

Adm. C.: A sense of gratitude completely overwhelms you, and a sense of wellbeing and happiness pervades to such an extent that you lose sight of the little things some people consider important.

Anyhow, we went to Noumea. Actually, in those early days of the war there was very little debriefing. As I remember, I talked to members of Admiral Halsey's staff, but I talked to J. B. Colwell more because he was a very close friend and because of any desire to impart any knowledge that we had attained that would be of help to others. I think the briefing and debriefing of later years has grown out of all proportion -

Q: It's certainly reached the high point now in Vietnam, hasn't it?

Adm. C.: It certainly has. You can't do anything without (a) being briefed, and after that (b) being debriefed.

As I remember, we had a very pleasant couple of days in Noumea and then I was told - I think while I was still there - that I would go back to the Naval Academy. I thought that I would have been reassigned in a combat area, but the feeling was that I should be rehabilitated, although I didn't realize that I had to be.

Q: It takes a longer period than one realizes!

Adm. C.: Well, I was surprised that I wasn't immediately reassigned because most of the people who had survived the sinking of Helena were immediately reassigned to new construction with, I suppose, the thought that during the new construction period there would be ample time to be rehabilitated.

However, I was assigned to the Naval Academy and, in one respect, I think it was a very wise assignment both from the point of view of my particular abilities and from the point of view of giving me a slight period to get myself adjusted again - although, as I said, I didn't feel any need for it.

Q: You went back as ordnance instructor, did you not?

Adm. C.: Yes, I did, and that is what I had reference to in terms of being able to impart some of the experiences and some of the new developments as I had seen them in operation. And, because of my experience, I was able to have a very practical approach to ordnance as it was being taught at the Naval Academy.

Q: This is the best kind of instruction, isn't it?

Adm. C.: I would hope so. I felt, as you often do when you come to a new job, that there are certain things that desperately need changing, and, having been so wound up in my job on board Helena that I could sense the problems as they developed in the ordnance equipment. I felt that the way it was being taught at the Naval Academy was not, at that particular time, practical enough and I was made head of the First Class Committee. Most of the tests and examinations that had been conducted in the Department had been the essay type, and I felt that it was more important that they learn a lot of things, and I also felt that it was very necessary that their broader knowledge be tested objectively, rather than subjectively, if I use the terms properly. So I instituted at that time the multiple-choice and true-or-false tests for the first time at the Naval Academy in the Ordnance Department. I think they'd been used in other departments before, but I remember the first one and the first class came after the test and said: "My God, how did you dream up such a test?"

I said, "Because, if you knew all those things, you knew the answers perfectly, in my view you would be a better gunnery assistant when you left the Naval Academy to assume your duties aboard ship, and from a practical point of view I feel strongly that your life might depend on it."

Consequently, I felt that it was important that they be given difficult examinations. Then, of course, we could always put them through a normal distribution curve and come up with a reasonable mark.

It was a challenge to me because I had never really made out examinations. I had been helped as a line PG at the Naval

Chew #3 - 115

Academy by both "Rivets," Admiral Rivero, and J.B. in mastering what I thought at that time was a very difficult ordnance course. That provided me the academic background and with my practical wartime experience I thought I would really be able to help the midshipmen.

Q: Were they all keyed up? I mean in an atmosphere of war they probably had a different attitude from what you knew as a student there.

Adm. C.: I think they were, and I tried to play on that. After all, I had just come back. I told you that I spoke to the midshipmen and told of my experiences, and then it was after that that little article was written in the Naval Institute Proceedings, which was a condensation of my remarks to the midshipmen. And they were all made in an effort to have the midshipmen themselves recognize the seriousness of what they were studying. I was particularly enthusiastic because of my experience.

Q: Were the wraps off, security wise, in terms of radar and things like that? Could you talk about and teach them?

Adm. C.: I could talk pretty much about radar. I could talk, of course, about all of the fire-control equipment, generally speaking. Really, the only areas that touched on sensitive security were those of the coast watchers, which I really didn't have to get involved with. As I remember, when I talked to the midshipmen I skirted those areas rather carefully, because at that time it was very sensitive that we had Australians and New Zealanders and, of course, American coast watchers who were extremely vital in providing us with information. I think I told you that the air raids the night of the Battle of Guadalcanal came on a more precise schedule as advertised by the coast watchers than we were able to get target services from our own people. I was tremendously impressed with them, but at that time I had to keep away from that subject.

But the practical aspects of ordnance, as I knew it and had experienced it, I was able to impart I think, a degree of enthusiasm which probably was not available to someone who had been a professor and had come into the service to teach.

Q: This indeed was wisdom on the part of the authorities who assigned you there. This was the era - a new era - of servo-mechanisms. Was this something that you dealt with extensively?

Adm. C.: I think you're asking me questions of technical nature that probably Lloyd mentioned. Of course, when you speak of servo-mechanisms you're speaking of follow-up mechanisms.

Well, I don't quite understand your question. My primary concern was teaching the midshipmen the fundamentals of the fire-control systems as they were then installed aboard our new construction cruisers and destroyers. They were pretty universal. They had been developed primarily by the Ford Instrument Company. There had been modifications and there had been improvements, but essentially the principles were the same. Our courses included other systems, such as the Bofors system and the lead computing sights, which we had been very successful in testing. As I remember, even at that time, the VT fuse was pretty much tabu to talk about.

Q: It was.

Adm. C.: When I came back to the Naval Academy I don't think we ever discussed it.

Of course, the war was still on -

Q: You were there for two years, were you not?

Adm. C.: Well, not quite.

Q: September 1943 to May 1945.

Adm. C.: Yes, that's right. It was almost two years, and at the end of the first year I began trying to get away!

Q: That's a usual thing!

Chew #3 - 118

Adm. C.: Yes, that's a usual thing, and I went to Washington and said that I thought that with my experience it would be much better if I could get to sea as I had, from my point of view, contributed all that I was able to contribute in my practical experience, my technical knowledge, which was not of the highest, I might add, but my practical experience probably made up for it. And, since I had done my bit at the Academy, I thought my experience in the war area might be better utilized by letting me go to sea.

I was unsuccessful the first year. They said that my services were required at the Naval Academy, which I couldn't quite understand -

Q: What did they do with you during the summer months?

Adm. C.: I went on a cruise. We went to Trinidad and into the Gulf of Paria and had our exercises down there -

Q: Which was protected by booms -

Adm. C.: That's right. It wasn't much of a cruise.

As a matter of fact, the summer months are sort of dim because by that time I had decided that this was not the place for me and I wanted to get back to sea.

So I went to the Superintendent and said:

"Admiral Beardall, I want to be released." And he said:

"Well, your normal tour is two years, but at the end of that time I want you to remain here as my aide."

Q: To succeed Felix Johnson, was that?

Adm. C.: No, it was to succeed - it could have been Ted Torgerson. I've forgotten just who it was. Anyhow, I said:

"Admiral, I don't want to do that." He said: "Do you realize what you're saying, young man?" And I said yes, I realized, "I fully realize what I'm saying, but I don't think that it is fair to me. I want to get back to sea and I feel that that is the proper thing."

He said: "Well, of course, you know if I insist you will have to stay."

And I said: "Admiral Beardall, I do not think you will do that," and he said: "Maybe you're right." He finally said, "OK, you can go."

So I went over to the Bureau, I went to the destroyer detail desk, and I said:

"I think I'm fully qualified. I've had destroyer duty. I would like command of a destroyer."

I can't think of the detail officer's name, but he said to me: "I can't do it. I'm willing. I'll give you command of a destroyer tomorrow because I think you're qualified, but you're nailed to the cruiser desk. They feel that your wartime experience has been in cruisers and they feel also that the level of expertise has been diluted in the cruisers and since you are experienced in that line of work, you cannot have a destroyer."

I said: "OK. Who the hell do I have to go to see?"

And he said: "You can go to see anybody."

I said: "Fine. I'll go see the Chief of the Bureau of Personnel," who happened to be Admiral Fechteler.

Admiral Fechteler had been one of my instructors when I was at the PG school. He was a commander and I was a lieutenant. I walked into the office and said:

"Admiral, I want command of a destroyer and they tell me that I'm going to be assigned to a cruiser. I've had enough trouble getting away from the Naval Academy. Let me have a destroyer?"

He said: "No, I won't, but I'll tell you what I will do, Jack. I'll give you your choice of any cruiser that is going into commission. I want you to understand the reasons. It's not arbitrary. We do feel there has been a dilution in the type of people that have gone to cruisers. Your experience is all in cruisers and, believe me, we need you."

I suppose, although I was not flattered, I accepted that explanation, particularly when he said I could have any ship I wanted.

Q: I suppose wartime didn't permit the luxury of diversity of experience, since you had to focus where you were qualified?

Adm. C.: Well, that seemed to be a logical solution, although there were other people who had not had exactly that experience and had had diversification in assignment, but apparently this was the policy of the Bureau at the time and I was unable to crack it.

So he said: "All right, you can have any ship you want. By the way, there's going to be a new _Helena_. It will not be a light cruiser such as CL-50, but it'll be one of the new heavy cruisers and it's building in Boston, and you will be ordered as exec."

I said: "I think that's only fair and I look forward to it with enthusiasm."

So I left the Naval Academy –

Q: May I interrupt at that point and ask you to give me a picture of the Naval Academy in wartime and the differences, if there were any, the streamlining, as contrasted with your own time as a student?

Adm. C.: To be perfectly frank, there were accelerated procedures. As we all know, the curriculum had been shortened to three years. I don't think the academic pressures were any greater. I feel that probably the academic pressures were less because people were needed in the fleet. Not that the standards had been lowered. I don't think that was the case, but just psychologically the desire to have people join the fleet because the war was still very much on very probably had the effect of making it, not necessarily easier, but making it faster, and by making it faster producing the end product without some of the strains that were necessarily attributed to desire for academic excellence.

I don't know whether that's an accurate appraisal, but it would seem to me to be the case.

I felt that the Naval Academy had produced excellent graduates for the purpose for which they were needed, as junior officers in the fleet, at the time. As I say, I didn't find it too different.

I lived in one of the apartments over by the hospital, not in Perry Circle, but on the Naval Academy side. Most of the people who were at the Naval Academy, a great many of them at least, had had combat experience and had been pulled in. There was a gaiety possibly among the faculty - not a gaiety, that's a very poor word, but a feeling of appreciation 1) that they were here, 2) that they thought they were doing a good job - it was a very satisfying job, I thought -

Q: People lived intensely, I suppose?

Adm. C.: People lived very intensely. I remember the parties at the Club were always a little more intense. It was not so much eat, drink, and be merry, for tomorrow you may die, but at the same time -

Q: This was an actuality!

Adm. C.: This was an actuality and one that was very noticeable, I thought. Other than that particular attitude, I thought that the Naval Academy was kept pretty much on an even keel, and, as I say, except for the accelerated curriculum, the standards were maintained, but because of this feeling of necessity for people in the fleet perhaps the academic pressures were not quite as great. At least, I felt it that way, although in my particular job in the ordnance department I felt that I demanded very high standards because I felt that this was a practical application that, as I said before, might eventually save their lives.

Q: What percentage, would you say, of the instructors were civilians at that point?

Adm. C.: I can't remember, but if you remember a lot of the civilian instructors who had Reserve status were put in uniform so there might have been a misleading figure if I had said how many people wore civilian clothes. There were quite a few who when the war started, having had some Reserve status either from NROTC or from some other activity, immediately put on uniform and became instructors at the Naval Academy. Just what the percentage was at that time, I really wasn't in a position to know.

The Ordnance Department was almost all uniformed line

officers, although some had been Reserves. I can think of one right now and I'm sure you will know him. He's Pierre Bernard, who's President of the Annapolis Banking and Trust Company. He was at that time a lieutenant commander. He's a graduate of the Naval Academy and when the war started, he came back in and was an instructor at the Naval Academy. There were several others in that category, even in the Ordnance Department. What the percentage was, for example, in Foreign Languages, I'd have no idea. In the Ordnance Department they were practically all uniformed line officers, either Reserve or regular.

I cited that example of the banker, and then there was another one, Fred Billings, who was also a rather prominent - I guess he was a banker with Mellon Bank or one of the bigger banks in New York. He was very active in recruiting for the football teams - even that wasn't lost sight of completely and, of course, as you remember, during the war, because of the athletic programs that we had in the services, we had excellent football teams and excellent sports participation in all lines of sport. We had some of the more prominent tennis players. I think Hunt was there at the time and he had been a Davis Cup winner. During this period we excelled in all sports.

Q: Well, there was a general intensification of life and this would apply in the sports world as well.

Adm. C.: I think so, and I think it was very noticeable.

To carry on with the thought of any great differences, I think that the differences I've enumerated, the accelerated feeling of desire to get people into the fleet, the possible - in my view - easing of academic pressures, because of that, but the life of the Naval Academy went on in its same way and I think this is probably a tradition that is a hang-over from the British, because, as you know, during the war there were sometimes very severe criticisms of the British because of their "business as usual" attitude even in the midst of war and battle. In this particular aspect I think it was good.

Q: It helps to preserve one's sanity!

Adm. C.: It helps preserve one's sanity and it helps in terms of having the Naval Academy not change - not that I don't think change is good - change drastically out of all proportion to the need for change. It is a very leveling influence, and I thought a good one.

Q: Now, shall we resume with <u>Helena</u>? She was in Boston.

Adm. C.: Well, the precommissioning detail was in Newport and the crew was assembled in Newport.

Q: The ship was actually building in Boston, though?

Adm. C.: The ship was building at the Bethlehem Shipbuilding

Company in Quincy, and as executive officer I was responsible for the assembling of the crew and the pretraining details of the crew.

Q: What kind of a complement was she having?

Adm. C.: Oh, she was going to have a big complement. The heavy cruisers at that time had a complement of close to 1,700, and we had a good nucleus of trained men. There were only one or two from the old Helena. Most of them had gone to one of the cruisers that were later sunk, and another group had gone to one of the carriers - just which one I've forgotten.

As a matter of fact, there was a humorous approach. I heard this story much later, but this rather experienced crew having been sunk on Helena, when they were on the next ship, which also was eventually sunk, somebody said, "What do we do now?" And this guy from Helena said, "Follow me," as he jumped over the side!

Q: I've heard tell that it was a policy fairly quickly learned not to assign the bulk of a crew from a ship that had sunk to another one?

Adm. C.: I think that was a policy that was developed after this, and I think it was a very wise policy. I think also that it's perfectly true that if you have a group of experienced people you don't want to put them all together. You ought to let their experience be diluted among the other units of the fleet that probably need the benefit of their wartime experience.

Q: Yes, because you had a lot of draftees coming along.

Adm. C.: We had a lot of draftees at that time and we had, of course, a lot of very inexperienced people.

But, as I said, our precommissioning crew in Newport was an enthusiastic crew. However, I think by that time you could see the signs of the end of the war.

Q: Among the officer complement, were there many from the Naval Academy?

Adm. C.: No. As I remember, the percentage of Naval Academy graduates at that time had fallen off so that our precommissioning detail probably had only about between 8 and 10 percent from the Naval Academy. Of course, the captain was, I was the exec, two of the heads of department were, the gunnery officer was, the engineer officer was not. Then, as they went down through the assistants and the division officers, the greater proportion were not Naval Academy graduates.

I always had a very strong feeling about non-Naval Academy graduates because I felt that they were just as good and,

God knows, I'm a blue-and-gold all the way through, but they were just as good as the Naval Academy graduates. I think you can take a mild pat on the back by saying that maybe it was because of the leadership, if you want to call it that, the example of the Naval Academy people and the nucleus that they formed, but my feeling was that the Reserve officers who came in, some of whom integrated later into the Navy and some of whom, as you know, have now made flag rank, were just as efficient, just as good, and just as enthusiastic. Oftentimes, even a little more innovative perhaps than we were.

Q: Did you have any particular problems as the crew assembled?

Adm. C.: No. As I remember, we had very few problems. We were at the stage in the war where, as I said, I think you could begin to see that the end was in sight, although, of course, at that time the atomic bomb hadn't been dropped.

Q: This was probably July, was it?

Adm. C.: When I went to Newport it was about June of 1945, and we put the ship in commission in August of 1945.

Q: Before the surrender?

Adm. C.: No, the war was over. The surrender was - when?

Q: In August.

Adm. C.: Yes. I'm trying to think where we were on the surrender day. I think we were in Newport. It was just at that time. But, strangely enough, even though it was after the surrender we went through the full course of sprouts at Guantanamo. I think the only relaxation for the rather intensive period of workup was that we didn't have to work on Sunday. But we had the same shake-down training, the same rather intensive schedules. I had a very interesting experience there.

As I say, we were commissioned, we went to Guantanamo for workup under the same rules and regulations that all the ships at that period had gone through, except for the relaxation of Sunday, and my captain who was Arthur H. McCollum had been an intelligence expert and he was called back to Washington. Oh, let me go back a little bit.

Prior to that time the gunnery officer had been taken ill. This was during our shake-down training. So the captain called me in and he said:

"Jack, you're an experienced gunnery officer. You can handle both exec and gunnery officer."

And I said: "Yes, I think I can. That won't be any problem."

I think this is unique in the history of our Navy. I became the exec and the gunnery officer by official letter from the captain. Then, about a week later, during the midst of our shake-down training, he was called back to Washington for the Pearl Harbor hearings and he said:

"OK, Jack, I turn over the ship to you."

So I was then the captain, the exec, and the gunnery officer during the remaining period of shake-down training and, as I remember, I brought the ship back to Boston.

Q: Mac was at the hearings two or three weeks, wasn't he?

Adm. C.: He was there twice. I've forgotten the precise number of days, but I was then captain, exec, and gunnery officer, and, I might add, I enjoyed it tremendously.

Q: Catapulted into the three jobs!

Adm. C.: Catapulted into the three top jobs.

Of course, with the surrender - and I'm sure everyone you've interviewed has certainly corroborated this statement - the war was over and the feeling was completely different. It wasn't immediately noticeable, but <u>Helena</u>, the CA-75, after her shake-down and her workup, came back to Boston and was promptly sent to England where we were, I thought, to become the flagship of Admiral Connoly - I've forgotten who, but we never saw a flag officer aboard. We worked with the destroyer division and in a few minor exercises with the British. But the pressure was then off and by that time the point system was beginning to come out and who was going to be released and who was to stay really became the major problem.

Q: That large complement of 1,700 diminished!

Adm. C.: Well, it had't quite diminished. We had an interesting cruise and that operated, I think, decidedly to our advantage. We stayed in England for a few weeks and then we went down to the Mediterranean, where we were again technically to become the flagship of either CinCNelm or his equivalent. But that didn't materialize either and we were ordered to Asia.

Of course this gave us a very interesting sort of beginning leg on the round-the-world cruise. We went through the Suez Canal, where I learned for the first time a term that is used quite commonly today, "posh." And I suddenly understood the meaning of posh, because it was hot as hell going through the Suez Canal and posh meant "port outbound, starboard homeward bound". No one wanted to be on the sunny side either going to India or returning.

Q: What was the purpose of the Far Eastern tour?

Adm. C.: It was to go out and take up a position in China because of the unsettled conditions there. Being the exec, I wasn't really privy to any "eyes only" orders. In fact, everybody wondered why in hell we were going to China.

We stopped in Singapore and had a very pleasant time.

Q: Would this Far Eastern mission be related in any way to the captain's long experience with the Far East?

Adm. C.: No, I don't think so because by that time Captain McCollum - he was with us in England and the Mediterranean, but he was relieved shortly after we arrived in Tsingtao. He was relieved by Victor Blue. It was sort of fun - I loved it - because Captain Blue said:

"Well, Jack, you've been the captain, exec, and gunnery officer. I'll sit by and you run things and if I don't like it I'll tell you that I don't like it, and if I think it's all right, why, continue."

So I thoroughly enjoyed my service under Captain Blue.

But to get back to my story. We arrived in Tsingtao, and at that point, the point system - that's not meant to be a play on words - was becoming uppermost in everybody's mind, "when am I going to get home?", followed secondly by a related question, "what are we doing out here?" After a stay and some operations in the Tsingtao area, which was rather limited, we went to Shanghai and tied up between the buoys off Garden Bend. There we stayed almost five months.

I think, in answer to your question, it was a little early but maybe this was a precaution for what was beginning to happen in China at that time.

Q: You mean the Communists coming down from the north?

Adm. C.: The Communists coming down from the north. I can amplify that later during my second command, which was also in China.

We found, or at least I found as exec, that it was a very difficult job to maintain the morale of the crew, because there we were between the buoys, we didn't get underway, we had to have a very rigid schedule to keep people occupied, we weren't shooting, we weren't doing the things that we had trained so hard to do, and everybody was interested in when they would go home.

Q: The Magic Carpet was in -?

Adm. C.: The Magic Carpet was in full swing. I found it a very difficult time. I set up a rather rigorous schedule for myself. I used to go over and play squash every afternoon at one o'clock, then we would come back and play bridge in the evening.

Q: Sports were very important.

Adm. C.: Very important and the facilities were very limited. As I remember, there was only one golf course in Shanghai that was playable at that time. There were no football fields or baseball fields. The crew did improvise a few, I think, somewhere. But we had a great deal of difficulty. The primary occupation of the crew was probably dealing with the Chinese merchants who set up on the third deck. We had agents who were tailors and agents who were furniture-makers, and we had agents who were jewelers - as a matter of fact, some of them became my fast friends. I'll digress a bit.

The jeweler who was the ship's jeweler was T. Y. Lee who later became very famous in Hong Kong and just recently died. I received a letter from his nephew saying that he knew the admiral would be saddened by the news of the death of the venerable T. Y. Lee, who had been a friend of many, many years. Of course, he was a very successful man later on in Hong Kong. He built up a tremendous business. In addition to being a fine old gentleman, he was considered an expert on jade. He took me one day, many years later, in Hong Kong and said:

"I don't believe in stocks and bonds, but there's nothing like this," and he showed me a jade collection, ranging from precious gems all the way down to commercial jade. It was fascinating, but, as I say, that was really the main occupation plus rigorous sort of make-work drills and keeping the ship spotless.

It was a very, very difficult time in my career and I think a very difficult time in the career of most of the officers who were aboard ship. Fortunately, we were the flagship of Task Force 77 and Admiral Willard Kitts was the task force commander, and we were able to go down to Hangchow and to take trips. We went obviously to Peking, Tientsin.

Q: Did you get over to Japan at all?

Adm. C.: Never did get to Japan, never. I think a lot of us wanted to go to Japan and we thought we would be sent there, but we weren't. I went as far as Guam, where I was relieved as exec.

But, getting back to the period in Shanghai, in retrospect and reading Tuchman's book Stilwell and the China Experience, I couldn't help but realize the accuracy of her research. I thought it was rather startling. At that particular time, if I remember correctly, inflation was rampant. You had to have literally thousand-dollar bills to buy anything. As a corollary, you probably know that Nationalist China has nothing greater than a one-hundred-dollar bill, which is $2.25 right now. They don't make any. They learned their lesson the hard way and if anybody wants to counterfeit $2.25 bills, that's up to them. The 5,000 and 10,000 denominations, some of which I still have I think tucked away somewhere, were indications of the turmoil of the country.

The mayor of Shanghai was later evacuated to Chicago and lived the remainder of his life in Chicago. Of course, with my name "Chew" it was interesting. For example, the task force commander Admiral Kitts, used to entertain, as you would expect, and he would have the exec of his flagship, and one particular afternoon he came in and looked at the seating, then turned to his aide and said:

"Hey, Bill, you can't have Admiral Kitts, then a Chinese General Wang, then Commander Chew, then another Chinese.

You've got to split up the Americans and the Chinese."

And his aide said: "No, that's the exec of your flagship!"

Later on, in Taiwan, my name caused quite a stir.

But, getting back to the period in history, you could see the turmoil in China. I went back about a year later. At this time, as I remember, the Communists were still way out west. They hadn't got to the northern part nor were they working down. The next time I went back, they were actively on the march, and the second time was before the Nationalists left and went to Taiwan. But the handwriting was on the wall, very much on the wall.

Well, as I said, I had that period in China. It was a very difficult one. Those members of the crew who had the requisite number of points were far more concerned with getting home than they were with the activities of the ship. We had obvious, I suppose you'd call them, altercations or problems with liberty. We found that if engaged in a fight a Chinese skull was not as rugged as ours. We had problems of that nature that were settled in the normal way. The Chinese authorities were very cooperative.

I have a - I don't really know what it is, but I got it somewhere - that was given to me by President Chiang Kai-chek the Christmas we were there. That made it even more difficult. Here was Christmas and we were spending it in Shanghai, not knowing precisely why, particularly since we didn't move from between the buoys.

There's one interesting anecdote that I'd like to tell you. As we came up the river into Shanghai in *Helena*, the pilot was

was of French extraction. He had been a Yangtze River pilot for forty or fifty years. As you know, Shanghai is at the mouth of the Wang-po - you turn up into the Wang-po and the famous Garden Bend is in the Wang-po River. But, coming up the Yangtze to the Wang-po, and up the Wang-po River, he was a marvelous shiphandler, superb, and after the ship had been moored between the buoys he was sitting in the wardroom and we were discussing the fact that the war was over and, obviously, all of us who had fought the Japanese had a hearty respect for them but at that particular time a tremendous hate. They were cruel, unjust, bigoted, and I had just expressed that view in connection with my experiences in the other Helena. And he said:

"Commander, I want to tell you something. You just talked about the Japanese, but the Chinese, if aroused, will make the Japanese look like patsies. Don't you ever forget it."

Well, I've never forgotten that remark, and then, of course, I have seen some of the results of their purges and they can act with a nature that's just as decisive as the Japanese and, possibly because of their vast numbers, it goes a little unnoticed. But I've never forgotten those words and I've often thought of them in terms of what happened in Taiwan. Chung Ching Kuo came there and "took care of things." But it was an interesting observation and one that was, I felt, based on long experience and was probably pretty valid.

Q: What is it predicated on? Is it the concept of the individual?

Adm. C.: I think it was predicated on - I really don't know what it was predicated on. I think it was more a matter of his particular experience in watching when Chinese were cornered what they would do in terms of what the Japanese had done. It was more a remark based on experience and whether it was predicated on any philosophical or psychological fact, I don't know. But he said it with such conviction. I tell you why I say this. You know, the American view prior to World War II was always the "little Jap", you know, with the big teeth, with a big sword -

Q: And the bow!

Adm. C.: And the bow, but with a knife ready to go. While the concept of a Chinese was a happy-go-lucky guy who just loved everybody, was poor as hell, poor but honest, and wouldn't cheat anybody out of anything. Well, anybody who knows the world nowadays knows that probably the best bargainers in the entire world are the Chinese, without any question. I would put them up against the traditionally accepted leaders in the bargaining trade, the Jewish race, without any question, and frankly the Jew would, in my view, unquestionably lose his shirt. This I found to be a very accurate appraisal but, as I said, this was such a reversal of the previous view held by most Americans that all Japanese were really hideously cruel, while all Chinese were lovely sort of simple souls who wouldn't hurt a flea. He was so vehement in his opposition to such a view that I thought it worth recording.

As I say, I've never forgotten it. I can see the man sitting right there this minute in the wardroom telling me. I can't think of his name, I'm ashamed to say. It was not a revelation, certainly, but it was an interesting fact that I tucked away and I feel that he was right.

Well, to get on with my story. We finally survived and were headed - incidentally, we did have a trip to Hong Kong while we were on the Asiatic Station. We operated basically, initially, from Tsingtao, then went down to Hong Kong, then went back to Shanghai.

Q: Was Hong Kong even at that time an R & R place?

Adm. C.: Oh, no, there was no such thing as R & R. Actually we had gone there I think, purely as a diversion. The results of the war were still very obvious. From the harbor you could see all the bomb damage on the buildings on Victoria Peak. There was still other bomb damage throughout the city. Hong Kong is an amazing place. An attache years later told me his view of Hong Kong. He said, "It's lucky there's only one Hong Kong in the world. The world couldn't stand two of them."

Even at that time it was beginning to thrive. It was the merchant center of the Far East. They were digging out from the rubble and establishing their tailors and their jewelers and all the rest of it that makes it the fascinating city that it is today.

So, we had a trip to Hong Kong. We were able to go to the new territories - no, maybe that was a little later. It was not an R & R center but it provided us with much needed relaxation. We went to Guam and I was relieved by a classmate, Jack Minor, who was later a flag officer, is retired and lives over in Arlington. That was in March of 1947 that I was relieved, and I came back to take command of Stickell, a 2,200-tonner, the 888.

Q: Was she building or was she already built?

Adm. C.: No, no, she had been in commission for a number of years. She was not one of the last, but she was one of the middle of the 2,200-tonners. I became her commanding officer in March of 1947. I took command in San Diego where, incidentally, housing was rather difficult and I bought a house.

During the initial period of this rather protracted deployment, and I sometimes laugh at people - not laugh, but I'm better able to appreciate their views for long deployments in Vietnam. This was a long deployment, when you consider that we left Boston in the winter, just before Christmas of 1945, and I didn't get home until March of 1947. Meantime, my family had to pretty well shift for themselves. The home port was initially on the East Coast and then it was shifted to the West Coast. My wife and children lived in Berkeley, California, after they moved from the East Coast to the West Coast on their own.

But, as I say, I finally got back to the West Coast, took command of the Stickell in San Diego Harbor, and within a very short period I was ordered to Honolulu for ASW training, the whole division, Stickell, Anderson, Baussell, and Agerholm. We were all ordered to Pearl Harbor primarily to serve as targets for submarines and to improve our own ASW. It was a forerunner of one of the ASW groups, although at that particular time it wasn't recognized as such.

Before we went to Honolulu we went to Bremerton and had a six-week overhaul. That was just after I took command of the ship.

Q: Were your ranks depleted on Stickell?

Adm. C.: No. As I remember, we had rather an adequate crew. The Magic Carpet was pretty much over by then. We had almost a wartime crew.

Q: It had been determined who was going to stay in the service?

Adm. C.: Pretty much - well, not necessarily, because there

Chew #3 - 142

were those who still didn't have enough points to get out, even at that time. So there was an element of the crew that was not the essentially career Navy, but they were a pretty experienced group, and I enjoyed my command.

I'm jumping ahead of myself, but anyhow we were sent to Honolulu for ASW and that was a very pleasant deployment because we worked with the submarines, and we'd go out and come in fairly early, and, although my family wasn't there - it was another separation, we were able to play golf on Saturday and Sunday and keep ourselves healthy and busy. It was truly an interesting and busy deployment.

Suddenly, we were ordered to China again. That one I didn't quite understand -

Q: How did you react to that?

Adm. C.: Well, I think with a natural reaction. I thought, my God, I've been separated from my family all these months, I've just been home a few months - six weeks in the yard and about a month or so in San Diego - and here I am going back to China.

Q: And it wasn't possible to take them?

Adm. C.: Oh, no. I wondered what the reason for it was. Again, looking back upon history, it's obvious but that's in retrospect.

Chew #3 - 143

Q: This was 1947?

Adm. C.: Yes, and again, as I said, the handwriting was beginning to show on the wall as to what was happening in China. I will relate an interesting episode that took place because I think it has bearing on how books are written and I've always been interested not in writing, but in sort of wondering how people dream up the stories that they put into books, and I know damned well it isn't all imagination, there must be some basis or some foundation for the stories, as good as they are.

We were told to go to China, so we set sail. We were in normal column formation. As a tidy sailor, I like to be well closed up. I was sitting up on the bridge one evening with my feet up on the coaming with the officer of the deck, George Merkle, who was a very fine ex-enlisted man, a lieutenant. We heard the loudspeaker on the ship ahead - you won't believe this - say:

"Will the man who took the captain's strawberries lay to the bridge?"

I turned to the officer of the deck and said: "George, let's close up a little. This sounds interesting."

The wind was from directly ahead, it was a nice evening at sea, about sunset. We closed up to within 200 years so we could hear the louspeaker. Shortly thereafter, there was another announcement"

"Will the man who took the captain's strawberries lay to the bridge?"

I said, "This is going to get better." About fifteen minutes later there was another announcement:

"There will be no movies tonight unless the captain's strawberries are returned."

And, of course, this was the basis for the story in the Caine Mutiny. And here it was actually happening, and I'm sure that Herman Wouk

Q: And you heard it out in the ocean!

Adm. C.: Indeed we did. It's interesting that three of the episodes in the Caine Mutiny were similar to things I had been privy to. One was the captain's strawberries, one was when an ensign assaulted a commander - I've forgotten just what the circumstances surrounding that were - and another one had to do with alcoholic beverages in a boat. However, I've never seen nor spoken to Herman Wouk but wasn't the book fascinating?

Getting back to the Stickell, we arrived in our favorite home port of Tsingtao, where we had been for quite a few months in Helena. This time our services were a little better. The war had been over a little longer. We were able to do a little shooting for practice, but not very much. We were sent on sweeps, once all the way up into the Gulf of Po Hai. I had one interesting experience there. At that particular point the Communists were about down to Hu Lu tao, which is on the Gulf of Po Hai, and we were sent up to take a look.

I can remember them vividly, the fortifications, the pillboxes, the walls - speaking of walls, we were going up into the Gulf of Po Hai with very limited radar facilities. We had our own radar, of course, but there were no beacons or anything. And we were in a dense, dense fog and lost, so we slowed down to wait for the fog to lift. The shoreline was flat and I didn't trust it, although I could get the reflections from the mountains on my radar, I didn't know precisely how far away the shoreline was.

Suddenly the weather lifted and, there, coming over the mountain was the Great Wall of China, and that made the determination of our position very easy as we were right opposite Shan-hai-kuan. I think there's another name for it, but Shan-hai-kuan means where the mountain meets the sea, and that's where the wall of China ends as it comes down into the Gulf of Po Hai.

We didn't go ashore at Hu Lu tao. We simply went up and looked, and, as I said before, the place was bristling with soldiers, at that particular point the Communists had gotten down about that far.

We went in to Ch'in-huang-tao, which was the coaling port of a well known mining company. The manager had been returned - the British manager - but even then people were thinking about getting out. One of the observations that he made was: "Captain, it's interesting and I think you'd be interested to know that all during the Japanese occupation of this mining complex, the records were kept beautifully, the equipment was maintained, and when we came back at the end of the war it was just as if nothing had happened. We were able to take over, so complete and so adequate had been their administration of what was a very big mining industry."

As a matter of fact, most of the coal for Shanghai comes from Ch'in-huang-tao. I saw a Chinese destroyer in Ch'in-huang-tao with a deckload of coal, and they were taking it back to Shanghai and were going to sell it.

We stayed there for only a week but, as I said, you could see that they were preparing and had already evacuated their dependents. The manager had been there prior to the war as an assistant and then came back at the end of the war and took over from the Japanese as manager, and, I think, left shortly thereafter when the Communists came through.

Unlike most China sailors, I never got into Chefoo, but thought that we were fortunate in being able to go up in the Gulf. Hu Lu Tao is a very grim-looking place and the fortifications and the pillboxes were very, very visible at that time.

Q: Did you have contact with our naval attache on this occasion?

Adm. C.: No, I had no contact with anybody on shore. In fact, to my positive knowledge I never saw the naval attache.

Q: He was very much concerned with the safety of American

citizens.

Adm. C.: I can understand his concern, because it was very obvious -

Q: And I thought maintained a fairly close contact with our ships.

Adm. C.: Possibly he did. He may not have had contact with this particular ship, but I'm sure he was well aware - we were fairly well aware of what was going on, and although our home port for all intents and purposes was Tsingtao, we were able to get up the Gulf. Peking by that time was untenable, as I remember. Of course, it was, because Hu Lu tao is south of Peking.

We went back to Hong Kong. As a matter of fact, I was relieved in Hong Kong after 16 months in command of Stickell. Except for the few weeks in Bremerton and the few weeks in San Diego, it had been a compound deployment, so that by this time I was particularly anxious to get home. And frankly, although in later years I became aware of the situation, at that particular time I could not have predicted the eventual retreat to Taiwan. As a matter of fact, I didn't know what was going to happen. I don't think very many people did, to be perfectly frank, because, if you remember, it was about that time that the various missions - I've forgotten whether Marshall went to China then and who was the ambassador?

Q: Hurley.

Adm. C.: Hurley, yes. From our point of view, it was terribly confused. Before being relieved we went to Okinawa and took up station as SAR ship in Buckner Bay.

Q: What kind of ship?

Adm. C.: A sea-air-rescue ship, primarily for Air Force planes flying in and out of Okinawa.

I think one of the more humorous aspects of our deployment in Asia in Stickell was the question of venereal disease. As you, I am sure, are well aware, prior to the war venereal disease was handled on a very, on not what you'd call a cavalier basis but it was certainly handled as a disciplinary matter. If a man had venereal disease he was restricted. Of course, during the war, there was a more advanced way of looking at it. It became a matter of education to prevent venereal disease.

Well, my exec was a Reserve officer who had his master's degree in English and had taught. He was a very talented young man, and thereby hangs another story that I'll tell you later. But he was a writer. He didn't like to handle the ship, and I loved to handle the ship, so we got on beautifully. I said:

"OK, Norton, you run the administration and write all the papers and answer all the letters and all that stuff, and I'll run the ship from the bridge. But, you know, we've got a problem. We're going out to China and we've got to have a venereal disease program. It says so in the Seventh Fleet regulations. What do you suggest?"

He said: "I have an idea, Captain. I'll sit down and I'll write a book." And he wrote a little booklet. He was talented, he was an extremely talented illustrator. So he illustrated this little book, with lots of cartoons, various examples of what to do and what not to do. It was an educational treatise.

We reported duly to the Commander, Seventh Fleet, and were promptly asked for our venereal disease program and proudly presented it. And they said:

"This is simply marvelous, just superb. We're going to adopt it throughout the Seventh Fleet. You're to be highly commended."

We went home feeling very good. We went to Tsingtao and then we went to Hong Kong, and the statistics for the first three months of our deployment came out. The <u>Stickell</u> not only led the Pacific Fleet, it led the entire U. S. fleet in incidence of venereal disease! It just so happened at that time -

Q: The leaflet boomeranged!

Adm. C.: - we were in Okinawa, and I said:

"Well, men, I guess we're going to revert back to the old system. I realize that I can't restrict you, but to protect you from getting further infected, I'm afraid that you will be unable to go ashore. You can call it any damned thing you want, but we're going to straighten this out in one hell of a hurry. We're not going to be the leading offenders in the U. S. Navy for venereal disease, and this time we're going to do it my way."

Well, we were away on isolated duty. I wasn't under the watchful surveillance of the medical officer on the flagship, so we had a little more stringent program which entailed deprivation of liberty, which, as I said, was against the rules. The next month our venereal rate fell off considerably. The last quarter I think we were within one or two of the lowest rates of venereal disease in the Navy.

I always have been slightly amused by this because this was a fine educational treatise and told in great detail what you should and what you should not do, but unless some teeth were put into it, I found that it wasn't completely successful.

Q: I suppose it only stirred their imagination that much more.

Adm. C.: I think it stirred their imaginations probably and they felt that here they were in China, they might as well enjoy it while they could.

It wasn't a very long cruise because, my total time on board was from March of 1947 to July of 1948, and of that time practically the entire year was spent deployed, with the exception of that short time in Bremerton and even shorter time in San Diego.

I had an interesting experience coming home. We still had NATS then, which was the Naval Air Transport Service, but it was about to be converted into MATS, which is now the Air Transport Command, ATC. I got a ride from Hong Kong to Guam and I got bumped in Guam. I received my orders back to the Naval Academy at that time -

Q: Which must have been highly pleasing.

Adm. C.: Oh, I was just delighted, having been there once before and having loved it. Not only being a native of Annapolis, which really had very little to do with it, but after such a long separation - this had been an unduly long one, in my view - I was delighted with the orders and couldn't wait to get home.

So, I got as far as Guam and got bumped. I couldn't get a ride on the Naval Air Transport Command at all and I was traveling under orders, but I guess the Magic Carpet was still in effect and apparently there were higher priority people than I. I waited on Guam for two or three days and finally there was a Marine transport plane, an old C-54, and I talked to the commander and I said, "Where are you going?" He said: "I'm going right back to El Toro." So I said: "Oh, good. That's great..." My wife was in San Diego at the time, "Would he give me a ride back?"

He said, "Sure," so we had a couple of McArthur seats.

One other officer had bummed a ride with him.

We got in this old C-54, roared down the runway at Guam, and there are mountains, and the crew chief pointed to this spot out there and said, "See that old charred spot? That's where a Marine transport went in here a couple of weeks ago." I'm a congenital coward in an airplane. I hate them, just loathe them. I suddenly looked out and there was the engine gloriously on fire and, having just seen the charred spot, I said, well, I guess we've had it, and I heard the chief saying, "What the hell do you think I'm doing? I'm pulling the fire bottles." He pulled the fire bottles and it worked. The fire was extinguished, the engine nearly fell off. We circled around, landed. I was glad to touch ground, got out, waited dutifully until I was able to get on NATS, flew back to San Francisco, and, there in San Francisco when we landed - or wherever we landed on NATS, I've sort of forgotten - was that Marine aircraft that had beaten me back. They had flown out an engine, changed the engine, and it had beaten me home. It was at El Toro, which is the Marine air base. I thought that was pretty remarkable. But I must add I was scared because it's a terrifying thing to look out and see the engine, as Bob Newhart says, "gloriously on fire."

Returning home from my deployment in Helena, I was met by my wife and in keeping with my remarks on long deployments, my young son, after the initial greetings, said: "You're Jack." I said: "Yes, and I'm your father too, God damn it!"

These little vignettes of returning from a long deployment always amuse me. Did I mention about the WAVES?

Q: No.

Adm. C.: Well, when my son said, "You're Jack" I knew I'd been away too long. Also, when a WAVE passed me on Market St. in San Francisco after the sinking of Helena, she saluted smartly (a good looking gal) and I was so taken aback that I failed to return the salute, stopped, stared, and remarked, "I'll be God damned." I had never seen a WAVE.

Stickell later on was modified from a standard destroyer to a radar picket!

I received a letter two months ago asking me to participate as an ex-commanding officer in the ceremony turning her over to the Greek Navy.

Q: Is she serving now as a radar picket?

Adm. C.: That I don't know, but she's in the Greek Navy.

Q: Under another name?

Adm. C.: Yes. As a matter of fact, I could go and look up the name if it were of any interest. The last commanding officer very thoughtfully provided us with a brochure of the turnover ceremony and a list of all the old commanding officers and a history of the ship. She had a very distinguished career and I hope she continues her career in the Greek Navy.

Q: You wanted to add another incident on the Chinese mainland?

Adm. C.: Yes, I thought it was significant.

As you remember, I mentioned the fact that a couple of the Chinese Nationalist destroyers had taken deckloads of coal from Ch'un-huang tao and were taking them back to Shanghai and selling them for an obvious profit.

Q: Black market.

Adm. C.: Yes. There was a case while we were there that I thought was fascinating. If my memory serves me correctly, and it doesn't make any difference as to the precise title of the official, but he had to do with the Shanghai Light and Power Company. Whether he was the manager or whether he was a director or the president, or whatever he was, he was accused of bribery and it became rather a celebrated case in the courts and was covered as adequately as it could be in those days by the press. It had to do essentially with cumshaw! All China sailors are familiar with the term. He was tried in the Shanghai courts and acquitted, and the basis for the acquittal was the fact that this is the way we - we, the Chinese - have been doing business for centuries and cumshaw is a recognized fact of life. Therefore, he had committed no crime.

I think it's interesting from the point of view that our influence, for example, in Japan has led to their judicial system closely following ours.

Q: They've westernized it?

Adm. C.: A westernized type. I feel that right today, were there to be another trial of a similar nature, the verdict would probably be the same and that there has not yet and, in my view, in the foreseeable future will not be a notable westernization in China because I think it's harder to change the Chinese way of thinking than any of us would like to recognize.

I think this is an interesting incident because it came right out in the papers, and this guy was acquitted because cumshaw was a recognized way of doing business in China. You can carry that on, and the business of integrity gets pretty thin.

Q: Integrity, as we know it.

Adm. C.: As we know it. And I simply record it because it may have historical significance in the future.

Q: Back of that attitude stands, it seems to me, the attitude toward the individual, the individual in the western world and the lack of that in the eastern world.

Adm. C.: Absolutely. I would agree 100 percent. I thought it to be less true, probably, on Taiwan, where there is to a degree an absorption of western ideals.

Q: That is, among the ruling group?

Adm. C.: Yes. Possibly a result of some of them accepting Christianity.

Q: It's the Christian influence. Madame herself.

Adm. C.: Madame herself and, of course, the President himself. And a number of his trusted advisers. Yet, on the contrary, the Japanese have never embraced Christianity - I think I'm correct - to the degree the Chinese have. Yet, their ideas of integrity are certainly more similar to ours and parallel to ours. It may be of course, that we've left such a mark on them as a result of our occupation, that they have assimilated it to a greater degree than the Chinese.

But it is not a result of religious guidance because the Japanese in some ways, I think, are rather interesting, even if they're not religiously exclusive - if I may use that term - because they have a tendency to cover their bets. You can be a good Buddhist, practise a little Shinto on the side, and maybe throw in a little Christianity.

Q: Well, they've always had a kind of a dual religion.

Adm. C.: Dual religion and I don't think they would stop at dual, because if they needed another cover, why, they could accept a third religion, particularly the advantageous aspects of it, if there are any.

I found that very interesting and I digressed on the story of the Shanghai Light and Power Company because I think it has possible significance.

Now, where were we?

Q: You're on the way back to Annapolis.

Adm. C.: Yes. We finally made the trip back and I was able to pick up my wife and children. The first time we were there was during postgraduate school, the second time was during my wartime experience in the Ordnance Department, and this time I was ordered back, and although I wasn't told precisely what I was to do when I got back, I was assigned to the Executive Department.

Q: No teaching?

Adm. C.: No teaching, which rather surprised me. I was a commander then, and I was given a battalion. I think the rationale was that I had taught, I had now had experience in command, I was needed in the development of the midshipmen's moral and spiritual wellbeing - not spiritual in the sense of religious, but in the sense of traditions of the Navy - more so than I would have been in teaching.

Q: And the ethical area?

Adm. C.: Ethical is a better word, moral and ethical. I welcomed it. I found it intensely interesting. You were working more closely with the young men than you would have been in the class, because after all the classroom contact is once every two or three times a week. But this way I could see the young men practically every day. My office was in Bancroft Hall as a battalion officer.

At that time, there were some midshipmen who had served in the Navy, and had decided to come to the Naval Academy - one or two even after having been commissioned as Reserve officers, but quite a few with enlisted experience. So this was a very experienced Naval Academy in those days.

My first year, I was the tennis representative, having been a tennis player at the Naval Academy. I worked with the team in addition to working with the people in my battalion. I served a year as a battalion officer, and then was moved to the head of the Leadership Department. It seems to me somewhere along in there I made captain.

I was the executive officer the last year. I was there

from July of 1948 to March of 1951.

Q: You were there under Admiral Hill, then?

Adm. C.: Yes, under Admiral Holloway and Admiral Hill.

My first year was as battalion officer, so that I was pretty well able to live with the midshipmen, to go down in the evenings and consult and guide them as best I could, listen to their problems, and get to know them.

The second year I was made head of the Leadership Department.

Q: What does that entail?

Adm. C.: That entails - well, I think there was a very unique approach to the problem of developing young men in the traditions of the service to make them effective junior officers in the fleet. The Leadership Department was based on this principle: first of all, to understand human behavior you should have a basic knowledge of psychology, enough to give you a working knowledge; then, the second phase of the leadership program was the study of a book, whose name now escapes me, but it was basically precept and examples - stories of naval heroes, how they reacted to any given condition; and the third, which followed rather logically, was a course in naval justice, earlier called Courts and Boards and, as I will later tell you, at that particular time the Courts and Boards were revised to the Uniform Code of Military Justice.

So, my second year I was involved in that particular program, and it was quite a change, but I had known the midshipmen rather intimately and was glad to head this particular facet of their education.

When I was told I was going to take this job, somebody said we really don't teach them enough psychology. West Point teaches a great deal more and we ought to teach them a lot more and cut back on the Courts and Boards and possibly cut back on the precepts and examples. It was a little book called Naval Leadership by Precept and Example and it had been written by the Naval Institute. Anyhow, I said: "I'm not a psychologist and I don't know whether they need any more or any less. Why don't you send me to Johns Hopkins and let me study for the summer. I'll take intensive courses and then I'll come back and I'll give you a recommendation on what you ought to do." And they said great, go right ahead.

So I went over to the Bureau of Personnel and they signed me up for courses at Johns Hopkins, and I commuted daily all during the summer. I took two courses, one in basic psychology- the other in educational psychology.

Q: How did you find going back to the books at that stage?

Adm. C.: I found that I could still handle it. I got As in one course and Bs in the other, and there were a lot of bright young kids, but I felt that it was well worthwhile. I was delighted to have done it. It provided me with a fund of information, hopefully not just a little bit and a dangerous thing, but a fund of information that I felt enabled me to make the recommendation that, in my view, we didn't need any more basic psychology. We had enough. Part of the recommendation or decision, if you want to call it that, was based on the fact that the two professors I had - both were Ph. D.s - their approach to the problems was completely different. One was an M.D. who had gotten his M.D. from Harvard and his Ph.D. from Hopkins, I think, or the other way round, he had the clinical approach. He wanted to go into your mind and find out where the wire was crossed and, if your behaviour was a little bit odd, there was, in his view, a God damned good reason for it. The other one would put everything to the normal distribution curve, and anything at this end of it was abnormal in one way, and anything at this end was abnormal in the other way.

And when you realized the background for these two men, you could understand why. One had worked for his doctorate by studying the prisons of either Illinois or Indiana -

Q: His field work was prisons?

Adm. C.: His field work was prisons, so he looked at normal behavior as the middle of a curve and abnormal behavior as something else, and he believed in that. And yet the other man believed just as strongly in the opposite approach. I

Chew #3 - 162

must admit that I was instrumental in having the doctor hired by the Naval Academy as a consulting psychiatrist, and I think he was quite helpful.

Q: You leaned to his theory!

Adm. C.: I leaned to his theory, I'm afraid, a little more than I did the other.

Q: Through this contrast you saw a certain amount of faddism to the whole thing?

Adm. C.: To the whole thing, and I felt that I was far better qualified to come back and head the department. It was not a department because it was in the Executive Department, which was under the Commandant of Midshipmen. I'm sure it's since been assimilated by somebody else or is taught in a different way, but at that time it seemed to me very logical that you should teach a little basic psychology, then give your dosage of precept and example to show how a guy should do it, and then, God damn it, if you didn't do it, show what happened to him. That was extremely logical to me.

Q: A more common-sense approach!

Adm. C.: It was fairly common sense, I thought. As I said, at that time the old naval Courts and Boards were really misplaced, and I can't think of the priest's name, but he was the one who made all the studies on justice during the war and came in with a great many recommendations. He was at the Naval Academy and talked to me at great length prior to making his recommendations which eventually, I think, became the groundwork for the revision of Courts and Boards into the Code of Military Justice, which I'm sure, as you will recognize, liberalized quite markedly the justice system throughout the services, and made it uniform which I thought was good.

So, my second year was spent as the head of the Leadership Department, and then my third year at the Naval Academy was as executive officer of Bancroft Hall, which is now called the deputy commandant.

My boss was Bob Pirie and we were great and good friends, mild antagonists on the squash courts where we played every noon, and became fast friends throughout the remainder of our naval careers.

Q: How did you find Admiral Hill as Superintendent?

Adm. C.: Oh, I was devoted to Admiral Hill. I had some very interesting conversations with him. There's one aspect of my tour at the Naval Academy that I think is significant. If anyone asked me right now what I contributed, in any small way, which you always hope you will, it would be my help in developing the Honor System.

The midshipmen, as I said, at that particular time and

it was, say, 1950, included some who had been enlisted men in the Navy, and one or two had been officers in the Navy prior to coming to the Naval Academy. They were a very mature bunch. Prior to that time, the Naval Academy had no formal honor system. We were all supposed to be officers and gentlemen and, as such, were not expected to lie, cheat, or steal, but it wasn't formalized. And there were a couple of very idealistic young men who came to me in my capacity as both the head of the Leadership Department and later as exec and said:

"Captain, really we feel that the Naval Academy should have an honor system that is if not the equivalent of, similar to that at West Point."

I became very deeply involved. The first honor system was evolved under Admiral Hill's superintendency and I was instrumental in developing it. I say this with pardonable pride because most of the midshipmen wanted the same system that was in effect at West Point and I didn't!

I had many discussions with them about the West Point System or Code. Obviously an honor system should cover the three cardinal sins, lying, cheating and stealing, and this, of course the West Point Code did. However, I had three basic objections to their system.

First, I felt they had expanded on their code to cover other offenses. I was told, for example, that a Cadet going on leave in New York could be made "honor bound" not to take a drink. This seemed completely unrealistic to me and far beyond the basic concepts of preserving honor and integrity.

Second, the Honor Committee composed of cadets, made disciplinary recommendations that were binding, i.e. dismissal.

The third that I had was the requirement not only to turn yourself in - report yourself for one of the above infractions, but to turn in anyone else observed committing them.

In my discussions with the Midshipmen I was able to convince them rather easily, that whatever system we adopted should be rigidly limited to the basic honor offenses - lying, cheating and stealing. I think the ridiculous example I used was that if it applied to drinking, why not apply it to "talking in ranks" or "failing to get a haircut."

Today with increased participation by the students in nearly everything, I might have had difficulty in combating the idea of having the Honor Committee taking disciplinary action itself, but at that time I was able to make the point that decisions of such gravity were command decisions and should be made at the top and not by students even though they were the Honor Committee. For this was the Military Way of Life for which they were being trained.

The real problem, it seemed to me, was that of reporting contemporaries - classmates. From a practical point of view the requirement of turning yourself in for an honor infraction was unrealistic and against human nature. If you were the kind of a guy who was going to commit such an offense, the chances were remote as hell that you could be made to feel honor bound to report yourself. There were no real problems in reporting subordinates. Certainly there were gray areas - for example - was he borrowing a stamp and forgot to tell you, or fifteen cents, or five bucks, or was he really stealing. Or you see someone gazing over another man's paper. Is he copying the paper, cheating? Do you know? But if he was a subordinate the chances are a report would have been made and the investigation and decision as to punishment left to the authorities. No honor system seemed necessary under those circumstances. The old adage of being an officer and a gentleman which served us so well all these many years seemed adequate.

So, as I said, the real problem came down to the contemporary relationship complicated to a certain degree, by the gray areas pin pointing an honor infraction. For this reason honor committees of representative midshipmen seemed necessary. The purpose of the committees was to investigate any report, determine if an infraction had occurred, and if it had, make its report to the Executive Department. The nature of the punishment, if any, was then solely a matter of determination by the Academy authorities. The most important point was the individual making a report to the Honor Committee had the approbation and support of his peers in bringing to light a possible infraction.

So this was, in general, the system that was adopted. It may have been modified by now, but I think it was a fine start.

Q: Admiral Hill was very much interested in building morale through sports and that sort of thing.

Adm. C.: Very much.

Q: Will you comment on that?

Adm. C.: Yes. As I said, my first year I was the tennis representative so I was fully aware of his interest. He was active himself. He always came out every afternoon to watch the teams practice. He was interested in one other very active program which was to evaluate midshipmen as to their future capabilities and potentialities.

At the Academy the aptitude-for-the-service program had really just come into being. It was simple enough for a first classman to grade a second classman or third classman, but it was very difficult - and this was a part of my argument - for a first classman to evaluate his own contemporaries. There have been various theories on this. One, for example, that was prevalent in earlier days was that submariners who were more their own contemporaries were harder on each other than larger ships where the senior evaluator was far above the lower level that he was evaluating, and consequently had a tendency to be more lenient. That's the other side of the coin. But this aptitude-for-the-service thing was based on conduct marks, which were purely arithmetical marks determined from conduct reports, and from - a mark that was a combination very similar to a fitness report system, - of your attitude, I've forgotten the exact terms now, but your attitude, your military bearing, and general aptitude for the service. That was commonly called, and I'm sure you're familiar with the term, the grease mark. As you progressed from plebe through youngster to second and first class, your grease mark multiple was given more and more weight when averaged with your academic marks to determine your class standing.

Interview No. 4 with Vice Admiral John L. Chew, U. S. Navy (Ret.)

Place: His residence in Providence, Annapolis, Maryland

Date: Thursday morning, 14 December 1972

Subject: Biography

By: John T. Mason, Jr.

Q: Admiral, it's good to see you this morning. Last time, you concluded your remarks with an account of your tour of duty at the Naval Academy when you were there in an executive capacity. Now, I think, you want to say how you extricated yourself from this assignment in order to go to sea.

Adm. C.: My departure from the Naval Academy this time was accomplished a little more readily, purely as a matter of luck. Normally, the tour of duty at the Naval Academy, if there is such a thing as a normal tour of duty, is approximately three years. I knew I was expected to leave in June of 1951. About the middle of February I received a call from Admiral Murray Stokes, who had been my executive officer on the first Helena, and he said:

"Jack, would you like to go to London? I'm going as Admiral Carney's chief of staff and I would love to have you go also — "

Q: Was this CinCNelm?

Adm. C.: CinCNelm. " — in a capacity on the staff." With June Week staring me in the face for the third time, I jumped at the opportunity and said, in essence, when do we leave. He said:

"You'll have to leave in March and consequently you won't finish out your three years," and I said that would be delightful, "I can eliminate all the problems of June Week that normally are those of the executive officer, and I will be delighted and ready to leave whenever you say."

At this time, my wife had a blood-pressure problem and naturally I came home and said:

"Hey, we have been asked to go to London, what does the doctor say about you?" and she said, "Let's go."

So, in March we departed from the Naval Academy and arrived in London. I think any foreign duty is always interesting and, from my point of view, great fun. This was my first real exposure to Admiral Carney, who was then CinCNelm, and I can't tell you how impressive a man I thought he was.

Q: A living dynamo!

Adm C.: Absolutely. He never ceased to amuse me with his wit, his quickness, his facility with words. I would labor over a dispatch as a staff officer, and he would sit down and dictate it and his would be so much better than mine that I have always felt a little ashamed of myself. One of his favorite stories that I have never forgotten was we were discussing some of the problems attendant on CinCNelm and its association with the JCS-RE and he felt things were being done backwards. He said:

"Jack, damn it, this reminds me of a tonsillectomy through the rectum!"

During my service on the staff I was in the Joint Plans Division and that section was Army, Navy, and Air Force, and we were concerned with the joint planning with the Army in Europe and the Air Force in Europe. At that time, there was no such thing as SACEur. There were the three commanders, who were called the JCS-RE which meant the JCS-General Handy and, I believe, General Norstad, who later went on after Eisenhower to become SACEur.

We were in London from March until September and then CinCSouth was established and Admiral Carney became CinCSouth.

Q: With headquarters in Naples?

Adm. C.: Yes, such as they were. As a matter of fact, the headquarters at that time were on an AGC. I think it was the Adirondack. We had not even moved ashore. After a few weeks or possibly longer, we established a headquarters in downtown Naples and moved the staff ashore.

Q: Didn't Carney have the villa of Lady Hamilton there?

Adm. C.: Yes, he had Villa Nicki, which I can tell you another story about that occurred later on in my career.

Most of our problems at that particular time were involved in disestablishing the JCS-Representatives Europe and establishing what later became the Supreme Allied Commander, Europe, SACEur.

Q: These were administrative problems?

Adm. C.: No, these were actually study problems because at that time Admiral Carney preferred - and I think it was the Navy's position at the time - that the JCS-RE were adequate. After all, this was basically a logistic-type command and there wasn't a need for a centralized command in Europe. I think as a matter of record and if I remember correctly, Admiral Anderson on the staff of Eisenhower was instrumental in establishing the centralized control and it was his study that eventually prevailed, although in my capacity as a member of the staff of Admiral Carney I was generally opposed to it.

Our stay in Naples was again, I thought, interesting. We were there, for example, when there was no PX, there were no facilities. As I mentioned, the headquarters were on the ship. We lived on the economy. There was a DOD school established for our youngsters.

I remember going up to Heidelberg as a member of a study group. Captain Laird was the head of the study group and we had a joint team, including a Colonel Tabb from our staff, and here again we were still opposing the centralization of control which eventually came to pass with Eisenhower in command in Europe. It was interesting to me - if I can remember the precise relation - General Eisenhower argued, I believe, that Admiral Carney should not be an American commander with responsibilities in London and Allied commander with responsibilities to NATO. It seemed strange to me that he ended up doing just precisely that, being the American overall commander and the Allied commander as well.

Our stay in Naples was really touched off by the decision to establish SACEur and divorce Admiral Carney, who was then both CinCNelm and CinCSouth, and reestablish CinCNelm as the U. S. command back in London. So, we arrived in March and stayed in London until September, moved to Naples in September -

Q: Of 1951?

Adm. C.: Of 1951, and then when SACEur was established and the U. S. command reestablished in London moved back to London in June of 1952. So we were really in Naples under

Admiral Carney only nine months.

I went back to London and Admiral Wright had been established as CinCNelm and, as I said, Admiral Carney had been divorced of that responsibility and remained in Naples.

Q: When you were initially in London and when you returned, since you were Joint Plans, did you have some concern about the Berlin situation and the Russians on the horizon?

Adm. C.: Yes, we did. As I remember, it was a little early then to anticipate the full impact of - or at least we didn't visualize the problem. We could see it in the offing, but it was not imminent enough to really do a great deal about it at that particular time. As you can see, my tour there was broken up, with the six months in London, the nine months in Naples, and then approximately a year back in London under Admiral Wright.

At that time my wife had a very serious illness, which I mention only because it had a bearing on where I went later on, what my assignments would be.

Q: Well, and it had a bearing at that time on you.

Adm. C.: Of course, yes. But interestingly enough, it affected my naval career to a certain degree because during my stay in London I had been selected to go to the Naval War College. As a matter of fact, I can say in all honesty I

Chew #4 - 175

was rather disappointed because at that time it was considered that the National War College was the place to go-

Q: Having just been set up a few years before!

Adm. C.: Having just been set up a few years before, and consequently I was told I was going back to the Naval War College. I wrote a letter to the Bureau and, in essence, said:

Dear Bureau (I think I addressed it specifically to Admiral Bill Cooper, who's a good friend of mine),

Dear Bill,

I've been on a Joint Plans staff. I've been in London and my title was something like Assistant Strategic Joint Operations Plans Officer, and I think my title was somewhat the same in Naples. Then when I returned to London I was a Project Officer for Special Matters in the Joint Plans Division, and if I am going back to the Naval War College to learn how to plan and how to get along in joint matters, I think it is a waste of my time and the Navy's time also.

He wrote back and said he was inclined to agree with me and if I didn't want to go to the Naval War College I didn't have to, and he would assign me to a ship -

Q: He didn't give you the option of the National War College?

Adm. C.: No, and at that time I'm not so sure whether I would have taken that either.

In the meantime, my wife had had a stroke and it became obvious that she would be an invalid probably the rest of her life, and to go to sea seemed impossible. I thought, after having asked for it, it was going to be a bit unusual to turn around and say now that I've asked for it and you've told me I can go, I really can't go, but such happens to be the case. Admiral Burke arrived in London and solved my problem by asking me to go back with him, the Director of the Strategic Plans Division, Op-60 - " Maybe he was already Op-60 at that time. I think he was, and he said: "It's a killing job, a hard-working job, but at least you'll be close to Bethesda and will be available. Would you like to come back to Op-60?"

Naturally, having Admiral Burke ask, I was flattered. I later learned how difficult it was to work in Op-60 and I'm sure that any number of people will verify the fact that the hours in the Strategic Plans Division, although it was at one time supposed to be a steppingstone to promotion, were probably the worst of any in any section of the Navy Department.

Q: But you'd had a bit of experience in that type of thing in working for Admiral Carney. I mean, a similar drive.

Adm. C.: Yes, I had. I think Admiral Carney frankly was able to sometimes get things done a little more quickly even than Admiral Burke, but Admiral Burke was a tremendous driver and obviously it was a great privilege to be sent back to -

Q: Before you launch into that, I would like to ask one other question about your service with CinCNelm. Was CinCNelm not concerned about Middle Eastern affairs in those days?

Adm. C.: Oh, I'm glad you asked that question because CinCNelm's bailiwick extended all the way to Burma, and indeed we were concerned about Middle Eastern affairs. One of the highlights of our tour, really, in CinCNelm - this was when I had gone back to London -

Q: The year in London?

Adm. C.: Yes - was an inspection trip to the Far East and it was fascinating. We flew with Admiral Wright to Naples and then over to Malta, where he consulted with the then commander in Malta, Lord Mountbatten. And, as a matter of fact, I had the opportunity to discuss under the wings of the plane the philosophy of the RAF versus the USAF with Admiral Mountbatten.

Admiral Mountbatten, knowing that we were having our problems in Europe between the Navy and the Air Force, as we often do, said:

"You know, the reason the RAF and the Royal Navy get along

so well together is not necessarily because - or, putting it conversely, is not necessarily because the Army and the Air Force get along well together in the United States and the Royal Navy and the Royal Air Force get along together so well, the Royal Air Force sprang from the Royal Navy and the U. S. Air Force sprang from the U. S. Army. But the Royal Air Force actually, in addition from springing from the Royal Navy, had its procurement pretty well as an off-shoot of the Royal Navy's technical knowledge in the manufacturing business. And it was because the Royal Navy controls so much of the industrial capacity of great Britain in terms of developing armament, guns, sights, that they also eventually began to control - or, at least, to have a say in - the operation of the Royal Air Force.

"Of course, your Air Force sprang directly from the Army and consequently they seem to get along better with the Army than they do with the Navy, while the RAF had its allegiance to the Royal Navy."

I thought this was very interesting.

Q: The RAF virtually absorbed the Fleet Air Arm, didn't it?

Adm. C.: Virtually, yes. Of course, the Fleet Air Arm originally, I think, was at least suited-up naval officers, then, later on as times changed, the fliers aboard the carriers were actually RAF pilots.

Chew #4 - 179

Q: And aren't there those, in this country at least, who ascribe the lesser status of the British aircraft carrier, in contrast with ours, to the fact that this happened?

Adm. C.: Quite possibly so.

I found Lord Mountbatten, and obviously he is, an interesting man. I met him back in London again I think once after that, but I've forgotten when.

Q: His American deputy at that time was Jimmy Fife, wasn't he?

Adm. C.: Yes. As I said, this trip, which started out as an inspection trip - Admiral Wright really wanted to go all the way to Burma, but I think at that time they changed the line and we didn't quite get that far. But we did go from Malta to Cyprus, where we spent a night and discussed, not in any great depth, but in at least a cursory manner, the situation on the island. We flew from there to Dhahran, Saudi Arabia, where we spent a couple of days, basically looking over the situation.

Q: With the Aramco people?

Adm. C.: With the Aramco people, and that's where I saw the examples of the carnage that was left by the sheik's entourage when they used the guest house at the Aramco compound.

Q: Did we have a Persian Gulf station at that time?

Adm. C.: I think we did, but we didn't visit it because that was really, as I remember, an arm of the Sixth Fleet that this was not a responsibility per se of CinCNelm, although eventually it would come under that particular command.

We left Dhahran also by plane and flew to Karachi. This was purely an inspection trip. I use the word "inspection" advisedly. We were in Karachi, or in Pakistan, approximately a week and were fortunate enough to go up to Peshawa, which is the beginning of the Khyber Pass, and took a trip up the Khyber Pass to the Afghanistan border. That was truly a memorable trip in terms of our heritage. You could think of Kipling and you could think of old battles that were well memorialized by a stone saying that the 31st Khyber Rifles - I use that number, but I'm not quite sure what it was - fought here, and the Northumberland Fusiliers fought here, and all the various British organizations fought here, and here, and here. In honor of Admiral Wright they had sentries who stood on sort of blocks or stones all the way up the Pass with their rifles at the ready, and after we got all the way to the head of the Pass approximately, the Khyber Rifles put on one of their ceremonial dances, and I might add that after they twirled and jumped and spun they really put the average modern gymnast to shame for just sheer endurance.

It was interesting also to me to find that there were quite a number of blue-eyed people, natives, with their long beards in that area, and naturally I asked the question, and the answer I got was that they were possibly descendants of the lost tribe or Pathans - I think Pathan is the proper term - and they were indeed an interesting throwback. But thinking back as school kids, what could be more fascinating than to go up the Khyber Pass and see and hear Gunga Din sort of pouring the water out of the bucket for you. Possibly, he did that somewhere else, but it was truly a memorable occasion for me.

We came back, had conferences at Rawalpindi, and I think at this time - of course, there's always been the basic animosity between Pakistanis and Indians -

Q: Religious, basically?

Adm. C.: Religious basically. Of course, we all know Mountbatten was the man who was responsible for segregating, or for breaking off East and West Pakistan - East Pakistan, which is no more a part of Pakistan - based on purely religious lines. We discussed the defense of Pakistan in limited matters with the Pakistani high command, which was at Rawalpindi. I don't know that anything significant was really accomplished, but it was interesting to exchange views with them. They were apprehensive even then, and I think at that time, too, the Kashmir thing was a source of trouble.

Q: Yes, they were planning a plebiscite.

Adm. C.: Yes. We came back from Peshawa, as I said, by Rawalpindi and returned to Karachi, where we picked up the <u>Pittsburgh</u>, which was a cruiser in the Sixth Fleet, and rode her down to Ceylon. It was a break from air travel, at least from my point of view, and one of the few times that I was aboard a warship during my entire cruise with CinCNelm.

We stayed in Ceylon about a week, and went up to Nuwara, which I believe is spelled Nuwara Eliya, but is called Nuwara. This was purely a recreational visit, Nuwara being the summer resort for Colombo. Of course, we went over to Trincomalee and looked at the installations over there.

Q: Was the Royal Navy using them at that time?

Adm. C.: I don't think so. We had nothing there at that particular time, as I remember. It was available, but they were beginning to roll back there. We visited Mountbatten's headquarters up in the hills of Ceylon.

Q: His headquarters as they came to be?

Adm. C.: Yes. Well, no, his headquarters during World War II and they were sort of preserved as a, not a shrine, but certainly as a place of interest. As a matter of fact, I remember playing golf at Nuwara and it was about 7,000 feet up and I theoretically felt that I could hit the golf ball farther but it didn't seem to work that way precisely. It was most enjoyable. It was very cold and brisk at night. We sat around an open fire. It was a thoroughly delightful weekend.

We returned to Colombo by car and departed there for Madras.

Q: On the *Pittsburgh*?

Adm. C.: On the *Pittsburgh*. We stayed there for a short time. It was my first exposure to India. There were still the remnants of what has been commonly called, is commonly called, colonialism. The British race track was operating beautifully clockwise, ours go counterclockwise, and life seemed to be, as you would expect it. Of course, in India there were signs, as there are, as I later found out, in most Asian countries of abject poverty and considerable affluence. Interestingly enough, the trip to Madras doesn't loom large in my memory and frankly I think I was perfectly happy to leave via the *Pittsburgh* on our way back to London, where we stopped in Aden for a short inspection tour of not over a day. Then we left for London by air.

Q: At that stage of the game, was the American Navy at all interested in island bases in the Indian Ocean, or were they still the exclusive province of the Royal Navy?

Adm. C.: I think I can answer that unequivocally. We had very little interest in the island bases in the Indian Ocean. It only became evident with the complete withdrawal of the British Navy from that area, or certainly the pullback, that we evinced any interest. I was familiar with that later on in my capacity as Op-44, which was involved with bases, but at that particular time I think we had very little interest and expected that to be the province of the Royal Navy.

Q: But this was the postwar era and did we not have some knowledge of the fact that the British were going to withdraw?

Adm. C.: I think we had the knowledge but I think from the practical point of view we sort of still hoped that they would be able to handle it. I don't know whether that's an accurate appraisal of it or not but it did not seem to me that we were there looking, for example, at the Seychelles or at any of the islands that we have later been interested in, for whatever reason, whether it happened to be for a communications station or an actual base.

As I remember it, Aden was fairly tense at that time. Whether it was a side effect of the total Middle East problem or not — oh, I remember. The British were beginning to withdraw from Aden. In fact, there were very few units left there and this was one of the reasons, I believe, that we had gone there, to sort of take a look at the situation. It was felt, I think, that they could still handle the situation there, but whether at that time the complete withdrawal was anticipated or not I don't know - or at least if I did know I've forgotten.

Q: During that year you were in London, did you make any specific plans in terms of the developing animosities between the Arabs and the Jews, the new state of Israel?

Adm. C.: I'm glad you asked that question because, as I remember, during my stay there we had plans for practically every contingency, except the one that actually occurred. Now that's hard to believe, but that's the truth and I remember it well. We had plans for the Israelis beating the hell out of the Egyptians, the Egyptians beating the hell out of the Israelis - we had all sorts of plans. But the actual situation that came about - when was it - about two or three years later - as I remember, we had no plan for. Maybe in the interim, in that great joint planning group, such a plan was developed, but I thought it was of interest to note that during my time there that particular situation frankly was not foreseen.

Q: Now, that prompts another question on my part, something that has long intrigued me in terms of these plans that the Navy and the other services make. When you develop plans for a given situation and that situation does indeed develop, are the plans usable under those circumstances or do they have to call for much modification?

Adm. C.: I would think an honest answer to that is that practically any plan has to be modified, some to a greater extent than others, some to the extent that you don't even recognize the original plan. And I think there's probably a very good reason for that. The situation has changed, the practical aspects have changed. The forces that were earmarked for some reason or other have changed. Of course, the plans are theoretically updated so that this won't happen, but, in fact, it does happen. Then, probably even more important is the political situation changes even more drastically, and this obviously has a tremendous effect.

Q: When that happens, when a situation develops and you are confronted with it, is it better to start from scratch at that point and make another one?

Adm. C.: That's a very good question, and I've heard people say it's better to have a plan than no plan at all. Of course, the corollary to that is that a plan is no better than the assumption on which it is made, and if those assumptions change or become invalid then the validity of the plan itself is put in jeopardy.

In fact, in answer to your question, I had the President of the Republic of China once say to me:

"Well, Admiral, it's better to have a plan than no plan at all, no matter how bad."

That's how he felt about it. I think essentially it is better to have a plan because even though you may not anticipate the actual combat operations - and this is particularly true of the Army - you have to have some sort of a logistic plan to get people there even if they don't do what was originally planned. So, for that aspect of it, I think planning is most important.

I'm not sticking up for planning because I was a planner once, but I think from a truly objective appraisal I would say yes, even though as one of the Middle East planners we developed plans for every contingency possible and didn't even hit the one that actually eventuated. Now, whether certain annexes of the original plans would be useful in a different situation, I would think yes. So in that respect, again, I would consider it better to have some sort of a plan rather than none at all.

Q: It causes us to focus on an area, whether we anticipate what develops or not?

Adm. C.: Yes. And, as I said before, the logistic aspects require a certain amount of prepositioning, possibly stockpiling, and this could be done to meet a situation that doesn't necessarily develop as the plan called for, and I think it would be very necessary.

Q: And the logistics of a situation don't change that much, do they, except for the development of technological things?

Adm. C.: That's right, and different concepts, of course, as we've gone from getting everything there by land, sea, or air to even stockpiling in logistic ships or that particular concept. But, basically, when you have material involved there should be some sort of a reasonable schedule to get it where it's going to be eventually needed, even if it isn't used for precisely the purpose for which it was originally intended.

Q: At that point in time, was there any evidence that the Russians might have intentions of pushing down into the Mediterranean and into the Persian Gulf?

Adm. C.: I think that possibility was always in the back of our minds, but in 1951 and 1952 it was a little too early. Later events, starting possibly with Sputnik going through the U-2 incident, and then, of course, crystallizing in the Cuban missile crisis, really shifted the focus to Russia. But at that particular time, as I remember it, although we'd think of it in the back of our minds we really had no plans whatsoever for that type of confrontation.

As I remember, chronologically, we were about to leave CinCNelm, but you reminded me of the trip almost to the Far

East, and then we left Madras and went back to Aden, and from Aden we flew back to London. I can't remember precisely what month that was, but it seems to me that it was during the winter and then, as I mentioned, Admiral Burke suggested that I go to Op-60.

Q: Yes. You left CinCNelm in June of 1953.

Adm. C.: Yes, and I arrived back in Washington within a short time and reported to Admiral Burke in Op-60.

On a listing it has my title as "head of the Joint Plans Section of the Strategic Plans Division." Initially, I was not. I was head of the Psychological Warfare Division of the Navy. Not only was I the head, but I was the only one concerned.

Q: This had to do with propaganda?

Adm. C.: This had to do with all of the aspects of psychological warfare, which was really pretty much the Army's bailiwick and the Air Force's and they, I might add, had rather extensive staffs with which I as the sole psychological warrior was supposed to keep up with. As a matter of fact, Admiral Burke once told me:

"Jack, you've set the Navy back years in psychological warfare!"

I said: "Have I, Admiral? I didn't really know how to

get it ahead."

My feeling was that psychological warfare within the Navy was a sort of losing business unless we could inspire propaganda shells or something like that. Our business primarily was to fight and we didn't have to think the enemy into doing anything. It was too much of a cut-and-dried business. If you were going to fight-fight and not try to influence anybody psychologically.

Q: If there was a contrasting point of view, what was it?

Adm. C.: Oh, well, of course, there was psychological warfare in the Army -

Q: No, I mean in terms of Navy activities.

Adm. C.: Everybody, I felt, recognized that there was a limited value because the other services had such sections of their staffs and it behooved us, as a joint operation, to at least participate in these activities. And if we had to support them, that's something else again. Of course, you could always support people by infiltration via submarine or an airdrop or something like that, so we had peripheral duties and I was the peripheral guy who was supposed to coordinate the Navy's psychological activities.

Q: I suppose we had some experience with that in the Philippines, did we not, with the watchers and so forth?

Adm. C.: Yes, indeed we did, but I wonder whether we would call watchers psychological. I think you get into the area of whether it's psychological or whether it's intentional - not intentional, I mean whether it's psychological or whether it's intelligence.

We had two officers in the section, Captain Parsons and I. One was the psychological warfare gent and the other was the unconventional warfare gent. Bill was the unconventional warfare -

Q: Was that tied in with CIA?

Adm. C.: To a certain degree, but it tied him in mainly with the unconventional warfare forces of the other services more than the CIA. In fact, we had very little to do in our capacities. We sat in a little cubbyhole way down the corridor and primarily were concerned more with, as I said, whatever support the Navy had to provide for joint psychological operations, because the capabilities of the Navy to indulge in psychological warfare per se, I felt, were very limited. And I think Admiral Burke felt they were pretty limited, too, although he used to needle me to keep me up to snuff.

I stayed in that office until there was a vacancy. One of the officers was transferred and then I moved up to the head of the Joint Plans Section. Thank God for me and the

Navy!

Q: That's when you got involved in those extensive hours?

Adm. C.: Oh, yes. Well, I was involved in extensive hours in the Psychological Warfare Division because the system of operation is such that when the Joint Chiefs of Staff meet, if they're going to discuss a psychological operation, the staff officer still sits around and waits until they come out to see what he has to provide for tomorrow's meeting or whatever piece of paper he has to prepare. And the same briefings go on for your own boss, the CNO, to prepare him for the meetings. So the hours in Op-60, which I was in from July of 1953 till July of 1956, were always long. As a matter of fact, very frankly I think Admiral Burke prided himself on their being long. His successor was Admiral Dennison, and even under Admiral Dennison it was difficult to shorten the hours because of the system.

Q: And also because of the man!

Adm. C.: Well, Admiral Dennison could cut through things pretty nicely if he really wanted to. I have the greatest admiration for him. He was a marvelous person to work for and had a lot of the same cutting edge in a different way as Admiral Carney.

Q: Give me a word picture of Admiral Burke at work in Op-60.

Adm. C.: I admire Admiral Burke and always have. I can't draw a parallel with any particular leader, but I must say that Admiral Burke could see the crux of a situation. I must say in all frankness that he was not as articulate as Admiral Dennison or Admiral Carney, but he knew what had to be done and he could tell people what to do. If he couldn't put the words down, somebody else could, and he knew when they were right. How that quality comes through I can't tell you, but I had the greatest admiration for him. He was a completely different type of leader than Admiral Dennison, completely different, and I imagine that part of it stems from the myth- not the myth, but his actual exploits during the war when he was a great operational commander. I wouldn't liken him to Patton at all, but still he was obviously inspiring to people who worked under him.

I think Admiral Dennison was inspiring in another way. His intellect alone was awe-inspiring to me. And frankly, Admiral Dennison was not easy to talk to in terms of small talk. I lived next door to him in Norfolk for a year and although we were good friends he would not be the kind that would regale you with funny stories.

Q: Would you tell me something about the work that you actually performed there in Op-60, strategic plans that were being developed?

Adm. C.: As head of the Strategic Plans Division, we worked on and in conjunction with the Army and the Air Force on basic war plans. To tell you the honest truth, I've forgotten the code name for it and I'm just as glad. We were always, it seemed to me, involved in some sort of a hassle with either of the other services as to the provisional forces, because in the final analysis this would determine eventually, if you can relate it to that, the provision of money for the ultimate provision of the forces. If you could get a plan, for example, that said you would have so many ships, so many divisions, and get approved, then in the JCS meetings you would have a viable reason for asking for appropriations, and that's why it was so important, and also at the same time, why there was so much dissension - and how we used to fight over words, words, words. In fact, it was really only when I served in the JCS that I realized the importance of preciseness. I'd always thought, you know, that a military man just said I want this, that, and the other, or I hope we need this, that, and the other and that was enough. But not in the JCS. It was very necessary to be precise. The terms that we've all heard were part of my vocabulary, how to waffle a paper - in other words, to say very little, how to slant it. I remember once many years later on when I looked at a paper and I said:

"You know, I worked in the JCS for three years and if this isn't the Goddamnedest slanted paper I've ever seen! You're talking to a guy who knows how to slant a paper."

And most of these were operations in conjunction with the Army and the Air Force in terms of developing force levels. That was one of our major concerns.

Q: Did you get into the area of Jupiter and joint cooperation there?

Adm. C.: No, I did not. I remember very vividly there was a commander in one of the other sections who was the force-level man and he said:

"Gee, just look! By the stroke of a pen I can cross out a cruiser," and, of course, this was just the beginning of the ultimate discussions that resulted in the JCS.

I would say that during that period one of the most important aspects of joint planning really was the development of force levels. I think it started with Admiral Carney, if I remember correctly. Wasn't that the time when we had a "new look" at the forces? Of course, Admiral Carney was CNO when Admiral Burke was in Op-60. I would say that 80 percent of our working time was spent on the development of plans as they affected force levels.

Q: This was in the regime of General Eisenhower as President and he put a lot of stress on the Joint Chiefs and their decisions?

Adm. C.: Yes, he did, and as a staff member in Op-60 I don't believe I ever attended a JCS meeting. I simply was used to brief in any particular area - that is, an area of my concern - or brief Admiral Burke who personally briefed Admiral Carney for his bout in the JCS. Then, after the JCS action your proposals or your papers would be modified in accordance with the decisions of the Chiefs. That was one of the reasons why the hours were so long. There were the deliberations there and the debrief that was necessary, often late, and I got used to it.

At that time I was living in Annapolis. My wife had died, and Admiral Dennison said, "Don't you want to move to Washington?" I said:

"No, I still have two youngsters to raise and, in my view, it's better to be in Annapolis and I'd rather stay here and go through the rigors of commuting, rather than move to Washington and upset their schooling."

Q: You didn't see much of them except on weekends, did you?

Adm. C.: I didn't see much of them at all, but as a matter of just side interest I ran a house. I was fortunate. In those days you could get someone and I had full-time help - a very pleasant black girl who came five days a week. Eventually, of course, I could send both kids to boarding school, but in the initial phases, why, I was able to run the house, get to Washington, get back, and it was a pretty full-time existence, including doing the marketing.

I might add that I was delighted because I'd been in Op-60 for three years when the detail officer called me and said, in essence:

"Jack, if you look at your record you may have been at sea a long time -" and I think I told you that earlier - "to begin with, but you've been ashore a long, long time as a captain and you've got to go to sea."

I said: "Great! When do I go?" And he said:

"Well, I have a destroyer tender for you and, with the situation of your children, possibly it would be better that you take that type of an auxiliary rather than an oiler."

I said: "Not on your life! I'm a naval officer and I'm going to go to sea, and I want the one that does the most sea-going. If you have an oiler available, in comparison to a destroyer tender that just sits at the dock, I want it."

So, he said: "All right, good. I have the Pawcatuck," which was the AO-108.

I was able to leave the Strategic Plans Division of the Office of CNO with happiness and report to the Pawcatuck.

Before going to the Pawcatuck, it might be appropriate to point out that during the planning processes and at that particular time one of the strong points of Navy arguments was that we were self-sufficient. We were proud of our underway replenishment groups, we steadfastly avoided talking about bases on foreign soil. Possibly from time to time this has changed, but at that time part of our pride was in being self-sufficient, and of course this develops the requirement for the underway replenishment groups.

Q: And I suppose this, in a sense, was reflecting a prevailing point of view anyway, which was anti-colonialism?

Adm. C.: Oh, absolutely, and it kept us from entangling alliances, so to speak. It was a very strong feeling and -

Q: How closely did this joint planning group work with the State Department?

Adm. C.: I'd better back into the answer to that one. I think in later years, when I was down in the Joint Chiefs of Staff, there was closer liaison with the State Department, but there was a section within Op-60 that had liaison with the State Department.

Q: So there was a feed-in?

Adm. C.: Yes. Later, that section was strengthened by the actual assigning of an officer to the State Department and, conversely, assigning a State Department representative within the Office of CNO, if I remember correctly. I do know that there was an officer eventually assigned to the State Department for that particular purpose.

So I would say that our liaison with the State Department was good, and there was a specific section within Op-60 set up for that purpose. But I can't over-emphasize the fact that really most of our fights and most of our concerns in the Joint Planning Group were the development of the force levels, which ultimately controlled the budget, or it was thought controlled the budget, whether it really did or not I thought at times was questionable. But the emphasis was placed on the importance of this- as it affected the control of the dollar.

Q: Now I suspect we can focus on your command of the oiler because later on you had more service in the Department and we might well at that point dwell on some of this earlier experience.

Adm. C.: Possibly, I was a little bit better educated when I later came back and so we probably could.

I was happy to be assigned command of the oiler. It's a unique experience. I'd been on cruisers and had destroyers, and really on ships of that size, whether they be destroyers or cruisers, or, obviously, carriers, you have quite a lot of help. If you're a skipper, you have a very competent executive officer and the heads of departments are up-and-coming people, all the way down through the division officers. When you go to an oiler, or at least in those days, it wasn't quite that way. There was experience, but there were few. Here was a big ship characteristically underpowered in comparison with a warship, but you basically had the captain, the exec, the engineer, the deck officer, a couple of watch officers, and that was it. So you had, I felt, tremendous responsibility and at the same time not as much assistance as you would have expected on a combatant ship. I know this to be true.

Q: I know this is an important command, the command of an oiler, and I know that it enhances one's career advancement, but why does it do so in contrast with command of a combatant ship?

Adm. C.: I think it was a pattern that had been established within the Navy that you had to have, prior to your major combat command, an auxiliary, possibly in preparing you for command of a large ship and to enhance your shiphandling capabilities. Even remembering that you'd been the officer of the deck on a cruiser many years before, I think the purpose was to get you back into the seagoing arena and then move you precisely and immediately to your major combat command. Now, let me quickly add that I think this practice has been discontinued. It was almost considered a necessary pattern to be followed if you were ever going to have any chance of promotion to flag rank.

Q: Yes, I've seen so much evidence of this.

Adm. C.: I could say practically unequivocally that that was the pattern. If you didn't have your preparatory command prior to your major combat command, your chances of selection to flag rank as a line officer were nil. The same way for aviators, if they didn't have a carrier. But certainly within recent years that policy has been markedly modified, and I think probably the finest example is the present CNO whose largest ship command was a DDG or a DDL, but a destroyer type before he made flag rank and then eventually became the Chief of Naval Operations.

Q: Well, Sir, when you were in command of the oiler, how much of your time was focused on fueling and refueling at sea and that sort of thing?

Adm. C.: Well, if you remember, in my previous assignment on a ship of this class, the Neches, I think I mentioned we did no fueling at sea. In direct contrast, practically all of our time in the Pawcatuck was spent in replenishing other ships. I think the only pictures I have of the Pawcatuck in the present day show her with normally a cruiser on one side and a destroyer on the other side.

Q: She was a unit of what fleet?

Adm. C.: She was a unit of the Atlantic Fleet. Actually, I

flew to Panama and relieved the commanding officer there, and then came back to Norfolk. If I remember I was only aboard from July till December.

Q: That's right.

Adm. C.: So there was not too much time for extended operations. We came back to Norfolk and then went to the Mediterranean where we were deployed in support of the Sixth Fleet. We made the usual port visits within the very limited time - of course, Naples primarily. As a matter of fact, I was relieved in Piraeus and, it seems to me, that other than performing our normal mission of replenishment at sea, we were in only the ports of Naples and Piraeus. I don't think we even made Villefranche. Maybe we did once. I've been in there before, so I've forgotten on which particular ship it was.

Q: Well now, obviously even an oiler has to refuel at times. Where did you get your supplies of oil?

Adm. C.: When we were here on the East Coast we normally refueled in Norfolk. In fact, we always refueled in Norfolk at the fuel docks up the river, and it was great fun bringing that big old lumbering thing in along the fuel dock-

Q: What was her tonnage?

Adm. C.: The _Pawcatuck_, loaded, I think was between 28,000 and 32,000 tons, with about one-tenth of the horsepower of a cruiser of 17,000 tons. So there was over twice as much ship with approximately one-tenth of the horsepower. At least she had twin screws and that made her easier to maneuver, and you had the fundamental principle of maneuvering that you have on any twin-or quadruple-screw ship. I enjoyed handling her.

We participated, I think, in one fleet exercise. I've forgotten whether it was in the Atlantic or the Mediterranean, but I do remember joining up with the fleet at night. We had a radar but it wasn't working, so we were sort of back to the old seagoing days and one or two of my younger officers said, "How are you going to do this?" and I said:

"Well, you know, we used to do this in days gone by without the radar. We'll do it somehow."

They were rather flabbergasted that we could join up with the fleet formation without the radar and arrive on station without hitting anything of major importance.

Q: To continue that question I asked earlier. When you were in the Med, where did you go to replenish?

Adm. C.: I think we replenished twice in the Med and I think we did it both times from contract tankers. And I think again this was probably in keeping with the principle of not being dependent on foreign bases. As you know, we had MSTS tankers and they were not at that time equipped for fueling at sea. Later on, I think they too were equipped for fueling at sea. We replenished from one of them, and this further reinforces my statement that I made earlier that we were still trying to show that we were not dependent on foreign bases.

Maybe we replenished once in Piraeus. I can't quite remember because we were there almost a week. But I do remember replenishing from an MSTS tanker.

Q: Was there any noticeable advancement in refueling techniques - any noticeable advancement from your previous assignment with the Neches?

Adm. C.: Well, of course, with the Neches there was no fueling at sea conducted.

Q: At all?

Adm. C.: None at all. We were basically a tanker running from point to point, and we had no refueling at sea capability.

Q: No, Well, by the time you served on this one, had there been any advance in techniques?

Adm. C.: Oh, yes, primarily in the technical aspects of the

fueling rig itself. For example, in the earlier days they were winch-controlled, so that you took the slack in and out. An operator on a winch stood there and, as the ships moved relative to each other, he payed in or payed out the gear to allow the hose to reach its connection without parting. There were later developments and, possibly in later years, even more refinements which provided a counterbalanced type system, where the hose suspension was automatically payed in and payed out. This was a big advance. We had one of those installed, as I remember, on the Pawcatuck. I think all the fueling gear on present-day oilers is of the later design that does not require a man standing on a winch paying in and paying out the gear.

And there were tremendous improvements in the quick-acting disconnects, improvements made in the coupling devises which, in the earlier days, were cumbersome and difficult to hook up.

Those were the specific improvements that I think of. This ship herself, except for the fact that she had two screws, was not unlike the Neches - more powerful. The old Neches had reciprocating engines. The Pawcatuck had a turbine. We usually cruised at pretty much maximum speed.

Q: Which was?

Adm. C.: It seems to me we could make about sixteen and a half knots. She was not difficult to handle, particularly with her two screws and, of course, making a dock, you could say "all engines back full" and then read The New York Times before she stopped. But I found it interesting. I found the very short six months fascinating because, let's face it, I liked command. I liked to run the ship. I liked to handle a ship, and you'd be surprised how many people don't, and some successfull flag officers who really never liked to handle a ship, at least in my view. Maybe I'm a bit overestimating my own capabilities, but I always fancied myself as a good shiphandler, so I say this with appropriate modesty, I suppose.

Q: Did you encounter any sort of handicap on board the oiler because of the Navy Department policy of rotating the skippers so frequently?

Adm. C.: I personally didn't no. The exec, of course, was there when I got there and there when I left and so were most of the crew.

Q: They were the permanent ones and the skipper was the transient?

Adm. C.: Yes. So from my point of view there was no, at least apparent, problem. From theirs, maybe tremendous ones. I don't know - that is, from the rest of the officer personnel point of view. But, as I said, it was a quick cruise, just from July until December. I suppose I knew that it was the preparatory command - and that's not the precise word that was used then - before I got my major command, and when I was told that I was to leave the Pawcatuck - as I said, I was relieved in Piraeus - I didn't have very much time and flew home and to the West Coast. It's obvious I didn't take much time because I was relieved of the Pawcatuck in December and I relieved the command of the Roanoke still in December. I flew all the way and had at least a few days with my children and ended up in Long Beach, where I took command.

I think I ought to preface my remarks on the tour in the Roanoke by saying that it was one of the most satisfying commands that a naval officer could have. I enjoyed my approximately thirteen months in that assignment and I think there were basically two reasons. One, as I said, I enjoyed handling the ship. I felt that my experience on the Helena had been of inestimable value. It gave me experience in a cruiser type. I felt that I had refined my capabilities in handling the Pawcatuck, and then to find myself in command of a brand-new light cruiser, I suppose you could say, was the epitome of my career. Let's also put one other point in the proper perspective. I think always you have a hope that you will make flag rank, but whether you do or whether you don't, again my view is that the command of a major combatant is your most satisfying period in the Navy, without any question.

I think I started out by saying that the first reason that I felt that it was going to be the highlight of my career was because I liked shiphandling, and the second reason was because I rather enjoyed handling men. So, in a nutshell, handling ships and handling men, I suppose, makes me an operator in the true sense of the word, and possibly not a thinker and a planner which I had been posing as for quite a few years. I was extremely happy.

I relieved Gene Sands in Long Beach, and we operated out of Long Beach for a period of a few weeks.

Chew #5 - 209

Interview No. 5 with Vice Admiral John L. Chew, U.S. Navy (Ret.)
Place: His home in Providence, Annapolis, Maryland
Date: Wednesday morning, 10 January 1973
Subject: Biography
By: John T. Mason, Jr.

Q: Good to see you in this new year, Sir, and to know that you're going to resume here with your very interesting story.

When we broke off last time, you had left the oiler, which you had commanded less than a year and taken over your major command, the light cruiser Roanoke.

Adm. C.: Well, it's good to have you, too, Jack.

I think one thing I forgot to tell you is something that very few commanding officers ever do and sometimes I wonder how I ever made flag rank. But at the change-of-command ceremony aboard the Pawcatuck, as I remember it, the commanding officer who was relieving me came aboard, we had the usual change-of-command ceremony, and, as the present incumbent, I read my orders and turned around and walked off. I apparently was so undone by the fact of turning over the ship that I forgot to ever be relieved. I simply departed the ship and, as I told you, I think, came on back to the States.

Q: Well, change-of-command can be an emotional experience, can it?

Adm. C.: It was a very emotional experience for me and I just completely forgot that my relief had to read his orders and he had to say "I relieve you, Sir" to complete the procedures. I just turned and walked off and I think about ten minutes later I was off the ship and on my way to Naples where I stopped on the way home.

I think I also told you that my next command, which was the <u>Roanoke</u> that I took in December of 1956, was probably the most satisfying, at least in my view, that an operating naval officer could ever have. If I were to look back - and, of course, you look back on various aspects of your career - the one I think that I enjoyed the most, was the most satisfying, the most fun, and probably the hardest work in some respects, whether the two go hand in hand is debateable, but at the same time I believe that I could say quickly that it was the most rewarding job that I had in the Navy and the one that I look back on with the fondest memories.

Of course, this rather divorces you from your family. This was purely a man's job and one for which, I think, as a naval officer you strive and hope to achieve probably more than any other job in the entire world. At least, that's the way I felt about it.

Q: A ship is a close-knit family and an entity in itself and you're in command.

Adm. C.: And I think, too, that the feeling is cumulative. The better you get the more pride you have, the closer-knit the family becomes. There's nothing like that old adage that nothing succeeds like success, but at the same time if you do have a successful ship the chances are that the morale is exceptionally high, sometimes even too high. I would like to explain what I mean when I say the morale is too high.

Q: Well, when you take over your major command you have a certain freedom because you've perfected your skills as a skipper, and this gives you freedom?

Adm. C.: Perhaps it gives you freedom, but it's freedom tempered with responsibility, and I would say except for those who strive to be Napoleons and those who strive to be the great strategists of our time, it's the most genuinely satisfying feeling in the world to have command of a fine ship. A destroyer is a fine ship in its class and, having commanded one, I'm sure I felt as rewarded at that time, but this was a beautiful thing. For some reason or other, it seemed to me more aesthetic almost than, for example, the ship that I had just left. It ploughed along at a very lumbering speed, but was still satisfying.

I felt, as I said, that the <u>Roanoke</u> was the culmination of a Navy career.

Our cruise was fairly eventful. We left Long Beach shortly after I took command and stopped in Pearl, as is the usual fashion, and then went directly to Sydney. Quite a few of the crew had been to Sydney at one time or another during the war and I had been very careful to explain that, in my view, it was a very fine liberty port. So when we got there we were all primed and had a marvelous stay, so marvelous that as we were leaving the quartermaster turned to me and said:

"Captain, look, we've won the gunnery "E", we've won the engineering "E", we've won the communications "E", we've won the battle efficiency "E", we've got "Es" on every gun, I have an idea. Why don't you write a letter to the Navy Department and say that we appreciate all these honors, but if they will let us go back to Sydney for one more week we'll give them all up and start all over again?"

And I said, well, I didn't feel that they'd view that with much favor but I appreciated the thoughts of the crew.

Q: What makes Sydney so intriguing?

Adm. C.: Well, it's a warm port. They were generous to a

fault. They invited the crew for dinner and to things that never happened even in the home port. There were group dances, there was entertainment for the crew, there was entertainment for the officers, golf and tennis, and people were invited into various homes, and there was always the romance that developed within a period of four or five days. We found it this way during the war, and I found it that way again.

On the way up from Sydney to Sasebo I asked to take the ship through the Solomons to try to point out to the crew where some of the more important battles of World War II had been fought, but due to time limitations we were denied the request.

Q: What was the purpose of your visit to Australia?

Adm. C.: It was simply a goodwill visit and to show the flag.

Q: You were en route to the Seventh Fleet, were you?

Adm. C.: We were en route to the Seventh Fleet. I think my timing is a little off. I don't think we left immediately after I took command because we continued through the gunnery year and finished that before we left for the Orient.

Naturally we were delighted at the opportunity to go to Australia because most of us who had been there recognized the fun, and it was strictly for fun as far as I could see. We had a few official functions, specifically in reciprocal lunches and dinners with the authorities in Sydney and the naval commands there. But it was strictly a sort of a second shake-down cruise really, and it was lovely.

We left Sydney, reluctantly I must admit, and headed for our base-to-be of Sasebo. Most ships are home-ported in Yokosuka nowadays, but at that particular time we were at least temporarily based in Sasebo.

This was my first time back in Japan and I must admit that I had mixed feelings. I had remembered the Japanese only as ferocious enemies, cruel, my experiences on the island had developed almost a genuine hatred, and here it was, the war was over, and we were going back to Japan. I remember talking to a friend before we left and I said:

"I wonder how I'm going to react to these people who have been our mortal enemies. Here we are going to operate from one of their bases. I wonder how I'm going to feel."

And this friend said: "Well, remember one thing. World War II was a bitter war, but probably the bitterest of all wars was fought between our own people in the Civil War, and I think it's within your capability to remember that and possibly look upon these people somewhat as the North looked upon the South or the South looked upon the North."

I found that to be very useful and I found it to be pretty much the truth. The Japanese possibly in their role as a defeated nation were more like us than any other Orientals that I've been associated with. I haven't associated with a great many, but in later years I went back to Japan, as you know, as Commander, Naval Forces, Japan.

But I viewed this whole trip with a great deal of trepidation.

Q: Isn't it rather remarkable that in such a brief period of time the feelings of our men who were involved in World War II changed so drastically?

Adm. C.: I think it's remarkable in this respect, but I think it also has to do with the effort of the Japanese. There were so many traits that were inherent that we liked - we liked their basic cleanliness, we liked their basic honesty-

Q: Their industry.

Adm. C.: Their industry, their stick-to-it-iveness, their ingenuity. These we like to think of as American traits, and we found them duplicated in the Japanese and I think as a consequence probably it speeded the process of healing the breach. At least, it did to me because I was impressed. I was impressed with their industry. I was impressed with their shipyard techniques. Later on I can explain what I mean more fully.

Q: Was there any evidence in that time of their harboring a sense of guilt over World War II techniques?

Adm. C.: I wouldn't be surprised. It's hard to say. I think the average naval officer with whom we had contact in the first days of our stay in Japan was a professional, somewhat similar to our earlier philosophy of naval officers. He didn't delve into the government's rights and wrongs. He did pretty much what he was expected to do, what he had been trained to do, and consequently didn't indulge in philosophizing as to the rights and wrongs of the war because this was what his country had directed him to do and he had been trained to do.

Consequently, it's hard to say. Frankly, I don't think they felt guilty at all. Later on, the higher-ranking officers that I talked to quite frequently and very openly about the war had no feeling of guilt. They felt that they'd made some mistakes and they felt frankly that they'd been taken by a better country. They knew it. They accepted defeat rather, I suppose you'd call it, stoically, but from a practical point of view they said, well, we lost, we might as well settle down now and rebuild. Even this aspect of their philosophy I liked. They recognized what had happened to them and they were going to set about rectifying it.

As you can see, I'm very fond of the Japanese.

Q: Most naval officers I've talked with are!

Adm. C.: Later on, when I was Commander, Naval Forces, Japan, the same feeling was greatly reinforced.

This time, as the captain of a ship, I simply knew some of the lower ranking officers in the Sasebo area and a few of the civilians, including the mayor. The usual thing. But we were in and out quite a bit, so I didn't have an opportunity to really discuss things as much as I had later on in my tour as Commander, Naval Forces, Japan.

During this cruise we were out on an exercise and received a typhoon warning. We ended up trying to run around the typhoon and ended up nearly in Guam. It was an interesting exercise in the command procedure because the carrier skipper, who was junior to me - there was no flag officer aboard at the time, was in tactical command of the formation. He elected to go around the typhoon, rather than out back across what I considered the less dangerous area of the storm, and we ended up running and running and running. I nearly ran out of fuel. I note this only to point out that in that particular time, even though the cruiser commander was senior to the carrier skipper, the tactical command rested with the skipper of the carrier.

There have been lots of discussions as to the propriety of this procedure, but I cite this particular instance because I think in this one instance, had I been doing it, we could have saved a lot of time and a lot of oil and a lot of money.

I think the other most significant happening of our limited stay in the Orient - and I cite this as an example of the overenthusiastic attitude and very high morale of the crew. We were allowed to go in to Hong Kong.

Q: This was R and R?

Adm. C." Strictly R and R, and after we departed Hong Kong, the communications officer came to the bridge and he was trembling. He said:

"I have a message from Commander, Seventh Fleet."

Q: Who was that?

Adm. C.: That was Admiral Beakley, whom I saw the other day, by the way, at Admiral Zumwalt's conference of all the retired flag officers.

The message read something like this: "Personal from Admiral Beakley to Captain Chew. You are a disgrace to the Navy. You ship has indulged in rioting, riotous living, and some episodes with the police."

I was so severely castigated that the communications officer was afraid to show me the message. Later I saw Admiral Beakley and he said:

"You deserved it. I was furious, but I still know you

have a great ship."

Q: How is the skipper supposed to control the on-shore leave?

Adm. C.: Well, the old theory of responsibility. He's responsible for the actions of his subordinates. It's very much like - this happened to be the responsibility for the crew - what happened to me in Long Beach, where I was coming in for a landing, having been out on an exercise, and I always handled the ship. I think I was a sort of rarity. When a pilot was mandatory he always came aboard, and particularly in Long Beach where I'd been in and out many times, the pilot came aboard and I said:

"Good afternoon, Captain, have a cup of coffee.," and he said: "OK, go ahead.: I said: "I'll bring her in." "Yes," he said, "you always do."

We had a very tricky landing to make. It was beyond one ship, inside a slip, and the pilot was sitting in the bridge chair and I was handling the ship. We got in beautifully. After saying "starboard engine back one third" we should have softly nestled into the dock. I would have turned the ship over to the exec to "double up all lines and secure". The bow, instead of swinging to the right, was swinging to the left toward the dock. My natural reaction was to say "starboard engine back two-thirds," which I did and, to my horror, I saw the bow swing even more rapidly to the left and we were picking up headway.

My immediate order was "all engines back, emergency full," which I gave, but in the meantime the ship had gathered such headway that it took off about 70 feet of the dock, including power lines, water lines, the dyke, and the overhang of the bow just missed one of those tremendous cranes which, if it had hit it, could have collapsed one of the legs and brought the whole crane down on us, which would have been a catastrophe. Fortunately, that didn't happen, but with the hissing steam from the broken steam lines, and the water, and the sparks from the cut cables, I really did it in.

My neighbor two doors up the street, Admiral James, was the ship yard commander.

Q: At Long Beach?

Adm. C.: At Long Beach. And when I got the ship secured - Admiral Fenno was the division commander at the time, Mike Fenno - I called him and I said:

"Admiral, I've creamed the dock," and he said: "Has the ship been hurt?" We were due to deploy shortly after that. I said: "No, miraculously enough, we have a real tough bow and my crew, I guess to protect me, has already been out and painted up the scratches and you can't even see it. I'll send divers down to make sure that the stem hasn't been bent below the waterline, but I don't think so because most of the cleavage was done above the waterline. The ship, miraculously, has not been hurt at all. I said "I'll give you a full report."

He said: "Oh, don't worry. Just give me a little administrative report. I know you handled the ship, and all of us have our problems."

I said: "Thank you very much, Sir."

Jimmy James came down and I said sort of who's going to pay for this, and he said:

"You know, Jack, I've always wanted to know what would happen if somebody knocked down those walls. I happen to have a little money in the ship yard fund, and we'll patch up the pipelines and we'll patch up the walls. It hasn't flooded the ship yard. We'll have it done and I guess it'll all be forgotten."

Well, the base commander was not quite as lenient. He wanted a full investigation, but Admiral Fenno stood up for me and said:

"He works for me and we're going to deploy within the next few weeks, and that's all I want done about it."

So I have Admiral Fenno and Admiral James to thank for really preventing me from having what could have been a very damaging investigation, because, as you know, out of an investigation always comes no good."

Q: The dyke was there because - ?

Adm. C.: The dyke was there because of the sinking of Terminal

Island. It was interesting because the dyke was higher at the inboard end of the pier than it was at the outboard end, and I hit it at the inboard end, where the dyke was the highest, and I cut out the high part fortunately.

I told you this story for a purpose, because what had happened was the bane of all shiphandlers' existences. The quartermaster - and that's what reminded me of it - who later, in Sydney said let's go back, was my trusted man on the engine order telegraph but at this time was on leave. Those cruisers had little knob engine order telegraphs, not the standard kind that you see in all the pictures that swing over and back. These were little knobs only visible to the operator. Knowing there was a possibility of making a mistake with this type of engine order telegraph I had put the officer of the deck on that station while my quartermaster was on leave as I felt that it was the most important station in maneuvering the ship. Having come in so easily and so nicely and gotten in position to back one-third, stop her, and double up all lines, when I'd given the order "starboard engine back one-third," he had rung up "starboard engine ahead one-third." When I gave the order "starboard engine back two-thirds," he had rung up "starboard engine ahead two-thirds." So instead of pulling the bow out, it had pushed the bow in and, of course, increased the speed tremendously. When I gave "all engines back, emergency full," there could be no mistake and he realized what had happened. Like everything else, it usually takes two people to make that kind of mistake. The talker heard me say "back one-third" and he relayed that order verbally to the engineroom, as was our standard procedure, and the engineroom failed to listen to the talker and followed the engine order telegraph. This, of course, caused the accident in which, fortunately, no one was hurt, but at the same time it did a tremendous amount of damage to the dock.

Q: The pilot could not have done any differently, could he?

Adm. C.: Well, if the officer of the deck had ordered, or rather rung up, the wrong bell, it would have made no difference to the pilot. The same thing would have happened to him. He might have detected it a little sooner than I did.

The end of the story is that that night, and my two children were with me in Long Beach, he came out to the house and said:

"Captain, I've ruined your career," and he cried. I gave him a drink and he's now a very successful investment broker somewhere!

Q: He left the service?

Adm. C.: He left the service for a very fine job. He was a young kid out of college, very enthusiastic about the Navy, but having had some connection somewhere or other, he was offered this job and found it impossible to turn it down.

From my point of view, he was right, he should have taken it!

I bring this story out in connection with my responsibility, because it was my responsibility even though I gave the correct orders. In the same way, it was my responsibility for the crew in Hong Kong later on during the cruise. I think the Navy feels that very strongly. It's a part of our indoctrination for command that you're responsible for the actions of your crew.

Speaking of responsibility, we had a bo'sun's mate on the <u>Roanoke</u> who was the heavyweight boxing champion of the Navy. He was a black man, and I felt that he was a real leader. This is germane to the race problems that we're going through today. He was the leader of the black members of the crew, and whenever there was any stepping out of line at all, I always went to this man and said "What do you think about it? How would you handle it?" and he would always handle it very effectively. I never had any trouble at all, and of course, in those days, you didn't expect to have any. But, as the leader of the minority group aboard ship, he was a splendid example of a fine sailor, and I find it difficult now to think that there is any discrimination aboard ship. Apparently the indications are, from some of the surveys that such conditions do exist.

Q: Going back to the <u>Roanoke</u> and the Far East -

Adm. C.: Well, as I said, this episode of tearing down

the dock occurred before we went to the Far East.

Our most significant military contribution during that period, I felt, was when there was the crisis in Indonesia, if you remember that. I've forgotten the exact cause of it. Admiral Davidson was aboard as the division commander. He'd relieved Admiral Fenno. And we were suddenly ordered down into the Philippine Sea, where we patrolled off Indonesia for about two weeks, ready to support, presumably, an amphibious landing if that became necessary. Obviously, nothing came of it but we had been positioned there as a support ship and stayed there almost two weeks. It was boring because the weather was terribly hot and muggy, and we simply steamed up and down. I cite that as a use of a cruiser in support at that particular time. We were ready and we were sent, we did our stint on patrol and then, the crisis died down and we were withdrawn. A great example of Naval flexibility!

Q: Sukarno got back in the saddle safely?

Adm. C.: That's right. Sukarno got back in the saddle safely and we came back to Subic. So our cruise in the Orient, in addition to being a very informative one for the crew, was fun for really all of us because we were able to get to Kobe for liberty and recreation. We were fortunate to go to Nagasaki, and the crew, of course, was able then to see - no, we didn't go into Nagasaki, but when we were in Sasebo a lot of people did go down to Nagasaki.

Q: Did you have any special educational program on board to make these various visits more meaningful to the crew members?

Adm. C.: I tried. As I remember, we put out a little paper on the port facilities and the history of the port in connection with the part it might or might not have played in World War II. But I frankly believe it was more oriented to the recreational facilities than it was to the historical aspects.

Q: Did they understand that they were, in effect, representatives of the United States when they went on land?

Adm. C.: I think so, yes, and I think the only ill effects of their representation were their high spirits that sometimes took over and caused minor infractions with the local authorities. But I think they all recognized that they were ambassadors of our country and behaved themselves accordingly, and except for that one instance, we had an exemplary record. I'm sure it was due to the fact that they did realize their purpose in being there.

It's sort of hard to sum up a cruise like that.

Q: Did it take you to Taiwan?

Adm. C.: No, the ship never went to Taiwan. Later on, I think the ship went up to Korea, but it did not while I had command. I don't remember whether we even got in to Yokosuka, which, of course, was the main base for all of our ships.

I was interested in Sasebo. I remember when we were there Admiral Burke came out and gave a short talk on the possible cutbacks in bases in Japan. At this time, it was pretty much a monetary thing and even while we were there they were thinking of closing Sasebo. They seem to have held on to it as time's gone by. And, of course, it's like the decision to close Yokosuka which came about a year ago, and that's been also let slip by the board.

The political significance I could say very little more about. There were not as many ships in the Seventh Fleet then as there are now with the Vietnam thing. We normally had one, or two carriers, at the most, a couple of cruisers, and about the same number of destroyers, as I remember, because at that time there was a continuous patrol in the Straits of Formosa, the Taiwan Straits, which during my tenure in the Taiwan Defense Command was reduced to a sporadic patrol.

Do you have any other questions about that cruise?

Q: No, I don't.

Adm. C.: When I was aboard Roanoke I received a letter that said "you're going to go back to CNO for duty." It didn't say where. One of my friends wrote me, interestingly enough, and said "have you asked for any particular job?" And I said: "No, I've never asked for any job in my life, except the exec of the _Helena_, and I figure it's too late to start now. I leave it up to them. They're going to send me back to CNO."

On the way back, I think it was in Honolulu, I saw Admiral Marshall and I believe I was supposed to go to work for him in one part of Op-04, which is the Deputy Chief of Naval Operations for Logistics. But then when I got there I found they made me the director of the staff of the Ships' Characteristics Board, which was still in Op-04 but a different section than I had been led to believe I was to go to.

It was an interesting job -

Q: Tell me what it encompassed?

Adm. C.: That's what I was about to say. Technically, it developed the characteristics that a ship - any ship - will embody once it's completed.

Q: This is looking forward to the construction?

Adm. C.: Yes. Before you actually begin the construction, you develop the plans for the ship that say what it's mission is, what it's supposed to do, what particular types of sonar will it have, if it's a destroyer, what guns will it have?

Chew #5 - 229

Will it have that many guns or that many people? Will the berthing facilities house so many men? How many men do you need to run this type of ship?

It was a fascinating job and it called for inputs from all over CNO to develop the characteristics of a ship. Now, of course, if you're going to build a motorboat it's fairly easy to say I want a 26-foot motorboat and I want it made out of wood or plywood or fiberglass, but if you're going to develop a destroyer you're going to say, all right, what should it have?

Q: At that time, it was something of a pioneering job, wasn't it? There were so many new missile-type ships and so forth coming up?

Adm. C.: I'm trying to think of the history of the Ships' Characteristics Board. I don't know whether it had been developed during the war or whether it was the development of some earlier office within CNO. But I do know that it was composed of representatives from all over the Navy Department and the purpose of course was to get a representative view. BuOrd said, "Gee, I want a ship that will carry ten people and will have ten 16-inch guns, sonar, and so on, for example, and the man from BuPers said, "We can't do that with ten people." The man from BuOrd said, "We can't put 16-inch guns on that kind of a hull," and the man from BuShips says, "We can't give you 60 knots with that size ship," and so on. So, it was an effort to develop a logical groundwork on which to design the ship, based, of course, on the mission that the ship was to perform.

We took that mission and said, OK, now how can we fullfil that mission and what type of ship are we going to build to meet the requirements.

Q: Am I not right in saying that there were a lot of new types coming on stream?

Adm. C.: Yes. There were a lot of new types coming along, particularly amphibious types. At that time, as you remember, the value of the amphibious force was pretty clearly recognized, not only during the war but in later possible emergency situations where you could make available within a short time -

Q: It was no longer innovative, it had become a part -?

Adm. C.: Yes, it had become very much a part of our Navy. I enjoyed the Ships' Characteristics Board. I was the Secretary and the head of the Board was Admiral Denney Knoll who was the director of the division. I think it was the Ships' Maintenance Division and under that division was the Ships' Characteristics Board.

In addition, of course, you really were trying to keep track of updating the ships, as new developments or even new

Chew #5 - 231

weapons systems were created. It was a question of whether you were going to take off the old gun and put on a new one, or update the generating equipment, or update the radio equipment. You were trying to keep track of the ship alterations and ship ordnance alterations changes, as well as develop the plans for the newer ships.

Q: Then you became a part of BuShips' FRAM program?

Adm. C.: Well, FRAM, of course, was a part of that program too. We were involved in the FRAM program as a major overhaul against the normal updating that goes along with what we used to call Ord Alts and Ship Alts. The FRAM program was a major updating beyond the normal updating that went along day to day with practically any ship, and I presume still does. It did during my time on the Roanoke and, of course, that's the last ship I had and that's quite long ago.

Q: How did you arrive at a set of characteristics for a new type?

Adm. C.: Basically by compromise. One of the standard sayings was: "Well, what the hell do you want, a rubber hull, you want everything in it?" We had a cartoon in the office that showed a ship that everybody wanted, it had everything. It had airplanes, it had torpedoes, it had guns, it had stabilizers, it had people -

Q: I've seen a drawing of a ship like that. Jimmy has one.

Adm. C.: I'm sure he does. Of course, this was almost a backdrop for our Ships' Characteristics Board meetings, because first of all you couldn't make the hull of rubber so that it expanded automatically, and as you put on a new weapon system it needed another 20 people to run it, and there was no place for the 20 people to stay and there was no food for the 20 people to eat. So, it was essentially a compromise, and that was pretty difficult to arrive at in order to have a ship designed to meet the mission.

Now, if the mission was a simple one, like a tugboat that's supposed to do nothing but tow, then you get into a very simple compromise of how big do you want it, how powerful do you want it, and how many people do you want in it? But when you start arming it, with what kind of an armament and what kind of missiles, is it going to have Asroc or is it not, is it going to have Tartar or Terrier or Talos, which were the three Ts at that time, then you get into manning problems that eventually expand to the point of the desirability of a rubber hull.

Q: This put you in touch with Strategic Planning and all the rest, didn't it?

Adm. C.: I don't think it did in terms of strategic planning because it was more a summation of the mission that was desired, and that possibly came from the strategic planners, so we were more interested in the mechanics of building the ship that would meet that mission, or be able to carry out that mission. Why the mission had been assigned we really weren't too much interested in. It was more the technical aspects of how to develop the ship that would fulfill all the requirements.

Q: Did you get involved in any way with the Polaris?

Adm. C.: No, I was not involved in any way with the Polaris because that was the Special Project Office under Red Raborn and J. B. Colwell was his first assistant. So, in answer to your question, no, I had nothing to do with it.

It seems to me we were involved in some of the alterations to submarines, but in no way were we concerned with the Polaris program.

Q: Well then, they invaded, in a sense, some of the precincts of your job?

Adm. C.: For that particular type of ship, yes, they did, I suppose, or possibly it was the other way around. I don't know.

I was there only from January of 1958, when I came from Roanoke, to September of 1958, so it was a period of only nine months. I can remember that the selection board was meeting -

Q: Because your fate hung on that!

Adm. C.: Well, I could have been in the zone. It was one of those 'iffy' things. It was not the year for my class to be selected. Although we were getting away from that. If you remember, just about that time they started the deep selections. It's always been amusing to me that here, in the later years, they say they're going so deep. Well, even back in 1957 and 1958 they were three and four and five years deep.

For example, in 1958 Admiral Rivero had been selected in 1955, "Red" Ramage had been selected in 1956, Bud Needham, Al Reid, and a couple of others had been selected in 1957, and we were still not within the zone. Ernie Hohtzworth was also selected in 1957, and then about six of us in 1958. The majority of my class were selected in 1959 and two were selected in 1960. So, from a practical point of view, our class underwent six years of selection. This happened to be the fourth year for me, but still not the year and I certainly didn't expect to be selected. I say that in all frankness and all honesty. I was prepared not to be. Naturally, you always hope to be.

I had in the office Gordon Chung-hoon, and Gordon was

a great one for knowing everything. I was sort of minding my own business about the Ships' Characteristics Board. I knew the board was meeting. I wasn't particularly concerned. I didn't even know the President of the board, whose name I can't recall at the moment. I remember we were sitting around after a meeting of the Ships' Characteristics Board and old Gordon said:

"I think the board's out. I'm going to call the White House. I know a guy over there." I said: "Goodie, go ahead." I went on back to my office and he came back in and said: "You made it!" I said: "How do you know?"

He said: "I called the White House, and they've got a guy on the list named Chow. There could be no other naval officer around your time that they could corrupt to Chow. It has to be you because the initials are J. L."

Q: It must have been Pete Aurand at the White House!

Adm. C.: I don't know whether it was Pete or not. I've forgotten, but I said, "I can't believe it," and then about ten minutes later they called from BuPers and said the list is out and you're on it.

I was so stunned, I just walked out of the office. I was in a driving squad, the driving squad that I told you of that had been with me twenty-seven years of driving experience of driving from Washington to Annapolis. I just walked out of the office and got in the car. I said, "I'm going to go out and sit in the car and wait till the rest of the guys come." It was about five o'clock then, anyhow. So I walked out stunned and came on home and had a drink. That's the story of how I learned of being selected to flag rank, via Gordon Chung-hoon.

Of course, as soon as I was selected it was very obvious that within a short period I would have to be transferred because this wasn't a flag billet, and I was told that I was going to be director of the Shore Establishment and Maintenance Division.

I sort of happily said: "What is that?" and they said: "Well, that has to do with all the shore establishment and the appropriations for it -"

Q: All the Navy yards and everything?

Adm. C.: Everything that has to do with the Navy's shore establishment, including getting the money, the appropriations, from Congress for all of the Navy's shore establishment, including Navy yards, naval stations, the Naval Academy, dockyards, training areas - any part of the shore establishment. And the monies are handled quite differently than are the appropriations for ships.

Anyhow, I knew absolutely nothing about it, absolutely nothing. I'd had one tour of shore duty, really, that amounted to anything and that had been at the Naval Academy. My tours at the Naval Academy and the one in London were not connected in any way with the shore establishment.

Q: You'd never had any political experience!

Adm. C.: No political experience whatsoever. I had really, up until that time, never even been stationed in Washington. But when you're selected for flag rank you're so happy about it that that part doesn't loom large. You think, "Oh, boy, if that's what they want me to do, I'll go and do it, and I'll do the best I can."

Q: It's a state of euphoria!

Adm. C.: Absolute euphoria.

My preparation for the job was to take a trip with the Assistant Secretary of the Navy to look at some of the bases that I was eventually going to have to administer and obtain monies for the maintenance of and for the development or expansion of, or the closing down, as the case may be.

Q: Who was that? Franke?

Adm. C.: No, it was Secretary Armstrong and he'd been newly appointed, so we were going to make an inspection trip of some of the bases. It seems to me on that trip we went to Subic, we went to Guam. I've forgotten where else we went, but this was my indoctrination into the development and maintenance of the shore establishment.

We made our trip obviously by air. It wasn't very long, as I remember. It seems to me it was about ten days and, other than the places I've mentioned, I've sort of forgotten where else we went. That was really the only experience that I had in that field of endeavor. I was a self-styled, perhaps and maybe erroneously, an operating naval officer, and I was rather shocked to find myself in this position, but it was a wonderful experience and an experience that stood me in good stead later on because my main job was to present the Navy's military construction bill to Congress.

Q: You were fighting in a time of reduced expenditures!

Adm. C.: A time of reduced expenditures, from January of 1958 to January of 1960.

It gave me a very, very intimate knowledge of Congress because I had to appear - the Military Construction Bill is unusual. First of all, you have to appear before the Armed Services Committee of the House to obtain the authorization.

Then you have to appear before the Appropriations Committee of the House to obtain the appropriation. Then you have to appear before the Armed Services Committee of the Senate. Sometimes they combined the Senate Armed Services and Appropriations committees, but, generally speaking, you appeared before four committees to try to obtain the one, authorization, and, two, the funds to construct anything on the shore.

Unlike the appropriations for ships, this was a very political thing. If you wanted to build a chapel, for example, at Pensacola - I remember that one quite well - it's hard for Congress to be against a chapel, so that's fairly easy, plus the fact that it conceivably could be very staunchly supported by the representative for Florida, who was Bob Sykes on the Appropriations Subcommittee of the House. But to try to get a swimming pool, for example, was to say the least, a horse of a different riding academy, because it was very easy to be against extravagance or pleasure for pleasure's sake. So, as a sort of cute way to try to get a swimming pool, we would call it a "survival pool."

Q: A survival pool!

Adm. C.: Yes. And this was true of an air station. You could give it a dual name, because you had to have survival training in it and, when it wasn't being used for survival training, it was used as a swimming pool.

Chew #5 - 240

It was easier, therefore, to get a swimming pool, for example, on an air station, I found, than it was on a naval station because there was no survival training on a naval station, as there was on an air station.

I cite these as sort of interesting examples of little things that went on.

We were very, very carefully questioned. I had obviously excellent help in the permanent staff of that division. One of my right-hand men was Tom Smythe, who had been with the division for a number of years and who helped us compile the lists of the items that we would present to the Congress.

Q: Did you have to have a dry run of your presentation?

Adm. C.: No. Let me first of all explain the procedure, because it is fairly complicated.

First of all, you had to decide within the Navy the priorities of the items that the Navy thought they needed, and within limited budget figures. Let's say, for example, that a military construction budget was going to be x million dollars. Then the Navy had to fight over whether you should have a carrier pier at Pensacola or a barracks at Newport, Rhose Island, or a new wing to Bancroft Hall at the Naval Academy, or repairs to the ship yard in Long Beach that was rapidly sinking into the sea. So there were meetings to determine within the Deputy Chief of Naval Operations for Logistics, under whom we came, the priorities within the Navy.

Once that priority list - and that was usually a battle, as a matter of fact, I had a lot of real tough words with my boss, who would say:

"No, I want a priority list of the items within the Navy" - this was Admiral Rollo Wilson, who I thought was one of the greatest guys I've ever known. He'd say:

"Jack, God damn it, give me a priority list." And I'd say:

"Admiral, I can't do it. I cannot give you a priority list because it's like this. If you "and this was my favorite story, I even told it to Congress once - "If you are left $50,000, or told you would be left $50,000, by your rich uncle and he wants a priority list, you can then come up with some of the things that you want. Now, let's just say you're a very sensible guy, you're not extravagant, you're not going to spend a lot of money, but your car is about on its last legs, so you want a new car. You're not going to be expensive and get a Cadillac. You're just going to get a Ford or a Chevrolet, and that's $3,000 or $4,000. Your house, obviously, is one of the important things. You're living in a neighborhood that's going down. You have this $50,000 and you think that you could possibly get a modest house in a better neighborhood, and maybe you can do it for an even $20,000.

Q: That dates your story!

Adm. C.: Yes, it dates my story. Let's make it a little more for the purpose of discussion, so that it makes it a little quicker. And so on, you go down the more important items. The house first, probably, and the car, and then possibly for recreation purposes this new house is going to be on a little stream and you want to get a small boat. Nothing extravagant, just with an outboard motor. You go on down the line, and finally come up with clothes and neckties and all the things that you need.

Then your old rich uncle suddenly says:

"Gee, I made a mistake. I don't have $50,000 for you. I have only $15,000 or $20,000."

Now, how the hell do you reorganize your priority list? Obviously, the big item has to come off, the one that you thought was your Number One priority. So every time you change the figure on me, I have to go back and do the whole list all over. I just can't take off at the bottom because if I take off the neckties it doesn't provide me with the necessary money.

I found this to be a very useful story, but still Admiral Wilson and I used to go round and round with our priority list.

I digressed there to show you the initial phases of a military construction bill within the Navy, to establish the priority list within the money you think you're going to get.

Chew #5 - 243

Q: Were you not also involved with a lot of converging empires within the Navy Department?

Adm. C.: Oh, yes. That's why I tried to say that, for example, BuAir wanted a new air station at Lemoore. They wanted another air station at New Iberia, which I labeled "New Siberia," and which has since been closed, by the way.

Q: That's in the bayou country of Louisiana?

Adm. C.: Yes, the cajuns and I had problems with that, too. But the first step was to develop the list within the Navy. Then there were extensive hearings conducted by the Department of Defense, the Assistant Secretary for Installations and Logistics. They went over it line item by line item, every single item within your list. There was one project that I remember well, over here in West Virginia. There's a radio project called the Big Dish. It was a radio-telescope type thing, and when you build something like that you have to build housing and you have to build the support facilities. Do you build a commissary or do you build a school? If it's out in the boondocks, what do you do?

As I said, the DOD would go over the list and they would approve and disapprove. They never added anything. They would always cut. That was the first review. Then, after the DOD approved your list, you had a review by the

Bureau of the Budget. The Bureau of the Budget went over your list, line item by line item, rarely, if ever, adding and usually deleting. This, of course, was to develop this particular phase of the Navy's budget.

After it had been approved by the Bureau of the Budget, then you had Congress to go through, with four sets of hearings. I presented those bills two years.

Q: How far in advance of your actual needs did this process have to begin?

Adm. C.: The planning was done in terms of, for example, the needs of the station in terms of how many people were going to be there over the next approximately five years, and if, for example, it were an expansion, did that justify the construction of a new set of barracks. Or, in another case, if the barracks had been World War I, which in some cases they were, were they so far beyond repair that a new set of barracks was required? That developed the requirement for the barracks.

The Congress was very careful to state that you should not use maintenance and repair money, M and R money, for construction. In other words, if you were really adding onto a barracks with your M and R money, you were violating the spirit and the letter of the congressional rules. So the requirement for a barracks or for a breakwater - I remember one of my first-year projects was to get the authorization and the money for a breakwater at Newport, which was eventually constructed. The requirement was well documented for the safety of the ships in the harbor at Newport. It was a justifiable requirement and, in the long run, it would save the Navy money from lost hours and possible damage from storms.

So, in answer to your question how long did it take us to develop the requirements, it was a requirement when it became obvious that we needed it. The construction period, of course, took a lot longer. A good example of that was the naval station at Meridian, Mississippi, which was, I might add, a favorite of Senator Stennis, being in his home state. The requirement had been developed by Op-05, the Deputy Chief of Naval Operations for Air, as a necessary requisite of the training program for jet aircraft. To build the station took about five years. So you had to project yourself, in some cases, four to five years, while in other cases the requirement, for example, for a chapel develops as a result of possibly increased personnel on the station or a more active chaplain or possibly the existing chapel may be beyond repair. It's hard to say how far ahead you develop these requirements.

Q: What about the sudden need for something, like that dyke which occurred before your time in this job, but like the dyke at Long Beach? The sudden apparent need for this.

Adm. C.: One of the line items of your bill is a fund to take care of emergency construction.

Q: A contingency fund?

Adm. C.: It's a contingency fund for precisely that purpose. In addition to the contingency fund for emergency, there was a line item for minor military construction. In other words, an item that did not require the authorization and approval of Congress. I think the limit was something like $15,000 or $20,000. In other words, if you wanted to build a shack out here at the Naval Academy to house athletic gear, you wouldn't have to go to Congress to get the authorization.

So there were these two line items, one for emergency construction, and the other for minor construction.

Q: In order to facilitate your presentation of this whole program to the congressional committees, did you engage in a rehearsal in order to make it a smoother presentation and to find any loopholes that might be corrected?

Adm. C.: I suppose you'd call it a rehearsal. I would get with my staff and we would go over the line items and the wording of the justification for the line items. Then I would come home and practise with my wife on how I would sound before the committees. But there was no dummy run before the

CNO or anything like that.

Q: You didn't involve JAG in it at all?

Adm. C.: No, the JAG was never in any way involved in this. After all, the items had been approved within the Navy by - of course, the final authority, the CNO. They'd been approved by the Department of Defense in its review. They'd been approved by the Bureau of the Budget in its review. So we had gone over this presentation before we got to the committees of the Congress two times formally, really, and informally within the Navy Department. So I guess you'd say that there was no rehearsal, other than the rehearsal that I did personally to prepare myself before a hearing.

Q: But you did run into some real sharpies in some of the congressional committees, did you not?

Adm. C.: I think I told you about Carl Vinson, who appointed me to the Naval Academy, saying "if this youngster doesn't do well we'll bust him back." I, of course, had just been selected and he well knew that. And it was interesting to know that even before I submitted the program to the committee for authorization, not money, I would go over personally to the staff and have the program reviewed.

Q: You mean the congressional committee staff?

Adm. C.: Yes. There would always be that initial review, and then I would appear before the chairman before the official hearing, and he would say:

"O.K. You know the committee has to take off a few things. What would you like taken off? I'll try to be as helpful as possible. What's your softest item?"

And I would say: "We don't have any soft items, Mr. Chairman. This is a considered list of the requirements of the Navy, and we want them all."

He'd laugh and I'd laugh, and he would say: "Well, if you have any that you think you can get along without, I'll be glad to knock them off because, after all, you know the committee has to take off a little here and there or they wouldn't be doing their job."

But he was a grand old man. So that was another sort of informal hearing before I even got to the committee itself.

Q: But not necessarily would it hold in the Senate or elsewhere?

Adm. C.: The Senate didn't do that. As a matter of fact, just as an item of interest, the head of the staff of the Senate my first year was Ken Ballou, who later became the Assistant Secretary of the Navy. He had a foot problem or he had a wooden foot. I've forgotten what, but he had a limp. The House was really more interested.

Q: Of course, that's where the appropriation had to originate?

Adm. C: That's right, but the authorization was equally important, and I found the appropriations hearings before the Subcommittee on Military Construction - you see, your presentation to the Armed Services Committee was to the whole Armed Services Committee for authorization only, then you went before the Military Construction Subcommittee of the Appropriations Committee for detailed hearings on each line item for the appropriation.

Q: What's the justification and rationale for that dual system? Why not just make the presentation to the committee that's empowered to do the whole job?

Adm. C.: There have been numerous discussions on that and, as I remember it, during the time the question came up if you're going to authorize it some of the members of the committee would say well, damn it, if we're going to authorize it we ought to give the money right along with it. The real purpose was this.

To allow the Navy - or the Army and the Air Force, as the case was - some flexibility. For example, if an article or an item had been approved, perhaps a barracks, all you have to go on is an architect and engineering study of an estimate of what it will cost. And you say, that's what we're asking for. As I remember, the breakwater was 5 million dollars - no, let me correct that, I think it was 7 million dollars, and that was the estimate that went down and that was the authorization that was approved, and the money was approved. It just so happened that that year there was a tremendous marshalling of heavy construction equipment that may or may not have had something to do with the construction of the throughway - Massachusetts throughway and some very big road construction - that I think fell through, so all this equipment and all these contractors were available. So the actual cost of the breakwater turned out to be less than the 7 million. If I remember correctly, it was somewhere around $5\frac{1}{2}$ million. So the Navy picked up a million and a half dollars. Now, if another item cost more than had been appropriated, if you didn't have another item authorized you couldn't have spent that additional money.

So the basic reason for the authorization and the appropriation was to provide a certain amount of flexibility and manipulation of the programs. Well, for example, Senator Stennis sent for me to come to Mississippi to explain why the airport at Meridian, which I think is known as McCain Field, why its construction program was not on schedule. Well, it just so happened that you couldn't get the contractors at that particular time to do the work, so you couldn't expend the money. He wanted it spent because it was within his constituency and was obviously helpful to the State of Mississippi. But that's an example of why the authorization.

He asked me that question. He said:

"The Congress has authorized this money, it has appropriated this money. Why hasn't it been spent?"

Q: That's the big question they're asking the President today!

Adm. C.: That's exactly right. This was on a much smaller scale, but we couldn't contract the work at that particular time and there was nothing that could be done about it. Of course, we tried to speed it up.

I think in later years they've gone along more to one line item, one dollar price. But you can see how that will completely destroy any flexibility.

Q: That was the Secretary of Defense's idea, was it not?

Adm. C.: Yes, and so the authorization and the appropriation went hand in glove.

I remember Mr. Sykes questioning me about the Pensacola pier. They were building a pier at Pensacola for the use of the training carrier which actually a couple of months ago when we were down there I saw. This gives me a sense of satisfaction. When I go to Newport, I can say, gee, I got the money for the barracks at Newport, and obviously if I haven't got it somebody else would. I was responsible for getting the money for the new wings on Bancroft Hall and for the renovation

Chew #5 - 252

money for the old wings, which was a very high-priority project because the wings had gotten to the state where it was more expensive to keep them up than it was to completely renovate them and put them in Number One condition.

I found it an interesting job. Actually, it was nerve-wracking to appear before these committees. Some of them were benevolent, particularly the Armed Services Committee. The Appropriations Committee was usually pretty rough, and the Chairman of the Appropriations Committee was old Shepherd of California -

Q: Who knew a tremendous amount about the Navy!

Adm. C.: Yes, and he knew a tremendous amount about his job. I don't know whether this is publishable for the record or not but it always amused me. In addition to amusing me it made it a very difficult job, because after the hearings, which would go on, say, from 10:00 to 1:00, then recess for lunch, and then from, say, 2:00 to maybe 4:30 or 5:00, God love him, old Chairman of the Committee, Mr. Harry Shepherd, would say, "You stay," pointing at me, and I think one day Jimmy James - I presented the program even for the Bureau of Ships, you see- was a backup witness and if the questioning got too detailed technically, the backup witness from the office that had presented the program - there'd be a backup witness from the Bureau of Personnel, for example for, the Naval Academy, although I normally didn't need a backup witness for that type of line item. I would need a backup witness for technical items that had to do with ship yards and so on.

Anyhow, Shepherd would say, "You stay. Admiral, you stay." Then he'd turn to his administrative assistant and say, "Get out the bottles," and he would put a bottle of bourbon and a bottle of Scotch on the table, and he would say:

"All right, now we've had all the formal hearings. Let's hear what the real story is on all this stuff. Have a drink." And he would insist that we have a drink, and he would insist that you have another. I remember leaving him and going home and studying my lessons for the next day's appearance when I'd meet this stern old guy who I'd been drinking with for the last hour and a half of the day, and suddenly he was a different man as Chairman of the Committee. In the afternoon he used to say:

"Well, you realize that this is a little different. We'll get to the bottom of all this stuff when we have a drink. This is off the record."

I thoroughly enjoyed him.

Q: He was noted for that. Did you in that job necessarily engage in social life in Washington which involved you with congressional people?

Adm. C.: None whatsoever. I had no contact whatsoever with any congressman. The only time I ever went to the Hill was to talk to the staff of the committees. I rarely, if ever, except to see the Chairman as a sort of a final polish-up before the hearings, I had no social contacts whatsoever.

Q: How did you deal with the blandishments of individual congressmen who were insistent upon retaining, say, a Navy yard in their bailiwick when it was scheduled for closing?

Adm. C.: Well, I think you have to give great credit to the committees. I can cite you a specific example of appearing before the Senate Committee to request the cutback of funds, as I think I mentioned before, for New Iberia, because it became obvious that we weren't going to need this jet aircraft field and there was a possibility that it could be reduced in scope with a significant saving of money to possibly a support airfield or an ASW aircraft field. Subsequently, it's been closed, so the justification really evaporated, but at this time I had to go back before the Committee of the Senate to get the authorization to reprogram funds on a reduced scale. In other words, the mission of the field had been changed. Therefore, I had to get new authorization at a reduced scope.

Senator Ellender literally gave me hell. He said: "here you come down here and build this airfield and displace all these people and now you're cutting it back. How the hell does the Navy know what it's doing?" I think he even mentioned the Cajuns and gave me a good fifteen-minute harangue. Senator Stennis got up and said:

"Well, after all, some of the things that you have charged Captain Chew with (or Admiral Chew, or whatever I was, and incidentally I was not frocked for this job. I made it a year later). You've castigated him, but some of the actions that you, Senator Ellender, have accused him of are attributable to other services, namely the Air Force, and he is here in an effort to save money for the United States Government." So he at least took up for me.

Now, in terms of individual congressmen who wanted items, the general attitude was that I did not have to go for closing because I was primarily in the area of development and only when I had to reprogram -

Q: You were an activist!

Adm. C.: Yes. It was more a question of support from an individual member of the committee, as opposed to his chairman. As I remember, Mr. Sykes was a great supporter of the chapel at Pensacola which the chairman sort of took a dim view of. But the only experience I had in closings was in the case of the reprograming for the reduction in scope of New Iberia, and there I was very actively criticised by Senator Ellender. But the committee as a whole protected me in that it was an effort to save money.

Q: Some individual congressmen apply a certain amount of pressure, sometimes a great deal of pressure, upon the Department as a whole when they're trying to save some installation in their district.

Adm. C.: Oh, I think this is very true. As a matter of fact, Mr. Sykes said to me one day during the hearings:

"I'm glad you're not a politician. You're trying to get the money and you're fairly agile on your feet. With the money you're trying to get you could swing a lot of votes. I realize the importance of these line items that are specifically for my district in Florida, i.e. Pensacola."

The pressures were really, as I say, more in support from the individuals.

Q: Yes, I can see. That's the other side of the coin.

Adm. C.: The other side of the coin, and I wasn't too much involved in reductions, except in this particular respect - and I mentioned it once before - where maintenance and repair monies were being used for basically military construction, of which the Congress took an extremely dim view.

Chew #6 - 257

Interview No. 6 with Vice Admiral John L. Chew, U. S. Navy (Retired)

Place: His residence in Providence, Annapolis, Maryland

Date: Tuesday morning, 23 January 1973

Subject: Biography

By: John T. Mason, Jr.

Q: Sir, we've reached the point in your story where you're departing from that very interesting assignment appearing before congressional committees on new naval projects in various parts of the country, seeing to the appropriations for them. Now, on April 18, 1960, you were assigned a new job as Deputy Commander of the Military Sea Transportation Service, again stationed in Washington, I believe.

Adm. C.: That's correct, and it was interesting, at least from my point of view. I believe, or at least strongly suspect, that my superiors were glad to see me go.

Q: Why? Because you could never supply him with a list of priorities?

Adm. C.: Possibly one of those reasons, but I was sometimes a thorn in his side and I think frankly he was delighted to see me go and I felt that probably as a rear admiral I had been basically fired, although, as I say, I'm not quite sure that it was quite as strong as that.

Q: Do you mean he liked a more amenable kind of person?

Adm. C.: Well, I don't know whether he wanted a more amenable kind of person, but he wanted someone who could do this thing and in my view it couldn't be done precisely the way he wanted it, although both the Secretary and the Assistant Secretary for Installations and Logistics had indicated that my appearance before the committee had been satisfactory. They thought I had done a good job.

Q: You seemed to have great rapport with Harry Shepherd?

Adm. C: Well, I had good rapport with Harry Shepherd and, of course, had even greater with Carl Vinson, but I really felt that after two years there was a desire to get somebody else. So I was told that I was going to MSTS as the deputy commander and chief of staff.

The one aspect of going to MSTS that I considered to be a definite plus was to work for Admiral Gano, whom I had known ever so slightly, but by reputation he was indeed one of the finer gentlemen in our Navy and one of the more level-headed, not necessarily easy-going, but a very fine officer, so I looked forward to a tour as his deputy and chief of staff.

Q: Would you give me at this point perhaps a kind of a job sheet of what this entailed?

Adm. C.: MSTS was the command that, as I think we so often advertise, had more ships than any other commercial line in the world. They were a conglomerate group ranging, of course, from the shuttle tankers to the special-requirement ships, survey ships, oceanographic ships, cargo ships that went to out-of-the-way places. Of course, the major part of the DOD transportation requirements were met by charter from commercial shipping lines, specifically the American shipping lines, and our job was to run the vast DOD ocean transportation system, which, as I say, was composed of what we called the organic fleet, i.e. those ships that had been commissioned in MSTS plus the charter ships plus the shipping contract, which was the primary way of getting goods overseas to our forces both in the Far East and Europe.

So there were really three types of operations, and, of course, MSTS was charged with the control of the organic fleet as well as arranging for shipping contracts, which was really commercial negotiation with the shipping lines to obtain the best rates possible for the shipment of DOD goods overseas.

Q: Were you limited by statute to American bottoms?

Adm. C.: Yes, unless there was some overriding and compelling reason that we might have to use on occasion a foreign bottom.

Then, in addition we operated LSTs that were crewed by Japanese and by Koreans. I may be mistaken on the Koreans. But MSTS, as we proudly said the largest shipping line in the United States, had this conglomerate type of thing where you had these three separate types of operations. There were no monies appropriated for MSTS. It had to pay its way, and the Army and the Navy and the Air Force were the customers. They had their monies appropriated for transportation and they paid MSTS for the services that were rendered. It was called an industrially funded operation.

Q: Did you have to have some residual funds?

Adm. C.: We had some residual funds, but they were funds that had been made and laid aside specifically for that purpose. In other words, had we been successful in operating at possibly below our tariff rates -

Let me go back. I think when MSTS was set up there was a fund and that fund was still there, which gave us a cushion so that if the cost of our operations exceeded the revenues that we obtained from the customers, i.e. the Army, the Navy, and the Air Force, then we had a fund that we could go to and keep from going bankrupt.

Q: I would think it would have been very awkward without a fund?

Adm. C.: Yes. We had this cushion, but essentially we were required to live within our means and, of course, like every industrially funded type of operation, if, for example, we started losing money we'd have to raise the rates. It was just that simple.

Q: So it called for some business acumen?

Adm. C.: It was unlike the Navy in that particular aspect. For example, the negotiations with the steamship lines were very businesslike, in which the tariff rates were established for the shipment of freight overseas in what were called the shipping contracts. The shipping contracts were made with the lines, based on their best estimates and our best estimates, and we haggled at great length over the shipping contracts trying to get the best price we could for our customers.

In addition to the shipping contracts which, as I say, were the basic means of getting general cargo overseas, we had charters, we had bare-boat charters —

Q: What are bare-boat charters?

Chew #6 - 262

Adm. C.: A bare-boat charter is when you take an empty ship and crew it and provision it and run it. You can take a ship that's being operated by a commercial line, for example, and charter that ship and then they furnish the crew and they furnish the operating supplies. That is a straight charter, but a bare-boat charter is when you go get an empty ship and crew it and provision it, fuel it.

Q: Crew it with enlisted men?

Adm. C.: No. That brings up another point. In MSTS one of our more important staff members was the industrial relations equivalent of the chief of staff.

The central office was in Washington. There was a staff similar to but not precisely like a naval staff. It was tailored to meet the requirements of MSTS. For example, I was the deputy commander and chief of staff, there was an assistant chief of staff for maintenance, there was an assistant chief of staff for operations, there was the equivalent of an assistant chief of staff for industrial relations - and when I say "industrial relations" this involved all of the hiring and firing of the civilian crews of the ships that were manned not by Navy personnel.

When I first got there there were still some transports that were manned by service personnel. Their captains were usually captains in the Navy, they were called the P-3s - one of them was the Rose. They were named after Army generals because, as you know, MSTS originally sprang from the Army Transport Corps, and there were great inequities because here, on one side of the dock, was a P-3 manned by a crew of enlisted men with naval officers running it, and on the other side of the dock, on exactly the same run, was a ship that was crewed and manned completely by merchant marine officers and crew.

Q: It must have made the labor unions very angry, didn't it?

Adm. C.: No, it didn't make the labor unions very angry. It made it the other way round, because at that time, as I remember, a captain in the Navy was getting probably about $8,000 a year, while across the dock there was a Civil Service MSTS civilian-crewed ship with a skipper getting between $18,000 and $22,000. And these were the negotiated rates that were the purview of the industrial relations officer.

So we were in the business of labor unions, the seamen's unions, in determining pay scales, in negotiations with the steamship lines in determining rates, in negotiating charters, so that it really approached a commercial operation, as the term "industrially funded" denoted-

Q: When you say "chartered ships," did this involve passenger liners?

Adm. C.: At that time it was pretty well recognized that the use of passenger ships as we know them for the transport of personnel to and from Europe and Asia was less efficient than the use of transportation by air, and we were in the process of phasing out the organic transport fleet. It was a slow process. As I remember, we held on to one or two for a while, then eventually those went, and at the present time there are no passenger ships in use by MSTS.

Q: There aren't many in use under the American flag!

Adm. C.: Very few. I guess there are none. They're all being laid up.

As I say, we had our basic fleet, the organic fleet that I spoke of, that were cargo ships that ran to out-of-the-way places not covered by normal shipping lines and were manned by civilian crews. You can identify MSTS because it wears a blue-and-gold stack mark to differentiate it from a U.S. ship in service, and the designation is not USS but USNS, standing for United States Naval Service ship. I think at one time we had as many as sixty or seventy ships of various shapes and sizes, from survey ships and a considerable tanker fleet that really was for use in point-to-point traffic. However, some of them had underway refueling capabilities.

Q: They were in addition to the AOs in the fleet?

Adm. C.: These were not AOs in the fleet at all. These were basically commercial tankers, though some of them were not unlike the oilers in the fleet, and they were without exception manned by civilian crews, all Civil Service, negotiated wages just like any other union would. However, some of them had been trained for underway replenishment. Now, basically probably the underway replenishment was more generally used for replenishing a Navy oiler at sea, rather than going all the way into port and have the oiler go into ports, as a time-saving and money-saving device.

Q: That required special training for a civilian crew, didn't it?

Adm. C.: Yes, and they were very adept at it.

I found that it was a completely different world from the Navy, although I'd had this experience before Congress for two years. There I was presenting a program and trying basically to get money. Here it was a question of trying to run a shipping line effectively, economically, to provide service so that your customers - the three services - weren't unhappy or felt that they were being overcharged for their shipments overseas. You really had almost a commercial operation. As I said, one of the more important equivalents of an assistant chief of staff was the industrial relations officer. Equally important, if not even more so, of course, was the legal officer. In all of our claims, if we lost cargo under a shipping contract, we had legal problems that the Navy never thought of, and we had a very fine legal staff.

Our maintenance officer was a naval officer. Our operations officer was a naval officer. Our legal officer was a civilian, as was the industrial relations officer. Then, of course, we had the other staff functions, but it was quite different in this respect. It gave me an insight into business, and - I'll be perfectly frank with you, Jack - most MSTS commanders, when they retired from the Navy, were in some small way affiliated with the shipping lines of our country.

To go one step farther in this organization - whether it's been reduced in scope now, I don't know - but in addition to the MSTS headquarters in Washington, which was the parent command, there was an MSTS command in New York, there was an MSTS command in San Francisco, and there was an MSTS command in the Far East. The Far East command was based in Japan, where there was a flag officer, and they were responsible primarily for running the inter-area LSTs. I frankly don't know whether they've been phased out now or not, but I think they have.

There was a great deal of discussion as to whether they should be crewed by Japanese and, of course, the basic argument from our point of view was that we are furnishing a service that is far less expensive with Japanese crews than it would be with our own American crews. Consequently, we feel that it is in the best interests of our country to continue this way." But we had numerous battles.

Q: How did you settle that with the longshoremen, for instance?

Adm. C.: Well, that was the point. Because of the special situation and the fact that it was a semi-combat zone during the Korean War, we were able to maintain the use of the foreign crews for quite some time. Whether now they've been phased out or not, I don't know. They probably have. I wouldn't be a bit surprised.

Q: One hears from time to time that the Navy, as a whole, doesn't really give the merchant fleets of our country their proper status and so forth, but it seems to me that the MSTS was a kind of a bridge between the regular Navy and the merchant shipping men of the country?

Adm. C.: I think that's absolutely true and, of course, recognizing the need for merchant shipping in time of general mobilization or general war, it's always been MSTS' position that we should have a strong merchant marine. I think later a commander, possibly "Red" Ramage, was instrumental in getting additional ships subsidized or appropriated for, or however you get money for the merchant marine -

Q: By virtue of your position, you must have been very welcome at the Maritime Commission?

Adm. C.: We had very close relations with the Maritime Commission and, as I said, those who had served in MSTS very often ended up in some capacity with either the civilian shipping lines or with the Maritime Commission. Two or three officers who retired from MSTS went on to the Maritime Commission.

Q: Were you tempted, when you retired?

Adm. C.: No, because too much time had elapsed. I was there just a year, then I had another eight or nine years, and by that time, well, I guess I'd lost interest. I was really never too interested in going into business. Roy Gano went and, I think, worked for a while with one of the lines, and then headed the United Seamen's Service, which is the service that provides recreational facilities and clubs and things overseas for the merchant marine. As a matter of fact, my neighbor up the street, who's a retired admiral, is doing the same thing.

Q: You mean Jimmy James?

Adm. C.: No, not Jimmy James. Wally Schleich. He is very active in the United Seamen's Service. But I found this a completely different way of life. One sort of humorous aspect of it - I had been invited - well, first let me say that in all my naval career I had never worn aiguilettes, and here I was a rear admiral and I really didn't know how to put the damned things on, and, to show my complete ignorance, there was a reception at the CNO's house and the uniform was "white service." So I looked it up in the book, but I failed to read part of the fine print and it said "white service," so I wore service aiguillettes. When I got there, one of my friends said, "Jack, you're out of uniform."

I said: "What do you mean? I've got on 'white service.' It said 'Ribbons, service, aiguillettes.'"

And he said, "No, you didn't read the fine print. At a social function that is worthy of an official invitation, you should wear your dress aiguillettes."

So I was the only guy there in service aiguillettes, at the CNO's house, and I might add that it didn't bother me too much.

Q: You speak about another world. I would think that the whole realm of labor relations was another world to you?

Adm. C.: Oh, without any question.

Q: Would you talk about that?

Adm. C.: Well, I was involved only in a supervisory capacity. The industrial relations officer did a great deal of the leg work in negotiating with the unions. And, of course, the MSTS pay scales were regulated by the union, the Seamen's Union, but there was one thing they could not do. They could not strike against the government.

Q: Then!

Adm. C.: Then. They can now, I guess, but then they couldn't, so this was a very important aspect of determining the wage scales. I was surprised, for example, that the chief engineer of a P-3, which was one of the last remaining passenger liners, received almost as much pay as the captain, and far more than the captain of the Navy-manned ship across the dock, and obviously far more than the chief engineer of the same type ship with exactly the same equipment, who was probably a lieutenant commander or a commander.

These ships, whether they were service-manned or civilian-manned, all had a military department on them, usually composed of a Supply Corps officer, who was like the purser, and possibly a Navy nurse for medical reasons, or a corpsman. So that there were people of military stature who were able to take care of the needs of troops. If the ship happened to be loading out a battalion or a regiment of the Army there was a military person to whom they could speak, rather than having to go to the civilian captain or to the civilian chief engineer.

But, as I said, those were very quickly phased out and have gone the way of all passenger ships, that is, American line passenger ships.

Q: Did these inflated pay scales make it difficult for you to pay your own way?

Adm. C.: No, because the inflated pay scales were passed on to the consumer, just like any other business when the cost of operation went up, then the rates went up, and we charged the Army and the Navy and the Air Force more for the transportation of the same amount of goods. On the other hand, of course, they could feel that they were being put upon, and we had meetings with their transportation people, particularly the Army and the Air Force who were our big users, as you could easily see.

Q: But they had no recourse, did they?

Adm. C.: Well, we had a sort of a moral obligation. We felt that we were running a business, but we were doing the best we could to hold down their shipping rates. No, once the rate was established and approved, they had no recourse, but in the negotiations for the rates we did the best we could.

As I said, it was a very strange operation. Your every effort was directed towards running an efficient shipping line. Every effort was made to get the best prices for oil wherever we would buy to bunker, every effort was made to hold the wages down within reason. You have to have happy crewmen, and most of them were very happy because they had Civil Service tenure and were protected under the Civil Service laws.

Q: Did this mean that you didn't get as much work out of them?

Adm. C.: No, I wouldn't say that. I think they were basically just like any others, and some of them were very fine. We had, obviously, incentives and the usual "skipper of the year" awards. As a matter of fact, one of the first things I had to do was go out to Chicago, I think, and give an award to someone who had participated in a rescue at sea under very hazardous conditions, and he was given the MSTS award. His name completely escapes me and the name of the ship does, too, but I remember going out and giving a little speech and presenting this skipper with the award for conducting this rescue at sea.

So, as I've said, it was more like a commercial organization than anything that I had ever known in the Navy. And, after all, I had been involved in contact with civilians in my job in CNO, in the Shore Establishment and Maintenance Division, because before going before the Congress with a request for a chapel or a swimming pool or a breakwater, we had to have engineering studies, we had to deal basically with civilians to determine the costs, in order to go in with a sensible estimate of how much money we needed. So I had that experience in dealing with civilians, but actually the negotiations in terms of labor were done by Joe Acker, who was the assistant for industrial relations.

The legal officer was Morse, who was one higher than the highest G-whatever it is and a very fine man. Admiral Gano, as I said, was a marvelous boss. We worked very closely. I participated sometimes in the negotiations, more as a top negotiator than I did as the nitty gritty. That sort of reminds me of the technical people over here. Not that I was Dr. Kissinger! I wasn't, but I found that every now and then I did participate in some of the negotiations for shipping rates. You see, these were established on a Q basis, or a measurement-ton basis, and you negotiated with the East Coast people for a rate, and then the Gulf, and then the West Coast people. So you were pretty actively involved most of the time. And, as the rates changed, why, your rates changed. So it was a very viable, living business.

Q: Did it put you in touch with foreign shipping lines?

Adm. C.: Only to the extent that when it was impossible to get an American bottom we would then charter, usually, a foreign ship, if that were the only means available. This was covered in the rules of the game, so that when American shipping was not available we could charter foreign bottoms.

Q: At that time, there was quite a contrast, was there not, between the rates?

Adm. C.: Yes, we'd get them less expensively, usually, for the same job, but we were prohibited by law, generally speaking, unless there was some unusual situation that required a foreign bottom.

Q: Admiral, since you had experience with maritime shipping in this job, did you come away from it in an optimistic mood about the future of our merchant shipping, or were you pessimistic, as a result of this experience?

Adm. C.: I think basically I was quite pessimistic. From a practical point of view, I saw nothing but the myriad problems of the shipping industry, not the least of which was the tendency on their part to price themselves out of business. From an emotional point of view, I wasn't fond of the way they did business and, although nobody asked me to work for them, I think without question I would have turned it down, because I would not really have liked to become associated with the shipping lines. Now, I may say that in partial ignorance, but at the same time I felt very strongly about it. I might even go so far as to say that I thought that, generally speaking, it was a sick industry. Steps have been taken recently, I think, to possibly rejuvenate it and I would hope that with the development of newer, faster ships and all the rest of the things that modern technology can provide, plus the requirements for special ships - survey ships, oceanographic ships, which is a very sexy term now, I suppose, the industry could be rejuvenated to the point that it would become a successful type of operation.

But at that particular time, I felt very strongly that it was a sick industry, and not only did I feel that way but I didn't want to be associated with it myself even after retirement.

Q: Off tape, you gave me an illustration of the lengths to which some of the shipping officials went because of the circumstances under which they operated. Would you repeat that?

Adm. C.: I think it was interesting that when we were entertaining, on a modest scale, as you must in the service, almost without fail one of the shipping concern executives would send rather elaborate flowers. This continued and after a while I finally called him and said:

"This is embarrassing to me. I can't in any way reciprocate. You know well enough that in my capacity I'm going to do everything in my power to be as fair as possible, and sending flowers isn't going to do you one damned bit of good. Why do you do it?"

He was very frank and said - and he was a good friend: "Jack, the reason I do it is very simple. I know that it isn't going to influence anything that you do, but it provides an open door. You possibly drop a note of thanks or you call and say thanks for the flowers. It provides me with an entree, through your secretary, so that if I need to talk to you I can."

I thought that was a very interesting approach and, of course, knowing the tax laws, I could see that it was a very effective means of maintaining communication for the time when something might happen that he would need to get in contact with me. And in this particular respect he was right, because during the Dominican crisis there were areas that it was not safe for American ships to go. The Navy would know about that but the merchant marine would not necessarily know, and I was able to inform people as to where their ships should steer clear, and for this they were not only grateful but certainly very happy to receive information in order to avoid an incident.

So in this aspect of it it probably paid off. It looked to me like a very expensive way of assuring access to a secretary, but apparently this is the way business is done in the shipping industry, and this is one of the things which I was not particularly fond of.

Q: Did you travel to any of the branch offices, so to speak, of MSTS?

Adm. C.: Oh, yes. We went to MSTS in New York and inspected them, and then I think we went once to San Francisco. I was there only about thirteen months and, if my memory serves me correctly, I didn't take any trips overseas during that time.

The commanders of MSTS Lant in New York and MSTS Pac in San Francisco came into the office with their problems and we had discussions, as you would with any subordinate commander, and I think there was some sort of administrative inspection that we gave them. At least I remember going to New York and looking over their operation.

Q: Was there any particular problem that stands out in this period of thirteen months?

Adm. C.: The salient thing was the transition between the type of operations that had gone on in the past, i.e., the movement of tremendous amounts of supplies overseas during the war and the years following the war, and the Korean War, to a specialized type of operation, such as running oceanographic research ships, specialized ships - the transition from the hauling of a lot of freight to this type of operation and the general reduction in the hauling of supplies as the troops overseas diminished. Now, of course, this was before the Vietnam conflict, during which the whole thing escalated again so that the primary requirement was to get the goods overseas. As you know, most of that was done by chartered ships and I'm sure MSTS did all the chartering and negotiated the shipping rates. Along with that you have to negotiate the combat bonuses and everything else that goes along with labor relations in a war zone, in addition to the legal responsibilities, and the liabilities involved. So I'm sure it was a very complicated procedure.

So the problem was not so much a specific problem but the transition from one type of operation to another. Then, the general feeling that the merchant shipping industry had to be rejuvenated. I think later MSTS commanders, and I speak specifically of "Red" Ramage who did all that was in his power to try to get an adequate merchant marine, recognizing that in times of general mobilization it's an absolute necessity if we're going to fight a war overseas.

Q: Did you have any thoughts in those days about establishing a system similar to what the Russians obviously have with their merchant marine, which is almost an integral part of the Navy?

Adm. C.: No, I don't think we had any thoughts along those lines. Of course, you're getting into almost that type of operation, although not precisely, when you subsidize a ship. Although you don't actually control it, when you provide (1) the building subsidy, which reduces the cost of the construction of the ship, and (2) then you provide the operating subsidy, which reduces the cost of operation of the ship for the owner, you have a pretty strong hand in the control.

However, as I said, there were one or two lines that were not subsidized and were very proud of the fact that they were wholly independent business operations, able to get along without government subsidy. As a matter of fact, I rather liked to do business with them because they weren't mixed up in government, and consequently weren't thinking of their subsidies.

Q: When you were operating survey ships and what have you, you were more or less working in tandem with another branch of the Navy itself, the Oceanographic Office. What were the requirements there that differed from the others?

Adm. C.: Here, the ship was owned by MSTS and the crew was provided by MSTS, so that you had very tight operational control, but your ship operated sometimes in conjunction with the Navy and sometimes in conjunction with research organizations, such as Woods Hole or whatever outfit was interested in the research capabilities of the vessel.

I think the Navy and MSTS have always been closely associated without one getting into the other's business. It's almost like being on one side of the dock or on the other side of the dock. That's not a very good example. Their ships looked different. They have the blue-and-gold band and they have a civilian crew, and when they are associated with the Navy, such as in a re-fueling operation of a tanker, they go about their business, and the contacts are probably more sporadic than you would expect.

Q: In the case of operating a survey ship or what have you, did this also put you in contact with shipbuilding concerns?

Adm. C.: I had very little to do with shipbuilding at all.

I think, at that time, really the merchant marine building program was pretty dormant. They just weren't building any ships -

Q: Bumping along the bottoms!

Adm. C.: Bumping along the bottoms - except some of these smaller ships that were being laid down.

Q: I was thinking of the specialized ships, oceanographic ships.

Adm. C.: I didn't have anything to do with it. I think the design probably was controlled through the Bureau of Ships, and even though the ship was to be operated by MSTS, the requirements for the ship were developed by the Ships' Characteristics Board that I spoke of earlier. I really don't know. As I say, I had very little to do with it because at that particular time there were just a few of these ships coming along, and the rest of the building program was pretty dormant.

Q: Well, that was a very interesting chapter in your career.

Adm. C.: It was an unusual chapter. As I said, it was the first, and really the only, time that I had such close association with industry, and I think it stood me in good stead later on when, as you increase in service and rank, your associations broaden to other elements of the population, whether they be industrial or political. As time went on, some of my jobs branched from pure naval relations to those with politicians of other countries, governing authorities of other countries, and this experience, I felt, was broadening and beneficial for assignments in later years.

Q: Now we have an entirely different assignment coming up, a most unusual one and an innovative one almost.

Adm. C.: This to me was one of the more interesting times of my naval career certainly. I spoke of the deep satisfaction I had in commanding the Roanoke, but in a completely different way this one was probably as rewarding or even more rewarding because it was on such a different scale.

Q: And this began in June of 1961.

Adm. C.: Yes, and I remember the detail officer called me and said, "I've got a destroyer flotilla for you," and I said, "That is simply great. Where is it?"

He said, "It's in Norfolk, and it's called Destroyer Flotilla Four."

So I said, "That sounds simply marvelous to me. I'll be out of here as quick as a flash."

Well, we were living in Annapolis at the time and I was commuting to Washington, so I was delighted to get rid of the commute which, as I mentioned once before, I'd participated in for too damned many years. We moved to Norfolk for what turned out to be, again in my view, a fairly short tour because it seemed so short. It was only about a year and a half, and, of course, it was packed with all sorts of experiences which have really not changed my life but certainly made me more interested in the space program than the average naval officer.

Q: When you went there, were you aware of what it was?

Adm. C.: I wasn't completely aware, but I had been told that CruDesFlot 4 - it was not then CrusDesFlot 4, it was DesFlot 4 - was involved in the Mercury recovery program. Quite frankly I really didn't know much about it and I sort of said "Oh? What does that entail?" And I was told it was going to entail going out and getting the astronauts.

Just before I got there, Alan B. Shepard made the first suborbital flight.

Q: Was that a part of Mercury?

Adm. C.: It was the first Mercury flight and my predecessor, who was DesFlot 4, was the recovery commander. This was a strange sort of arrangement. My duties as DesFlot 4 were pretty much administrative. My flagship was usually a tender during the year and a half I was there. Because of ship overhauls, I had three of them. It was for most of the time the Sierra, which was built as a destroyer tender during World War II or a little before that, the Tidewater, which was a converted merchant ship but was a tender, and the Shenandoah, aboard which I had my offices for a short period because of ship overhaul schedules.

The ships of the flotilla were generally responsible to me for training and operations in the Norfolk area. Then they deployed to the Sixth Fleet and were gone, as far as I was concerned, for their normal deployment tours to the Med, then they came back and were in a sort of a logistic work-up type period in which we were essentially responsible for arranging and providing logistic support and looking after them while they were in the Norfolk area.

But really that wasn't my primary job, as I soon found out, because the Project Mercury Task Force Commander, which was my other title, seemed to take far more time and, in this capacity, we in the command and on the staff were involved not only with the actual recovery but with all the pre-recovery training, which involved development of the expertise in the crews for getting the capsule, the helicopters for the training and recovering the astronauts from the capsule, and development of the procedures that have come a long way since the first flights.

As you know, Shepard was recovered successfully by helicopter. The next flight was Virgil Grissom and in that recovery the capsule was lost.

Q: The door flew off, didn't it?

Adm. C.: Well, the door was opened. I'm prepared to say that and not because Gus is dead, but that's what happened. He opened the door before the sling had been attached, which resulted, by the way, in the development of a completely new system wherein before anything is opened - and this is true now of the moon shots and everything else - a big inflatable collar is put on the capsule to avoid just such an accident as happened in the case of Grissom's capsule. The helicopter actually had the sling attached, but the minute the water got in the capsule it was either going to pull the helicopter down or he had to let go, and that's what happened.

Q: All the instruments were lost?

Adm. C.: Everything. Everything in the capsule was lost, and in some respects we were very lucky that we didn't lose Grissom because he just got out of the capsule in time.

Of course, in the development of the early recoveries we still had rescue teams standing by, the dropping of the frogmen was essentially a result of the development of the collar and the continued use of the collar throughout the subsequent recoveries.

Q: That was a great development!

Adm. C.: A great development. We worked very closely with NASA, which was at Langley Field near Norfolk before Lyndon Johnson moved it to Texas.

Q: What was the basic reason for the move? More space, or what?

Adm. C.: In my view, it was that Lyndon Johnson was a Texan and he'd been the chairman of the space committee in the Senate and as the Vice President, at that time, he was interested in getting certain aspects of the space program into Texas. I think he was primarily responsible. Whether it had anything to do with the weather or not I'm not quite sure.

However, in the early days when we used to work with the practice capsules, the boiler-plate models, they were all from Langley, and our helicopter crews and our ship-recovery crews were all trained in how to pick up the capsule, how, hopefully, to prevent it from sinking. The standard procedure at first was that it could be picked up either by helicopter or, if the ship got there first, why obviously the ship would pick it up. That was the case in Glenn's recovery.

The first recovery that I participated in was Grissom's.

Q: That was in 1961, wasn't it?

Adm. C.: Yes. Then, after Grissom's, I think before Glenn went up - let's see, Carpenter came after Glenn - we sent up Enos, who was a little rhesus monkey and he was recovered in practically the same way as the astronauts were.

Q: That was in space, wasn't it?

Adm. C.: That was in space. That was the first. He authored it and survived, not for long, I was told. I think he died early thereafter, but he was recovered intact and the procedures were essentially the same for the monkey as they were for the astronauts.

I remember that after each shot there were always press conferences and on TV -

Q: Were you, in each case, at Canaveral?

Adm. C.: Yes. As a matter of fact, I almost felt that Canaveral was my home away from home because we went down about two weeks before the shot and stayed during the pre-flight countdown, and then, of course, conducted the recovery operations from the recovery room, which was a part of the control complex there at - it was originally called Cape Canaveral, then afterwards Cape Kennedy, but we knew it exclusively as Cape Canaveral. Then we'd fly back to Norfolk and prepare for the next flight. So, essentially, in the year and a half that I spent in command of Destroyer Flotilla 4 really my primary job was the Mercury Task Force 40 Recovery Commander.

Q: I think it's Grissom who talks about the training exercises in Pensacola. Was the Navy involved in that?

Adm. C.: Some of the exercises were conducted in Pensacola, yes. The helicopter training, although some were also conducted in Hampton Roads, and a lot of the capsule practice recoveries were conducted right there in Hampton Roads. But there were others that were conducted in Pensacola. I think the location was probably dependent on water conditions and the flight crews of the helicopters that were to conduct the recovery.

Q: Tell me about the spread of the ships in the task force, the rescue force. You had, what, twenty or so?

Adm. C.: I'm trying to think of the exact number. Of course, the heart of the recovery force was the carrier, and she was usually a CVS, an ASW carrier. The kind I later controlled as ASW commander.

The general rule was to lay the force out along the axis of recovery, with the carrier at the projected point of impact and destroyers down the line and up the line, in case of a short shot or a long shot. The forces deployed basically from Norfolk or, in the case of the carrier, sometimes from Mayport, depending on what carrier we had. We had voice control to all the ships and we were assisted by the Sea-Air rescue forces of the Air Force. They had what they called Hu-16s, which were seaplanes, in addition to some of the bigger four-engined landplanes from which they could drop paramedic teams.

During the first recoveries they reported directly to me. The commanding general at Canaveral, of Patrick Air Force Base, and also - well, our relationship really hadn't been clearly defined - was Lieutenant General Lee Davis, and there was a little friction at the conclusion of Grissom's shot because I bluntly said that Grissom opened the door before he should and, since he was an Air Force pilot, I'm afraid that that provoked a little interservice rivalry which, believe me, I had no intention of provoking.

Q: A fact is a fact!

Adm. C.: A fact is a fact. So there was a bit of friction built up, I'm afraid. However, since Grissom was unhurt we simply felt, ok, that's over and done with, let's get going on the next shot. The next shot was Glenn's and, as we all know, this was the first orbital shot in our history, and, there on the wall, is the antenna from the capsule. It was the procedure that once the capsule landed you cut off the antenna because it interfered with the hoisting slings. At that time the collar still hadn't been developed and, as you see, that particular recovery was made by the destroyer because it just so happened that Glenn landed near the destroyer and it seemed pointless to pick him up by helicopter when, here, you had a ship right there available within a very short distance. So they went over and picked Glenn up and picked the capsule up also. It was later transferred to the carrier and sent on in in the usual way. But they were very proud of themselves. They had trained for this and took a great deal of satisfaction in recovering the first orbital flight.

Of course, it was a great success. There were no harsh words by anybody. I remember, at the TV interview after the recovery, a reporter said something about "Do you have anything special to say," and I said:

"Well, you know, it's better to be born lucky than rich, and I have something that I have carried with me ever since World War II," and it was my wallet that was with me all the time in the water after the Helena had been sunk, and in it were two four-leaf clovers. And I said: "I would no more come to a recovery from Norfolk without my wallet and my four-leaf clovers than I would fly to the moon. I do not necessarily attribute the success of this to that fact. Obviously, it is the result of effective training and hard work on everybody's part, but I still wouldn't be without my four-leaf clovers."

Everybody laughed at me and thought that I was sort of a kook, I guess, but I still have my wallet and I still have my four-leaf clovers, and I think if I were going on a hazardous trip again I'd like to have my wallet and my four-leaf clovers with me.

Q: Glenn's flight was February 20, 1962. It had been scheduled for an earlier date, in January.

Adm. C.: Well, we were obviously dependent upon the weather. I've forgotten whether Glenn's was delayed because of mechanical difficulties or on account of the weather.

Q: Tell me why weather is such an important factor when the flight so quickly is beyond weather.

Adm. C.: The reason for it is that the separation of the escape device - you see, there was an escape tower on the capsule, so that in the very early stages, really before flight had been developed, if something happened the escape tower would blow and the astronauts could be recovered within the vicinity. For this you had to have visual contact. All the telescopes that were around watched this until the rocket assumed its normal flight.

Q: And this still pertains?

Adm. C.: Yes, I think the escape towers are still there. Whether as the reliability increased and they felt that it wasn't necessary to have this additional safety device, I've forgotten. I don't know whether they do it on the moon rockets or not. But all the Mercury flights had the escape tower, and this was for a preflight malfunction.

Q: I see, and weather is a factor there.

Adm. C.: There's always that factor, and in that event the tower would blow, the capsule would come down right within the locality, and for this reason you had to have visual contact until she had assumed her normal flight path and had nosed over down range.

Q: How did your units in the task force coordinate with the other ships at sea, in the Indian Ocean and around the world stationed in case of some accident?

Adm. C.: We had good radio communication with the ships, through relay stations..

Q: And they were under your command?

Adm. C.: I've forgotten whether the ships in the Indian Ocean were directly under my command or - no, I know how it was. There was a force commander in the Pacific who was responsible for the positioning of those ships, and it was through him that we could communicate directly with the different ships.

Q: They were only there for emergency?

Adm. C.: Only for emergency, absolutely, and, of course, they were never used. In fact, they've never been used in any flight so far. All we needed was the direct communication, which we had through the Pacific commander, and he was a naval commander. However, we had coordinating conferences to make sure that they were on station and properly located. And, of course, NASA, as you know, had the tracking stations -

Q: Did you tie in with them?

Adm. C.: Oh, yes. We had communication with the tracking stations to get the position of the flight so that we knew where the flight was. It was interesting. The recovery room was right off the control room, and during those first flights - I'm trying to remember whether Chris Kraft was the director or not, but I can see him standing there now. I have a couple of pictures that might be interesting of when President Kennedy came down after the Glenn flight to look at them.

All the consoles for the original Mercury, which, of course, were far less sophisticated than the present-day Apollo flight ones, but on a smaller scale they were all there.

Right off the control room was the recovery room, and the recovery room had all the communications to the ships. We had our plotting boards, our communications to our sea-air rescue units and to all of the various stations. We had voice communications, obviously, with the ships at sea and, generally speaking, they were excellent. If we didn't have voice communications we always could go to standard Navy very reliable communications.

Q: In those early flights they had tracking stations in the Caribbean Islands, did they not, which they no longer use?

Adm. C.: I don't know whether they use them now or not. Of course, the first tracking station was in the Caribbean, and I should be able to remember the other stations as they went around the world. There was one in Africa, there was one in Australia, and I've forgotten where the others were, but they were all tied in. From the one in the Caribbean, of course, you could get your first indication of a good solid flight.

Q: That was in Antigua?

Adm. C.: Yes. I think it's still there. Whether it's been deactivated and made into some other kind of a station I'm really not quite sure.

As you can easily imagine, it was a procedure that was always very tense. Most people tried to be calm, but it's difficult to be calm, particularly when you're participating in something like that. It was particularly upsetting to me because, after all, when the flight was successful my work just began. Obviously that was to get the guy back alive and also to get the capsule back intact. So during the flight when everything was going beautifully, I was apprehensive because my work hadn't begun, and at that time, as I said, I was the Task Force Project Mercury Recovery Commander. I did not report to anybody except NASA. I had certain guidelines that the astronaut was to be picked up within a certain length of time. This was a guideline for use, for example, in whether a helicopter could get there or whether a ship could get there. I've forgotten the precise period of time involved but it became very important later on in the Carpenter flight, and was the cause of considerable controversy and eventual realignment of the command chain for recovery. In some ways, it was unfortunate, but I felt that I was right in the ensuing decisions that I made in regard to the recovery of Carpenter. There were other people who didn't feel that way.

Q: Tell me about that.

Adm. C.: Yes. The Carpenter flight was pretty much the same as the Glenn flight.

Q: How soon after the Glenn flight was it?

Adm. C.: You don't have the date there, do you, and I don't either.

Q: No, but it was the same year.

Adm. C.: Yes, it was the same year.

What happened was that there was a little longer burn apparently, so that Carpenter landed - if my memory serves me correctly - some forty miles, or maybe even a little more, down-range, and it so happened that a ship was not there. By this time they had developed the rubber raft, not the collar, but the rubber raft, and he got out of the capsule and was in the rubber raft, perfectly safe, the capsule was floating. It was going to take the helicopters close to the limiting time to get there - the time that I spoke of earlier prescribed by NASA for the limit of the time he should stay in the water, and the HU-16s, which were the seaplanes, Air Force sea-air rescue squadrons, felt that they should have been permitted to land in the open sea and pick up Carpenter. I felt that, since he was safe, since I could get the helicopters there, very frankly I felt that the HU-16s could land without much trouble, but taking off in a heavy sea was a different story, and, in my view, it would have been extremely dangerous.

Well, it got close, and the time limit was just about to be exceeded when, in fact, the helicopters arrived on the scene, picked up Carpenter, he was fine, picked up the capsule, everything was all right. But I was bitterly criticized by the Air Force for not letting the HU-16s land.

I came back and I never shall forget, because I arrived back in Norfolk and Admiral Beakley, who had been the Seventh Fleet commander and was Deputy CinCLant under Admiral Dennison, sent for me and said:

"Jack, you did absolutely right. You're not an aviator, but I agree with you and I am an aviator of some forty years' standing. You were right in not letting the HU-16s land."

And I said: "Well, I'm glad to hear that, Admiral, because I'm going to have a battle," and I ended up having a battle. I was sent for by the Secretary of Defense to tell him why I'd done what I'd done.

Out of that controversy over whether I had been proper in allowing the recovery to proceed according to plan by helicopter, instead of allowing the seaplanes to land, there developed a fight in the JCS about the command arrangements for the recovery of future flights. The JCS resolved it by making General Davis, who was the Air Force general at Patrick, the DOD coordinator for all recovery operations, and making the Navy recovery commander report to him. Prior to that time, I did not report to General Davis at all, but simply was responsible for the recovery to NASA and to the launch team.

Q: Who was chairman of the Joint Chiefs? Nate Twining?

Adm. C.: No, Max Taylor, I think.

As I said, I went up to Washington to explain my views and I was obviously pretty well supported by the Navy, and I was very happy to be supported by such an eminent aviator as Admiral Beakley.

Q: How did MacNamara act?

Adm. C.: He listened, and said: "Well, after all, he's back safely. The Air Force doesn't agree with you, but the "proof of the pudding - "and nothing more was said.

But it was a tense time for me. I think I was criticized in some of the press, but, like everything else, Jack, it blows over and is soon forgotten!

Q: Well, in contrast, the aftermath of the Glenn flight was pleasant, wasn't it?

Adm. C.: Nothing but peaches and roses, everything was great.

Q: You went before the congressional committee?

Chew #6 - 298

Adm. C.: No, I didn't go before the committee. I stuck to my recovery business.

Q: You did report to the CNO and various other naval people?

Adm. C.: Yes, I reported to the CNO because, having had some experience in my life in Op-60, it was obvious to me that there was going to be a fight in the JCS.

Q: This again, after the Carpenter recovery?

Adm. C.: This brought on by the Carpenter recovery. Some action would have to be taken, so I briefed the people who were interested and, frankly, hoped that the situation that had been developed would be continued, but I later found out that it wasn't and I don't think that it made too much difference, except that it did give General Davis operational control - or his successor - and, had that been in effect at that time, he could have directed me to land the seaplanes, whereas under the system that was existing at the time he couldn't. Consequently, I didn't. It could have made a difference, had the revised system been in effect at the time of the Carpenter recovery.

Q: As a footnote, I take it that the Army has phased out the use of seaplanes now, too, has it not?

Adm. C.: I think it has, yes. Interestingly enough, the Japanese have developed a seaplane that they think is going to be a great   seaplane, but whether, in fact, it will or not, I don't know. They've spent a lot of money on it. They also visualize it as a possible replacement for this type of sea-air rescue plane, and even if it's not necessarily a very successful ASW weapon, they hope that it will be a very successful sea-air rescue type of vehicle. Whether it's proved to be that way or not, I don't know, because it's pretty much in the development and testing stage.

But, generally speaking, seaplanes have been phased out because they are less efficient, there's no question about it, and, except for certain specific types of work where your only landing medium is water, a landplane can do the job much more easily.

Q: And a helicopter!

Adm. C.: And a helicopter, of course, is even better. Those helicopter crews were marvelous. They had trained well, they were very proud of themselves, they were excellent pilots. My hat was off to them because, of course, with pardonable pride, they were naval helicopters. They were certainly johnny-on-the-spot. The only reason it took them so long was the fact that they had to go so far down range to get to Carpenter in this particular recovery incident.

I felt that I was right and was, to a certain degree, vindicated, at least by the people for whom I worked. The final outcome of the reassignment of responsibilities, I felt, was a matter for the JCS to decide, and they did.

Q: Did the Coast Guard have any part in this operation?

Adm. C.: Yes, it seems to me the Coast Guard were available for inshore type work. Of course, they patrolled the area. I'm trying to remember whether they were available in case the escape tower had to be used. I think they were.

Q: Oh, as it took off?

Adm. C.: As it took off, yes. But down range, no, the Coast Guard wasn't involved at all. It was all Navy and the Air Force squadrons that were assigned to me for that purpose.

Q: Since you worked so closely with the astronauts, perhaps you have some special observation about them you'd like to make?

Adm. C.: Yes, I do, because I taught Shephard as a midshipman when I was at the Naval Academy. I was always impressed with his ability. As a matter of fact, I like him and I thought the mere fact that he stayed with the program as long as he did is indicative of his dedication to that line of work in which he was certainly preeminently successful.

Grissom I knew only in my contact as recovery commander.

Q: He wasn't a Naval Academy man?

Adm. C.: No, Grissom was in the Air Force. Carpenter I was very fond of. I thought they were an impressive group of young men. Glenn, of course, was a Marine and I've always had, as I explained once before, a great deal of admiration for the Marines, both collectively and individually. I thought essentially they were a very, very superior group of people. If I had a favorite, I suppose it would have been Shepard, of the ones I knew, Glenn, Grissom, Carpenter, and Shepard. Although I didn't recover Shepard, I had frequent conversations with him and during the training he was most helpful because he, after all, had been the first to make a suborbital flight.

One of my wife's favorite mementoes is a four-leaf clover, which I told you about in one of my first interviews. It was a parting gift when I left CruDesFlot 4 and the astronauts each signed one of the petals of the four-leaf clover, so that she has Glenn, Grissom, Carpenter, and I don't know whether there's a paw print for Enos or not.

But it was a most interesting time to be involved in the space program. It was the beginning and, as you know,

President Kennedy came to Canaveral afterwards to view the scene of the crime. Vice President Johnson also came. After the Glenn flight there was a big parade through the streets of Cape Kennedy. As a matter of fact, I think I rode with the Governor of Florida, who was a participant in the parade. They were very interesting and very happy times, except for the one incident of the Carpenter flight and the friction that was developed on the method of recovery.

As must happen to all good things, it finally came to an end, and it was rather interesting because I was on the golf course on a Sunday morning and the telephone rang, and it was the detail officer - the flag detail officer happened to be a classmate of mine. He called and he said:

"Jack, it's time for you to leave. That's only a year's tour and you've been there a year and a half. I have a job for you as commandant of the District in New Orleans."

I said: "What in the hell are you thinking of! If you are setting me up for plucking, that, in my view, is one of the surest ways to do it. I've always been under the impression that the commandant's job is one of the jobs that are reserved for those more senior who are serving out their last days in genteel comfort." Incidentally, at the present time that policy has been changed somewhat, but at that time it was certainly true. So I said,"If that's what you have in mind, I'm not interested. I don't want any commandant's job."

He said, "O.K."

I said, "Really, I feel that I might be qualified to be superintendent of the Naval Academy, but I'm sure that will never come to pass." And he said, "No, it will never come to pass, but you're perfectly free to ask."

So I asked officially and was turned down. A short time later I was called and told I was going to the Joint Chiefs of Staff. I said:

"Well, having served for a number of years in Op-60 and having been associated with Op-60 in JCS work, I could probably be as useful there as I could anywhere else."

My introduction to the Joint Chiefs of Staff, I must say, was rather startling.

Q: We'll reserve that for next time.

Interview No. 7 with Vice Admiral John L. Chew, U.S. Navy (Ret.)

Place: His residence in Providence, Annapolis, Maryland

Date: Tuesday morning, 6 February 1973

Subject: Biography

By: John T. Mason, Jr.

Q: Admiral, again it's a pleasure to be with you. Last time, as you concluded the chapter, you talked about your rescue operations of the astronauts in the Atlantic and how you were about to have a new command.

Adm. C.: Thank you very much for coming. I always look forward to these -

Q: I do, too.

Adm. C.: You didn't let me finish! I always look forward with a certain amount of apprehension!

I think I was about to tell you the last time how sometimes the Navy works in terms of transfers.

As I remember, it was a very lovely Saturday morning and I was on the golf course, and the assistant pro came over in a little cart and said, "Admiral, you're wanted on the phone. They want you to call Washington."

So I got in the cart and went back to the clubhouse to see what it was. It was one of the people in the Bureau of Personnel and he said, "How would you like to go as commandant of the Eighth Naval District?"

I was flabbergasted. I had had what I considered a resonably active career, and my answer was:

"Well, I'll tell you. If you're lining me up for early plucking, obviously I'll go wherever you order me but, in answer to your question, since you've asked me do I want to go there, I most certainly do not."

He said: "Oh! Well, we'll look over the slate and decide where you can go."

As a result, a few weeks later I was told by Admiral Smedberg that I would go to the Joint Chiefs of Staff. This, from a practical standpoint, seemed like a far more interesting assignment to me.

Q: Kind of an open-end one, too!

Adm. C.: An open-end one. I was not naive enough to think it was all going to be great fun, and I knew that in Washington the pressures were rather intense, having witnessed it, as it were, from the fringe, in Annapolis on my previous tours. But I at least was relieved that I wasn't being sent off into the never-never land from which I would certainly feel there would be no recovery.

I think as a practical matter that policy has been reversed now and, generally speaking, there are younger officers being assigned as district commandants.

Q: There's no reason why it shouldn't be an important assignment, is there?

Adm. C.: Well, having been in Op-44 when I told you about my experiences in the shore establishment, one of the prime targets whenever a reduction in force was mentioned or a reduction in facilities was always the naval district in New Orleans, and from a political point of view, being somewhat the bailiwick of Congressman Hebert, there was always a little bit of trouble in having it closed.

I felt that although it would have been a very pleasant and, I'm sure, interesting job, it would hardly have been, to coin a rather bandied-around phrase, interesting or rewarding. So, with those thoughts in mind, I was very happy to receive the assignment in the Joint Chiefs of Staff, although frankly I knew very little about it. However, I did feel that my previous experience in Op-60 which, as you remember, was the section within the CNO that dealt directly with the Joint Chiefs of Staff, meant that I was at least going into an area that my background would possibly have suited me for and given me an elementary bit of training in.

I was fortunate in having my relief, Admiral H. G. Bowen, Jr., tell me that his house was available in Alexandria. I've forgotten the precise days, but I think the manner in which I arrived in the Joint Chiefs of Staff was rather significant.

We had moved from quarters in Norfolk to Admiral Bowen's house in Alexandria. We'd been there four or five days and were fairly decently moved in. My reporting date was probably a week later, and we were prepared to get the house settled and do all the things that you do before you report in on the job. Well, one day before my reporting time, the telephone rang, and it was my friend Barney Sieglaff, who was in the Joint Chiefs of Staff at the time, and he said:

"Hi, Jack, what are you doing?" And I said:

"As a matter of fact, I'm cutting the lawn. Why?"

He said: "Admiral Riley wants you right away."

"Well, I've talked to my boss, General Unger, on the telephone and he said that my reporting day as indicated in my orders is next week and that's perfectly satisfactory, and I have a lot of things to do around the house to get ready. Did you say report right away?"

And Barney said: "Jack, I don't think you quite understand. Admiral Riley wants you today."

"Oh," I said, "today? All right, I'll go and put on my uniform and report today."

He said: "Don't even bother to put on your uniform. Put on a suit of civilian clothes and get the hell in here." Those were Barney's exact words.

So I went up, took off my working shorts, put on a suit of civilian clothes couldn't find my orders, as a matter of minor information, and reported to the Joint Chiefs of Staff.

I was immediately told of the Cuban crisis and that I was to acquaint myself with all aspects of the naval operations immediately, and that that afternoon I was to attend the Joint Chiefs of Staff meeting in order to familiarize myself with the situation, as it existed, and to act basically as a naval action officer within J-3. J-3 was the operations section of the Joint Chiefs of Staff.

Q: At that stage of the game, nothing had been made public on the crisis?

Adm. C.: The tensions had been rising, as I remember, but nothing had been made public as to the deployment of the Soviet missiles.

Q: Nothing, except Senator Keating, I suppose?

Adm. C.: I believe Senator Keating had, and I believe it was rumored, and, of course, this was know in the Joint Chiefs of Staff at that time.

So there I was thrown into the Joint Chiefs of Staff meeting, and I might add that I arrived home that night, or the next morning, at one o'clock, having spent the entire day. Finally, one of the administrative people in the Joint Chiefs of Staff turned to me and said:

"Admiral, you haven't any orders. You haven't even been cleared to go into the meeting of the Joint Chiefs of Staff."

I said: "I realize that, but I think you'd better speak to someone else about it, because I was told to go and, believe me, I went!"

Obviously, at that particular time, the atmosphere in the Joint Chiefs of Staff was very tense. I became an action officer, along with my contemporaries, throughout the Cuban crisis - the Cuban Missile Crisis, I guess it was called. It seemed to me that we never got home at night. We were in the Pentagon practically every day until six, seven, eight, ten, eleven, or twelve o'clock at night. Finally, as the crisis heightened, we set a watch. Prior to that time, there had always been a captain on watch in the operations center, and as I remember, we thought it a little bit humorous that eventually it was considered that with the President being personally interested, as you could well understand, the captain was not adequate to answer the telephone, so there had to be a general or flag officer on duty at all times in the operations center for J-3. So the three of us who were deputies for operations, one who has gone on to be Chief of the Pacific Air Forces, General Clay, who was then a brigadier general - Lucius Clay, my other contemporary was General Tibbetts, who was the pilot of the Enola Gay, and my boss was General Fin Unger. He was Army, the other two were Air Force. There was also an Army deputy whose name escapes me right now, I know, General Burba. He went to Fort Meade and died just about a year or so ago, a very sound and able man who was one of the troop commanders on Project Big Lift, which was that mammoth airlift to Europe designed to test the mobility of our forces and their ability to react quickly to a crisis situation.

So the four of us did around-the-clock watches during the Cuban Missile Crisis.

Q: And the chairman of the Joint Chiefs was Maxwell Taylor?

Adm. C.: Yes, and Herb Riley was the Director of the Joint Staff. The Joint Staff, as I'm sure you remember, was organized along the lines of a conventional staff. The sections were the intelligence section, J-3, which was later taken over by the Defense Intelligence Agency; the J-3, which was ours, the operations section; J-4, which was the logistics section; and J-5, which was the plans section. All were headed by flag or general officers and all had flag or general officers as deputies. The operations section, as I said, had three - no, four actually. I had relieved a Marine, Paul Fontanna, as a service replacement, and I was in turn relieved by an Air Force general. It was a completely joint operation.

I was fortunate to be present during the deliberations of the Joint Chiefs of Staff that resulted in recommendations made to the President. I felt very much a part of the crisis, as it unfolded.

Q: Can you talk about some of the details of your job?

Adm. C.: The details of my job were trying to keep track of the naval forces and trying to inform the Chiefs of their capabilities, their reaction times, what they could do, what they couldn't do, so that they could draw logical conclusions from the capabilities on hand at any given time.

Q: This, then, kept you in direct touch with Admiral Dennison?

Adm. C.: Well, Admiral Dennison, of course, came up himself on numerous occasions, but I was in touch with CinCLant, Admiral Dennison and I worked very closely with the Navy in their war room or their operations center.

Q: This being Admiral Anderson?

Adm. C.: This was Admiral Anderson. For example, one of my jobs that I remember rather vividly was to develop a paper on what happens and how we react if another plane is shot down. As I remember, one was shot down, some sort of photographic plane. What do we do if another one is shot down? We would prepare the basic papers, which, of course, were only prepared at the staff level.

As I remember, one Sunday we had worked on a paper and I had to send it to State for coordination and I had to send it, of course, to the Secretary of Defense for International Security Affairs for coordination who, at that time, was Mr. Nitze. Each put his changes on it and when it came back it was sort of written as we had originally drafted it, which always amused me because it reflected the thinking of both and then came back to mine. I was unduly proud about it, but I might add that I got over that very quickly. The fact that I had written the paper, it had been changed by such illustrious gentlemen, and finally changed back to the original draft. I think lots of people have had that experience in a staff capacity.

Let me add here, parenthetically, that I always felt myself a very poor staff officer. I preferred operations. I preferred being aboard ship, if I could, running things rather than preparing papers, and I felt that essentially I was not very good at it. My writing was slow. I always envied people who could write a paper and have it come out without any misspelled words or any faults in grammar. I always felt that my writing was not very good. However, I was intensely interested in what I was doing and I think, in my small way, I made a contribution during this particular time.

Q: Can you add something, from your point of view, to the historical record, some of the interesting details about the situation as it developed within the Joint Chiefs and as it pertained to the CNO and the Secretary of Defense, and so forth?

Adm. C.: From my level which, as you can see, was fairly far down, I did notice certain areas of basic disagreement. One of the things that always concerned me considerably was that the Air Force colonel, who later made general officer and as a matter of fact I think lives in Annapolis now, Doug Steakley, was the almost sole expert on reconnaissance. Technically, he came under the operations division, or section, within the Joint Chiefs of Staff, but he had complete access to the chairman and, I think, complete access to the White House, and his recommendations for example on overflights, further reconnaissance, were generally speaking, uncoordinated either with the other services or within the Joint Chiefs of Staff. Of course, this was primarily because of the security aspects of it, but I always felt that, since he theoretically came under my particular office as vice chief for operations, it was a difficult way to run a railroad.

Q: He had some sort of a personal relationship with Maxwell

Taylor -

Adm. C.: A personal relationship with Maxwell Taylor and, I think, a very personal relationship with the White House at that particular time. I know Admiral Riley had his problems. I felt that within the framework of the staff structure, as it was constituted, we did about as good a job in keeping the principals informed of their options as anybody possibly could.

As I said, most of our staff work was done in preparing the various options that were available, and looking at them from the point of view of the capabilities that were on hand to enforce any course of action that might be developed from these options. This gets into a very complicated bit of writing. Of course, the Joint Chiefs of Staff discussed it verbally, but I remember sometimes when I didn't go to the Joint Chiefs of Staff meetings sitting and wondering what paper we'll have to generate tonight to try to answer some of the questions and alternatives that were discussed in the meeting that particular afternoon. Of course, as you remember, they met fairly constantly, day and night.

Q: I suppose one of the difficulties in developing these papers dealing with the various options was that you had no time to look at them in retrospect. I mean, they had to be done as of now?

Adm. C.: They had to be done as of now, they had to be done that night, and they had to be ready for the next morning, or even for later that night. That's the way we generally worked.

Q: And very often, we know from experience in life, when you put something down, it's as well to look at it later and re-read it.

Adm. C.: Of course, we never had that luxury. We never had the time to do that.

Looking back at some of the things, I think, as I say, that generally speaking the performance was pretty good. When it was all over, as you well know and I'm sure Admiral Riley has told you, there were a great many congratulatory messages flying around from the President and from the chairman. I frankly thought that they were sort of manifestations of relief more than anything else. I personally didn't think that they were necessarily warranted, but then I'm a sort of a basic military guy who feels that you do the job you're supposed to do and nobody's supposed to say, gee, that's the greatest thing since motherhood.

Q: Were you aware of the role of the Secretary of Defense in the whole picture and what this meant for Admiral Anderson?

Adm. C.: I was aware of it, but we were so immersed in our

day-to-day problems that I would not be qualified to comment on any of it. Of course, I knew of Admiral Anderson's problems and his role in standing up for what he believed in and allowing his commanders to do what they, on the spot, felt was the right thing. I was well aware of that. I might add that that attitude within the Navy of relying on its subordinate commanders was viewed at times with a certain amount of alarm by the Army and the Air Force, who felt that there should have been tighter control from the central command post and reliance should not be placed on people in the field. This was the basic philosophy, I think, that has always pervaded the Navy and possibly isn't quite true of the Army and the Air Force. Whether it's developed within later years or not, I really don't know.

Q: Wasn't this perhaps the first instance, full-blown instance, where the central command moved individual ships around?

Adm. C.: Oh, absolutely.

Q: And the central command was in the White House?

Adm. C.: It was in the White House, but it was through the Joint Chiefs of Staff. You see, the forces were not under the command of the CNO or the chief of staff of the Army or the chief of staff of the Air Force. They were actually under the command of the Joint Chiefs of Staff, and they operated through the Joint Chiefs of Staff, through the unified commander, who happened in this particular case to be Admiral Dennison, because all the activities were within the CinCLant area. But that was the normal chain of command, and that continued on through the Vietnam War, because the normal chain of command was from the President, to the Secretary of Defense, to the Joint Chiefs of Staff, to the unified commander.

Q: Yes, CNO lost his command of the fleet.

Adm. C.: The CNO lost his command of the fleet then and never regained it.

So this basic philosophy of telling every ship right rudder or left rudder was well publicized in, I suppose, the confrontation with Admiral Anderson and the Secretary of Defense. My training and my upbringing have certainly supported the contention that the man on the spot should be allowed to make some decisions, but, as we well know, with the increased efficiency of communications and the general watching-over-the-shoulder process that has been developed, it was almost impossible to have any individual unit or ship act with any degree of initiative of their own. I think this was the part that scared me more about the procedures that were being built up - that it was, at that particular time, at least, a completely centralized operation and one in which the forces themselves were allowed absolutely no initiative.

Of course, the whole problem was that they felt sure that had there been a rash action it was a very delicate situation that needed handling at the top, and any rash action by a subordinate down the line might upset this very delicate balance, and possibly jeopardize the whole operation, as viewed from the top. This was the only way to think of it. But it was very difficult for me - I could understand it, but I didn't agree with it. As I say, my feeling - and this was not based on any great analysis - was that when the crisis had subsided and all these congratulatory messages were flying around this was not my idea of how you run a military operation. In light of modern technology and improved communications, perhaps I was wrong.

Q: Off tape you were talking about the frenzied atmosphere in which you functioned. Admiral Ward told me the story of his role in the situation where he assumed command, I think on a Saturday, without any knowledge of what was taking place, and on Sunday flew to Washington to the Joint Chiefs with Admiral Dennison, during which time he was briefed on his role as commander of the fleet!

Adm. C.: As a matter of fact, I think I was in the JCS meeting when Corky and Admiral Dennison appeared, and I remember the briefing. Since Corky and I had been in Op-60 together, I thought, good heavens, here's Corky one day on the job and I appeared here last week and was thrown in in my civilian clothes without any clearance, which I didn't receive until about ten days later, by the way. This was the frenzied atmosphere which persisted and continued throughout the crisis itself, obviously, but as a result the watch-keeping capabilities of the Joint Staff were continued. Additional flag officers, fortunately, were made available - flag and general officers, so that right this minute within the Joint Staff I'm sure there is a general officer on duty in the operations center. Obviously this was an outgrowth of the Cuban Missile Crisis and it continued. During my year and a half in the Joint Staff, it never really seemed to subside. There was always pressure on people. If the pressure didn't come from the White House, it came from the fact that the Joint Chiefs of Staff met and they required a paper, and just the pure mechanics of the fact were that they didn't get out until five o'clock or six o'clock, or however late they deliberated, and the staff officers had to work after they'd received their guidance, so there was always a night job. The logical question is, well, why didn't you go home during the day. You couldn't because there were routine jobs to be done during the day. So most of us worked late at night nearly every night.

Of course, at the end of the missile crisis, it subsided to a certain degree, but, at least in my view, the frenzied aspect remained. I was fortunate in a lot of ways, at least in participating in what was certainly the historical aspect of the development of this particular process, and I'm sure it works. But it's hard for me to sit back and analyze it now, in light of my earlier training. I think that's about the simplest way of explaining it.

Shortly after the missile crisis, you remember, there was a confrontation with Castro on the water supply at Guantanamo. I can recall vividly what happened and I can almost see it, but I can't tell you precisely the date. As you say, it was within a month or so of the crisis and the actual tension had subsided, but there were still these minor irritations. Of course, the first one was when Castro shut off the water to Guantanamo.

The Director of the Joint Staff was Admiral Riley and he had a Deputy Director, who was an Army officer, and as Assistant Director, Jim Davis, who was a naval officer and he'd been commandant of the Guantanamo Naval Station at one time. So I thought it was very strange when early one afternoon General Taylor sent for me and said:

"We're having trouble in Guantanamo. I'm going to make you the action officer on Guantanamo, and we've got to go to a meeting in the White House this afternoon." So, over we went to the White House. As I remember, this was the following winter. I'd like to go back a minute to the tense time in the Joint Chiefs of Staff when Presient Kennedy was assassinated.

We were all in the office when the news came from Dallas, and we sat around and waited, and of course we increased security throughout the world, which seemed the logical thing to do as a precautionary measure. That, I simply add as a sidelight on what the Joint Chiefs of Staff would do in a situation like this. Whenever there was a crisis, for example, the Middle East crisis, the immediate questions came up what can we do, what do we have available, how long will it take, so and so to get there, can we support such an operation. And practically without question the first questions in a foreign crisis that the Secretary ever asked was how many nationals do we have there, how long will it take to get them out, what are the evacuation plans, and we were all involved in that particular aspect of the planning with regard to any type of operation. But the one I started to talk about was the water crisis.

I'd listened to President Johnson on TV, and it was very interesting to me to see just before his death how he reacted to things like this and how concerned he was about national politics, but he was also concerned about foreign policy in a different way. As I said, I was called before General Taylor and we went over to the White House. The President said:

"Well, now Castro's cut off the water, what are we going

Chew #7 - 322

to do about it? I think before we do anything, we ought to send somebody down there to look at it."

So, it was decided that they'd send somebody down to decide what the alternatives were. Of course, the alternatives were pretty simple. You could make yourself self-sufficient by some sort of a water-distillation plant -

Q: But there was none in being?

Adm. C.: There was none in being at the time. Or you could, hopefully, have the water turned on temporarily and go ahead with the plans for a water-distillation plant, or make other plans, such as barging the water in to Guantanamo on a makeshift basis, in order to avoid a confrontation over the water.

Q: The choice of having it turned on temporarily wasn't with you, was it?

Adm. C.: It wasn't with us, but there was always that possibility that there might have been a relaxation. Of course, it turned out that there wasn't...

It seems to me we got back to the office about seven o'clock at night with this -

Q: That was the decision made?

Adm. C.: The decision made by the President was to send somebody down. I'd gone back to the office and sat down to write my notes about what had happened so I could keep my records straight, and General Taylor sent for me. This was about eight o'clock at night, and he said:

"Any reason you can't go to Cuba?"

I said: "No, Sir," so he said: "Well, I want you to go."

"Aye, aye, Sir. When do we leave? Tomorrow?"

He said: "Oh, no, you leave tonight."

I've forgotten whether I had a uniform on or not, but I probably had civilian clothes on, and I said:

"I think I'd better go home and get my uniform and a few tropical clothes."

He said: "That's all right. I'll give you time enough to do that. Catch a plane from Washington National. It'll take you to Norfolk and a Navy plane will fly you down."

So I went home and got my summer uniforms, got on the plane within about an hour and a half. Judy just had time to drive me to Washington National, which wasn't too far from where we lived. I made the plane, got to Norfolk -

Q: It was fortunate that you could get a plane that night!

Adm. C.: I've forgotten whether this was a commercial plane or an Air Force plane that was to fly us to Norfolk. We got a Navy plane from Norfolk to Guantanamo.

This particular mission was really under the aegis of

the Secretary of the Navy, but General Taylor felt that the Joint Chiefs of Staff, since it bordered on the operational, should be involved, and I turned out to be the senior member of the crew that was sent.

Q: How many were there in the group?

Adm. C.: This was the interesting part. It was not a large group. There was a Marine, whose name escapes me. There were a couple of engineering types able to ascertain the possibilities of other water supplies: for example, was it worth boring in Guantanamo for a well. It turned out, it wasn't. The Secretary of the Navy's representative was Captain Zumwalt, and he was really the action officer for the group.

Q: He was the aide to the Secretary?

Adm. C.: He was the aide to the Secretary, but it was a Navy group that had been assembled by the Secretary of the Navy and I was simply the Joint Chiefs of Staff representative to keep the chairman informed and keep the Joint Chiefs of Staff informed, as opposed to the information line up to the Secretary of the Navy.

Q: When was it made apparent just what role one played in

this group?

Adm. C.: Well, General Taylor said, "you're to go down there and you're to represent the Joint Chiefs of Staff. This is under the operational control of the Navy, but I want a Joint Chiefs of Staff representative and I want you to exercise your God-given powers of judgment if it becomes necessary."

Q: But these were verbal orders?

Adm. C.: These were verbal orders. I had not a piece of paper. I had nothing. I simply was told at eight o'clock at night to get on the plane, and, if I remember correctly, it was an Air Force plane because I didn't need a ticket. Otherwise, I would have been provided with a ticket.

Q: The Navy had taken care of all this?

Adm. C.: The Navy had taken care of these details, since it was under the operational control of the Navy. Of course, one of the great problems was what do we do with the dependents, with the water situation being so critical, and do we retaliate by saying we'll take our dependents away. It was a very interesting situation.

We arrived in Guantanamo. We made a rather careful study.

I remember walking up to the fence and looking at the Cuban guards with the then-commandant, who was rather a salty old guy, Admiral Buckley of PT-boat fame. He said, "Come on, let's go look at them." I believe my picture was in the Cuban paper the next day as an American coming down to look at the water situation.

Our recommendations, which were written on the plane going back were essentially those that had been discussed in the presidential meeting to begin with. What were our alternatives? And it turned out that the decision was made to supply Guantanamo by tanker with the essential water that was required to operate the base, and then to build a water-distillation plant, so that it would become self-sufficient. And that was done.

Q: That required time!

Adm. C.: That required time, but in the interim tankers were cleaned and made available for the hauling of water from Charleston, or some place in the South, to Guantanamo for the emergency requirements for the families. Then, the next question was should the families stay. I've forgotten just how that came out, but I think -

Q: They were taken off, weren't they?

Adm. C.: Some had been taken off during the missile crisis, but some of the, I think, had come back by that time. The question came up whether they would all be allowed back, and they were. I think this was a year after the Cuban crisis and some of them had come back. My memory fails me but I think there were certain families there in limited numbers.

Then, of course, there was the question of domestics who came in through the gate and served in certain capacities, not only in the clubs but as cleaning women in quarters and so on. The question was whether they should be continued, and we made the recommendation that they be continued. It seemed to me that you achieved very, very little on a national level by denying a few charwomen, or maids, or something like that access to the station.

Anyhow, it was very interesting. We stayed about a week and made our study, then came back. Captain Zumwalt was the spokesman for the group, and he presented his recommendations to the Secretary, most of which, as I said, I think had already been decided on prior to our departure - that essentially the thing to do was to provide the water by other means on a temporary basis, and then build a water-distillation plant. It was in order to crystallize the thinking that we were sent there. The interesting part was that, later on, in the paper, whether it was at the end of our jaunt to Guantanamo or whether it was a little while later in connection with another problem, which I think it really was, President Johnson said:

"Well, I'm not a precipitate man. Remember the Cuban water crisis."

This was in The Washington <u>Post</u>. He said: "I didn't do anything rash in the Cuban water crisis. I just sent a little old admiral down to Guantanamo to study it." And I was the "little old admiral!"

Q: You touched on the fact that it had already been decided before your mission there. This leads me to a question about the apparent general practice of the Secretary of Defense of deciding things and then getting fact-finding commissions to substantiate his decision already made but not yet announced. Did you have any experience of this?

Adm. C.: Certainly in that particular case it was very evident to me that this had been done, that our trip down there was almost a pleasant interlude in the middle of winter, to go to Guantanamo and look at something with which we were all perfectly familiar. We had a perfectly competent commandant who was able to make recommendations. This was a part of what we were talking about earlier, that no one out in the field could be relied upon to give an objective view, that somehow from the center of all wisdom and knowledge things had to go out and them come back. It disenchanted me to such a point that I used the old quotation that it seemed to me a person's intelligence varied inversely as the square of the distance from Washington. This, to me, was a very concrete example of it.

As I say, our finding, I thought, could have been prepared by the district commandant. There was no particular expertise involved. Captain Zumwalt was a very competent naval guy, but he was simply assimilating the detailed information the various members of the team had collected, and when we went back and gave our report to Mr. MacNamara in person, and I was there and Captain Zumwalt did the talking, Mr. MacNamara nodded his head, agreed in essence with what we thought had already been decided.

Q: How did the man in the field react to all this, Admiral Buckley?

Adm. C.: As I remember, Admiral Buckley felt pretty much the same way. He said unless we want to go to war over the water supply, it looks to me like the only way we can get water is to have it sent in by tanker and then develop some sort of independent source. And, he said, "of course, my first recommendation would be to find out whether we have any water on the base itself."

Whether there had been drillings conducted in the past or whether they were again conducted or not, I've forgotten, but it was pretty firmly established that water was some millions and millions of feet underground, and it was impracticable to develop a well supply. So, the only other alternative was the development of the distillation plant, which was done. As I remember, they even had ceremonies when they opened the distillation plant, because it meant the end of the tanker runs and the fact that Guantanamo again became self-sufficient, as far as water was concerned.

Q: Going back to this practice of prior decisions, do you have any other recollections of MacNamara in this regard?

Adm. C.: Well, Jack, I'm ashamed to say that I should have thought a little more about this, but I honestly can't pinpoint any. There was that pervasive feeling that persisted, no matter what. Perhaps a better way of explaining it is that, for example, in the preparation of a paper, it seemed to me at the staff level that you pretty well knew what that paper was going to have to say before you sat down and wrote it; that if you wrote it in a manner that you might consider to be completely objective, it probably wouldn't get through the top anyhow. So you might as well write it the way you knew it had to be.

This we discussed frequently at the staff level. Of course, on the other hand, you could say, well, that's the guidance that you'd received from the top when you were told to write it, but it sort of reinforced my view that I didn't like being a staff officer!

Q: One couldn't be independent in his point of view?

Adm. C.: I don't think you could be independent in your point of view, no. On certain operational recommendations, you could, yes. But when we were dealing to a great extent at the policy level, no, there were too many people involved. I mean even in the example that I related of the paper on what do you do if another plane is shot down - you knew you'd have to have the coordination of State, you knew you'd have to have the coordination of the Secretary of Defense, ISA, you knew you had to have the coordination of the services as to their capabilities. So it became a question of how basically to write a compromise paper. I felt that very strongly.

Q: What was the Secretary of Defense's attitude towards the officers who served in the Joint Chiefs?

Adm. C.: I never really knew. To be perfectly frank, I think that he paid very little attention to the staff level. He was obviously dealing only with the Chiefs. He was quite frequently, particularly during the missile crisis, there with the JCS, being briefed on essential capabilities or evacuation plans, the limitations of what could be done and what couldn't be done. But his dealings were with the Chiefs themselves, and I think he was perfectly able to make up his own mind, often based on advice or recommendations from his civilian side of the house which, of course, in the case of Mr. Nitze was often very sound and very powerful.

Q: Since you were there, will you relate the version of the confrontation between the Secretary of Defense and the Chief of Naval Operations in the Cuban missile crisis?

Adm. C.: As I remember, it centered around the principle that I was speaking of earlier, of allowing someone on the spot to at least participate in a minor decision and not be told - I think the term was "you're telling them from Washington when to put the rudder over," and, as I remember, it had to do with the location of a destroyer that had somehow gotten out of position, and orders came directly from Washington to have the destroyer get the hell into position. This was a little more than Admiral Anderson could take because he felt that the people who were then giving the orders from Washington were not acquainted with the situation that existed at the time in the disposition of ships, and consequently were in no position to give this type of an order.

Q: And obviously he was right because it was a matter of refueling, wasn't it?

Adm. C.: He was right. It was a matter of refueling. Of course, he was right, but obviously this precipitated a tremendous confrontation which, I presume from what I read in the papers, eventually led to the appointment of another CNO. I think it was that simple, and I think a great many people admired Admiral Anderson for it. I know I did. I felt that in this particular area he was unique among the Chiefs.

I had a great deal of admiration for General Taylor because he was a bright man, but I felt that General Taylor was a compromiser of the greatest competence, if that term expresses it adequately.

Q: Do you think he was hampered by his close relationship with the White House, or aided?

Adm. C.: Jack, that's a hard question for me to answer. I would presume that he was aided by his close association, aided possibly from his point of view. Whether it was an assistance to the operation of the Joint Chiefs of Staff or not, I would hesitate to say. It probably wasn't! But I think the close rapport that you do have obviously must assist, and at the same time it probably takes away a little of your ability to act as you see fit, inhibiting to a certain degree your courses of action. I would hate to comment on that too much.

Q: From your observation of him and the decisions he made as chairman of the Joint Chiefs, would you say that he had an ability to rise above his own particular service and look at the total picture, rather than the picture as it pertained to his service?

Adm. C.: I would hate to be critical of General Taylor to the extent that I would say that he wasn't able to. I think he was. I think you have to look a little deeper than that. Philosophically, there are basic differences in Army thinking and, on the other hand, Air Force and Navy thinking. Obviously, his thinking would have been colored by his Army experience and his Army training.

I know this is a sort of a trite example, but Army planning and Army thinking, generally speaking, must be more detailed than the Navy's. Consequently, centralization is more possible. While a ship operating at sea or an aircraft operating from a ship at sea has to exercise, I would think, more initiative than you would in a military operation on land which, by its very nature, is dependent for support on all its preplanning. So that, philosophically, the thinking of an Army officer is a little different than the thinking of a naval officer. And I think the thinking of an Air Force officer is half-way in between, if I draw the right parallel, because his genesis came from the Army but his mobility has led him to tend towards the philosophy of the Navy.

In that context, I think General Taylor was able to rise above petty parochialisms, but I think his thinking was generally geared along the lines of the Army. I don't know whether I've made myself clear or not.

Q: You have, but do you imply by this that he had an understanding of the real role of the Navy, the operational role of the Navy, as something more than just a transport vehicle?

Adm. C.: Well, here again you get into the basic philosophy that I think practically all of us would agree to, that man is a land animal and the control of the land, of course, is the fundamental aspect in any confrontation in any war. The Navy as an adjunct, from the Army's point of view, certainly contributes to the land battle, but whether it controls the land battle begins to get into the philosophy of mobility and the weight of weapons and all the complexities of modern warfare, and with the philosophy of an army officer I think he had a tendency possibly to underestimate the capabilities of the Navy in terms of his own thinking.

I wouldn't go so far as to say that he was prejudiced. I don't think in my position I was able to make a judgment in that respect, but I did feel that from my observations in the Joint Chiefs of Staff meetings, which I was privileged to attend, that this philosophy every now and then would surface. Whether it was to such a degree that it was detrimental to the over-all good of the country or not, I wouldn't go so far as to say. Whether, had Admiral Radford been chairman of the Joint Chiefs of Staff, things would have been different, I don't think anyone can say. I really don't. I think people when they get into that position - and I've always felt this about the President - try within their greatest capability to do the best things that they can for the country and they tend to overlook parochial and interservice problems.

As I said earlier, most of the interservice problems developed on the money level more than they did on the philosophical level. At least, I felt that way.

Q: Admiral, you were with the Joint Chiefs at the time of the assassination of President Kennedy. Do you want to recall more about that? You said something a little earlier about putting our forces on the alert around the world. Was there more to it than that?

Adm. C.: Well, of course, the first reaction that everyone had was complete shock. The other aspects of it that had to do with possible civil disturbances - I've sort of forgotten about it, but we were immediately alerted as to this possibility and initial steps - I don't think that they were significant steps - were taken to avoid anything that might disrupt the country.

Q: Was there any feeling that this could possibly be part of an international plot or something of the sort?

Adm. C.: From our point of view in the Joint Chiefs of Staff, and I have heard the rumors that this could have been, obviously one of our jobs was to take a look at it and, although this didn't come into my bailiwick in the operations section, it was more an intelligence question, and I think it was examined at the time. If I remember correctly, we felt that there was no conclusive evidence of any international implication. But, as I say, this was not a matter within the purview of the operations section, so I was not concerned, other than to think in terms of what steps might be taken to prevent civil disturbances and to be alert for any international implications.

Q: In a few months' time, did you notice any change in directions vis-a-vis the Kennedy administration and the Johnson administration, as it pertained to military matters?

Adm. C.: I frankly don't think so. I think all of us felt the early days of the Johnson administration were sort of a continuation of the Kennedy thinking, and I think that even President Johnson himself later on said that this was true. When the next administration came there were obviously certain changes, but at that time I didn't feel any particular change.

The only thing that I can remember is that the very close personal relationship that somehow we all felt with the President didn't appear to be as close with President Johnson. He chose to deal more through the Secretary, rather than have the very close personal relationship that I think everybody felt existed with President Kennedy. Other than that, I noticed no great change. Possibly, there were ones with which I wasn't familiar or didn't have sense enough to perceive.

Q: I was thinking in terms of civilian influence in military matters. In the Kennedy administration there were so many close advisors to the President in the White House who were strictly campus-oriented, and this ceased to be so in large measure, anyway.

Adm. C.: In that connection, as I said, I think that President Johnson followed the chain of command a little more accurately than did President Kennedy. As I said earlier, he used the Secretary of Defense more, I thought, than President Kennedy and didn't have that close personal relationship. So, in that respect, yes, the personal relationship sort of disappeared, and it became more of a business organization or even more of a military staff function from the White House, which frankly I saw nothing wrong with, believe me!

Q: During the year or so that you served in the Kennedy administration, did you have any personal contact with the President? Were you called there from the Joint Chiefs?

Adm. C.: Yes, I had been to the White House on two or three occasions. I had sat in the Oval Room. I think the first times were during the Cuban Missile Crisis.

Q: What was your mission then?

Adm. C.: It was very much what I described earlier, an action officer to listen to the deliberations and go back and try to determine what the alternatives were and what the courses of action were and to make the recommendations, which had to be coordinated all the way back up the line again before they became the decisions.

Q: And the deliberations, at that time, were carried on with whom?

Adm. C.: During that time when President Kennedy had a meeting, why, there were the members of the National Security Council, and the Secretary of State, the Secretary of Defense, the Chairman of the Joint Chiefs of Staff.

Q: The Attorney General also?

Adm. C.: And the Attorney General, yes.

Q: During the period you served with the Joint Chiefs of Staff, of course, there were matters that pertained to Vietnam as well. Can you recall anything pertinent there?

Adm. C.: I think my most vivid recollection of that aspect were the daily problems arising, and how General Clay was sort of the action officer on Vietnam, as I had been the action officer in the Cuban crisis. Lou used to go off every day and talk about it. As I remember it, we were concerned with Laos and the infiltration into Laos. Cambodia hadn't reared its ugly head at that particular time.

Q: It was neutral, in name.

Adm. C.: That's right, but Laos was very much in our thinking. I, fortunately, or unfortunately, as the case may be, was not the action officer in that area. Lou Clay was, and I used to commiserate with him because he had the same problems that I had had earlier during the missile crisis - although we all had them, obviously.

I do remember a couple of things very vividly. During part of the discussions in regard to Vietnam it had been repeatedly said in the Joint Chiefs of Staff that we should not become heavily engaged on the mainland of Asia with ground troops. I've heard that said by the Commandant of the Marine Corps, I've heard it said by LeMay and his successor, I think, and I've heard it said by the CNO. It was pretty much an agreed position of the Joint Chiefs of Staff, that we should never be heavily involved on the continent of Asia with ground troops. Now, whether General Taylor completely agreed with this or not, I was not quite sure. I had the feeling that he did. And at that particular time, a very popular phrase had to do with selective reaction, we would react only with the degree of force necessary at the time to achieve our limited objectives, and that God damned "selective reaction" and "limited objective" was prevalent in the thinking on Vietnam. And it stemmed primarily, I think, from the Secretary of Defense, Mr. MacNamara.

Q: This must have been somewhat of an anathema to the military mind on the Joint Chiefs, wasn't it?

Adm. C.: It was an anathema, yes, and it was particularly irksome to General LeMay, whose basic philosophy of World War II, flying by the seat of his pants, had never really left him. He felt that if you had an irritant, you'd better go in and get the hell rid of it with the mostest forces in the leastest length of time. He was a strong proponent of that. In fact, I think that of the Joint Chiefs he was probably the most belligerent.

Q: During your period of service, Maxwell Taylor left the Joint Chiefs, did he not, and did he not go to Saigon as our ambassador?

Adm. C.: Yes, he did. He left the Joint Chiefs and General Wheeler became the chairman of the Joint Chiefs. Of course, General Wheeler was a very different type of man from General Taylor. At least, I thought so. He was far more human, far warmer, far more accessible, easier to talk to, easier to listen to and, frankly, from those pointed comments, he was much better liked. He had the wholehearted respect and admiration of everybody. I think he was less apt to let his Army philosophy become dominant. It's very difficult for a naval officer to rise completely above his training. It's very difficult for anybody to rise completely above their training, until they get to a position like the president of the United States, and even then, I think that philosophically his thinking had to be affected. But I thought General Wheeler was less affected, for example, than General Taylor. He was, as I said, much better liked. The Joint Chiefs of Staff was, I thought, a happier place to work in with him.

Q: You had the same Secretary of Defense, however?

Adm. C.: We had the same Secretary of Defense, but General Wheeler had that marvelous quality that I think any military leader should have, and most do, of looking out for his troops, of looking out for his staff, looking out for his Joint Chiefs of Staff. I didn't feel that quality existed in General Taylor at all, possibly because of his coldness, because of his nature, he thought very little of the feelings of the rest of the staff. On the other hand, I thought General Wheeler did, and, as a result, at least from my middle-level point of view, the Joint Chiefs of Staff was a better place to work in during the time that General Wheeler was chairman.

I think, too, that having been the Director of the Joint Staff, he was more acutely aware of the individual problems that existed within that body and was consequently able to take steps, limited though they may be, to make living conditions better. If there were ways of getting people home a little earlier and not sitting around waiting for something that never happened, he could perceive them, while that never entered General Taylor's mind.

I was very fond of General Wheeler. Of course, he was still chairman when I was in Honolulu, I know because he came out to see Admiral Sharp, and I had lunch with him a couple of times, and he was chairman then.

I felt there was a vast difference in the attitude of the staff under General Wheeler in comparison to the attitude under General Taylor.

Q: Riley must have been of particular help when the Joint Chiefs were considering the situation in Laos?

Adm. C.: Yes, he was because, of course, he was familiar with that situation. Wasn't he there during the evacuation from North Vietnam? As I said, I didn't get too intimately involved. Lou Clay was the action officer for Laos. At that time Saigon and Vietnam were still pretty much a Military Assistance problem with overtones of things that were to come. As I remember, in those years there were very few troops in Vietnam.

Q: That's right. The hamlet program was to the fore. Surely this was discussed in the Joint Chiefs?

Adm. C.: Yes.

Q: High hopes were held out for it.

Adm. C.: Very high hopes were held out for that, and, as I said, it was again and again stated that, no matter what, we shouldn't become involved in the mainland of Asia with ground forces. Our efforts should be limited to the hamlet program, to the Military Advisory Groups, to helping train the South Vietnamese so that they would be able to do their own thing.

Q: What was the general attitude, as you recall it, towards President Diem?

Adm. C.: As I remember, Jack, my assessment of the Joint Chiefs of Staff view towards President Diem was pretty much based on what I read in the papers. I really didn't know what they thought. I think they were apprehensive, possibly, but I can't recall anything that would give me the right to assess their views on him.

Q: I wondered whether the Joint Chiefs shared a point of view, which seems to have been true of the administration, that Diem was something of a dictator and, therefore, not exactly the man we wanted there?

Adm. C.: I was not privy to many of the meetings on this subject, but it seems to me I do remember one in which the Commandant of the Marine Corps expressed that view. Whether this was a joint view that was held by all the Chiefs or not, I'm not sure, but I do remember the Commandant of the Marine Corps expressing it.

Q: You mean expressing disapproval of him?

Adm. C.: Disapproval of President Diem, yes. But, as I say, whether this was the Joint Chiefs of Staff corporate opinion or not, I've sort of forgotten.

Q: Some time earlier you said, when I opened up the subject of Vietnam, yes, there were several things you remembered in connection with that and you mentioned one.

Adm. C.: Well, the one I really wanted to say and to me the most important was the reiteration of the ground troop involvement, which was said, not once, but many, many times. In fact, it became such common knowledge that I came home - and I spoke, as you must understand, very little to my wife about anything that went on. She thought I was an idiot because I wouldn't talk - but that was when I did say:

"Sweetie, there's one thing. The Join Chiefs of Staff are unalterably opposed to the involvement of ground troops on the mainland of Asia."

Q: Were you aware of any close contact between the Joint Chiefs and CinCPac at the time?

Adm. C.: I thought there were very good relations between the Joint Chiefs and the unified commander. As I remember, Admiral Sharp -

Q: No, Felt was still there.

Adm. C.: Admiral Felt was there initially, yes.

Q: He was there until 1964.

Chew #7 - 347

Adm. C.: That's right, and I left the Joint Chiefs of Staff in July of 1964. I think he had just been relieved and Admiral Sharp had taken over.

Q: I was thinking of Admiral Felt and his relationship with the Joint Chiefs.

Adm. C.: Admiral Felt used to come in quite frequently to be consulted on his views, and I felt that there were times when Admiral Felt - and I hate to say this because I can't think of specific instances that would justify my statement, but that there sometimes was a little friction between Admiral Felt and the views of the Joint Chiefs of Staff as to how the war should be conducted. Yes, I felt that, but I don't think I could verify it on a specific basis. I wish I could.

I think there's one interesting story about Admiral Sharp, which I'm sure you've heard probably from other sources, and I wasn't privy to it except as it came down through the staff grape vines that there was a great fight in the Joint Chiefs of Staff as to who would be Admiral Felt's successor as CinCPac. The Joint Chiefs of Staff, as I remember it, were split on the ultimate outcome, and it essentially was the recommendation of Mr. Nitze that swung it. I think it went up split from the Joint Chiefs of Staff, with the chairman voting not for Admiral Sharp, but for whoever the other one was, and it was through Mr. Nitze's recommendation that Admiral Sharp received the appointment. I think you could verify that from other sources.

Q: You mention a split decision on that subject. There must have been other split decisions of the Joint Chiefs. Did they try to avoid this?

Adm. C.: Tremendously. They felt that it weakened their position. Something like a personnel appointment I think they could with impunity have a split decision, but on a military decision the chairman and the Chiefs themselves felt that they should never go up with split views if they could possibly avoid it, because it weakened the whole military position and with that I think everybody agreed.

Q: But sometimes it happened, anyway?

Adm. C.: Sometimes it happened anyway, but generally speaking everybody recognized that this weakened their position as the military advisors to the President, and gave the Secretary of Defense the authority that sometimes they viewed with a certain amount of alarm. I'm sure of that. When you abrogate your authority to present a unified position to your superior, you automatically put him into the position of making decisions which, of course, particularly in the military field they felt was their prerogative.

Q: I would wonder if split decisions, or the lack of them, would not depend upon the nature of the chairman of the Joint Chiefs, in some measure? His ability to effect —

Adm. C.: A reconciliation?

Q: Yes, a compromise.

Adm. C.: I think you would expect that to be the normal situation, but when you have very deep philosophical differences why, you're bound to have a few problems that can't be resolved. Particularly with a temperament like Lemay's, you just can't solve them and they have to go forward split. But everybody recognized without any question the terrific desirability of having unanimity of opinion when the recommendation went forward to the Secretary and on to the President. There's no question about that.

Q: What was Curtis LeMay's value to the Joint Chiefs?

Adm. C.: I thought Curtis LeMay was very valuable. He was a proponent of air power to the nth degree. He was, I thought, sometimes even unbalanced in that respect, but at the same time, I think his basic honesty was unquestioned. He was a great believer in getting in there the "fastest with the mostest," let's get on with it, and in that respect I think he was refreshing because, as I said earlier, General Taylor was a great compromiser, and you had two very different schools of thought. It was refreshing to have such enthusiasm.

I thought he was a very useful member. He was recalcitrant and this, of course, is particularly true when they got into the real nitty-gritty of money. I was not involved in that aspect of it, but I could hear about it from the fringes. I saw General LeMay when I was in Japan after I left the Joint Chiefs of Staff and he was just about to retire then. I always sort of liked the old man, and I thought that he really made a significant contribution to the JCS.

Chew #8 - 351

Interview #8 with Vice Admiral John L. Chew, U.S. Navy
(Retired)

Place: His residence in Providence, Annapolis, Maryland

Date: Wednesday morning, 14 February 1973

Subject: Biography

By: John T. Mason, Jr.

Q: Good morning, Admiral. Last time, you dealt with your period of service on the Joint Chiefs of Staff. I think you have some additional items to add at this point. Perhaps you might begin with the establishment of the National Military Command Center, which was an outgrowth of the experience with the Cuban Missile Crisis?

Adm. C.: Yes. I tried to recall any significant happening that occurred during my tour in the Joint Chiefs of Staff in the hectic days of the Cuban crisis, we had what I think was called a Battle Staff and it was a very skeletonized organization of a captain or a colonel or a lieutenant colonel sitting at each desk - the Middle East Desk, the Far East Desk, the European Desk, the Local Desk - and there was a team captain also usually, a captain or a colonel. Each of the deputies for operations, the flag or general officers, was required to be available on each given day, so that we rotated, but we did not stand a watch in the staff room or the office.

Well, as a result of the Cuban crisis - frankly it was precipitated by a call from President Kennedy one night to ascertain the situation or the status of some of the forces, and the phone was answered by a captain and/or a colonel - I've forgotten which - and it was suddenly realized that to provide continuity, theoretically, there should have been a flag or general officer there, and it was instituted immediately. That was the beginning of the standing of the watches by flag and general officers. From that genesis the present National Military Command Center has evolved, because the staff was enlarged, each area was covered more thoroughly, and at the present time - I'm sure it's still in effect - there is a flag or general officer on watch at all times in the Pentagon. And frankly, I think that's as it should be.

The obvious question is why hadn't it been done earlier, and the reason was because it was an evolution of who was commanding the forces. Technically, of course, the commanders-in-chief of the various areas commanded the forces, but under the McNamara administration of the Department of Defense there was a tendency to bring the control into a more centralized condition, i.e., emanating from Washington. Consequently, if you were going to do that, you had to have the staff to be able to do it. And that was the genesis of the now functioning National Military Command Center, or the NMCC as it's fondly known.

I remember when we would stand watches we would have to make periodic calls to the commanders-in-chief to test the phone system. I remember calling Admiral Felt one day and saying:

"Hello, Admiral, how are you?" And he'd say: "Hello, Jack, how are you?" And I'd say: "It took you thirteen seconds to respond personally to this call. Congratulations! Let's do it in twelve next time."

A big of levity, but at the same time we had to make these personal checks to the commanders-in-chief at periodic intervals to ensure the continuity of communications.

One or two other points that I think I failed to mention. During my period in the Joint Chiefs of Staff another operation of considerable significance was conducted. I watched from the sidelines and was not intimately connected. It had to do with the airlifting of a complete division to Europe in an exercise status to test the concept of mobility of forces.

Q: Where transports were used?

Adm. B.: This was all by air.

Q: Yes, air transports. What were used?

Adm. C.: I think the basic transport of the Air Force then, which was the C-130. The C-130 had just come in. It was a very efficient plane and it was used by not only the Air Force, but by the Marines. It's been supplanted to a certain degree by the C-141 which is bigger, and also to a certain degree, I suppose, by the C-5, which is even bigger yet. But the C-130 was the standard cargo plane of the Air Force and this was used to transport the entire division by airlift to Germany and get them in place. It was a very successful operation.

As a matter of fact, the commander of the operation had been in the Operations Division of the Joint Chiefs of Staff, General Ed Burber. He was the commanding general, I think, of the troops that actually were flown to Europe and flown back. He later was stationed up here at Fort Meade and has since died.

Another rather significant incident that occurred during my time in the Joint Chiefs of Staff was the now rather famous Dominican Republic crisis.

I remember very distinctly one Sunday afternoon

being called I think by General Taylor and he said, "I want you to go over to a meeting at the State Department." The meeting, of course, was presided over by the Secretary of State, Governor Harriman was sitting on his right, there were representatives from CIA, DIA, which was the Defense Intelligence Agency, and the, I suppose, State Department area officers or desk officers of that particular area.

The question was, what do we do. As we all remember troops were sent to the Dominican Republic, basically to protect our interests and to protect our civilians. I was there as a representative of the Joint Chiefs of Staff to simply answer questions as to the availability of forces, i.e., naval forces, in case of submarine attack or some unforeseeable contingency. I might add that my part was very minor. There was discussion and I was simply asked whether, if submarines were sighted, the Navy would be able to take care of them with the forces available, and my answer was a categorical yes. That ended the contribution that I made. The discussion centered around what do we do when the forces are there and, basically, what will they do other than protect our interests and hopefully maintain order, and we'll try to get them out as soon as possible. That's exactly what happened.

Q: Did the discussion also include some possibility of enlisting the support of the OAS?

Adm. C.: As I remember it, at that time it had gotten a little beyond the OAS. No, wait a minute. I think you're right, Jack. I think the OAS was considered as a possibility, but it seemed to me that the situation had deteriorated so that it was necessary to do something quickly, and it was recognized that the OAS was a pretty cumbersome organization and would possibly be too slow to act. I think that's generally the case, as I remember it.

Of course, the rest of it is pretty much a matter of record. We sent the forces. They apparently performed with a certain degree of proficiency, marked proficiency, and were withdrawn when the situation was stabilized. I didn't get into the politics of it too much, as to who was right and who was wrong, but it was interesting to listen to the conversation at this conference because it was pretty well established and agreed to by all participating members that anybody in the Dominican Republic could have been had for a price. It was just a question of how much you wanted to pay and whom you wanted to back. I found that very interesting. I think the Secretary of State agreed to that. Governor Harriman agreed that anyone there could have been backed for a price. It was a question of just determining what horse you put your money on.

Q: One other item that you wanted to add. You said that while you were still with the Joint Chiefs it was obvious that a real crisis was developing in the Far East, in Vietnam. There were many signs.

Adm. C.: Yes, that's quite true. As a matter of fact, it was best brought to light by the fact that at that particular time, as I remember, our efforts in Vietnam were mainly concerned with Military Assistance Advisory Groups and the furnishing of advisory teams, but we were very concerned about the situation in Laos. The present commander-in-chief of the Pacific Air Forces and son of the famous General Lucius Clay of Berlin fame was Mr. Laos, and I remember that Lou daily would go and brief the chiefs and try to determine what the situation was in Laos, primarily as it affected the operations on the Ho Chi Minh Trail and the delivery of goods and war supplies to the Vietcong. If my memory serves me correctly, at that time it was not even admitted that there were any North Vietnamese regulars in South Vietnam, although probably there were. But, as I say, we were primarily concerned with the situation as it existed in Laos and how that deteriorating situation might affect the operations in Vietnam.

You could see the signs of impending crisis, but I think probably the catalyst was the Tonkin Gulf incident that occurred shortly after I had left. And to continue the story, I was sitting in my office, strangely enough, having just made one of those phone calls to one of the commanders-in-chief testing the communications facilities, when the phone rang and it was Admiral Smedberg of the Bureau of Personnel and he said:

"When are you due to be released from the Joint Chiefs of Staff?"

I said: "Well, I understand the tour is normally two years, but in answer to your question, I'm ready now." So, he said:

"I offered somebody ComNavFor, Japan, and they didn't want it. Do you want it?" And I said, "You bettcha! When do I go?" He said, as soon as I could be released, so I went to see my immediate boss, General Unger, and asked him if it would be proper for me to be released a little early, and he said yes. Then I went to see Herb Riley's successor, General Burchinall, who was Director of the Joint Staff. I asked him the same question, and he said yes. So I phoned Admiral Smedberg back and he said:

"Okay, I'll cut the orders for you to go as NavFor, Japan, Commander, Naval Forces, Japan."

Q: You were talking about General Unger off-tape, General Ferdinand T. Unger, who later was in command in the Ryukus, and he left about the same time that you did from the Joint Chiefs.

Adm. C.: Yes. Ferdinand - I guess that's how he got the name "Fin" - went from there and, as I said, later became the High Commissioner in the Ryukus. My numerical relief was an Air Force general by the name of McPherson, and Fin Unger's numerical relief was Lloyd Mustin. Lloyd was there at the time and I did everything I could to fill him in on what was going on. For some reason or other, Fin had gone away during I believe the last two weeks of my tour in J-3 and Lloyd was there, so I was in a position to try to fill him in on the operations section.

In connection with the Tonkin Gulf affair, which I think, as I said, probably was the factor that brought this all into sharp focus, when I left Washington we were fortunate enough to be able to go on the <u>Lurline</u>, my first and only passage on a liner, a civilian liner, and my family obviously was looking forward to it with great anticipation. Then we were going to stay a few days in Fort de Russey, where I was to be briefed by CinCPac and CinCPacFlt for my future assignment as Commander, Naval Forces, Japan. It seems significant to note that one sunny day, as we were on the beach, the first of the combat planes took off from Honolulu for the Vietnam theatre. Both my wife and I had tears in our eyes as the planes flew overhead.

The Tonkin Gulf incident occurred while I was in Honolulu and I was able to attend the briefings on it in Admiral Moorer's office.

Q: He was CinCPacFlt?

Adm. C.: Yes. It seemed somehow, not prophetic, but certainly significant, having been in Honolulu in December of 1941, that here I was in Honolulu when the Vietnam conflict had been brought to a head. As I saw those planes taking off from Hickham, you can imagine how my thoughts must have turned back to those days in 1941. I mentioned it and my wife mentioned it. We were seeing the beginning of the war, but I don't think either of us realized the magnitude of the effort that was to go into it!

Q: Who could!

Adm. C.: No one could. I had repeatedly recalled those prophetic words of the Joint Chiefs of Staff that never should we get ground forces involved on the continent of Asia, so I felt possibly a little bit more secure than I should have.

Q: Do you recall how Admiral Sharp felt about it at that time?

Adm. C.: I think Admiral Sharp felt exactly the same way. He felt that naval and air forces could do the job that was required at that particular time.

We flew from Honolulu to Japan and arrived on the first Sunday in July. I was to relieve Walter Price, who was going home to retire.

There is an interesting story about NavFor, Japan, and the house that was occupied by the previous commanders of Naval Forces, Japan. It was the old Admiralty House of the Japanese Navy and it was out on a very pleasant bluff in Yokosuka, overlooking the Tokyo Bay side. A tremendous old, rambling, Japanese-style house, with tatami mats and the whole bit. As a matter of fact, it had a swimming pool but the primary purpose of the swimming pool was to furnish a water supply in case it ever caught on fire, and there was actually a fire engine stationed there with limited capabilities, just for that purpose. The interesting aspect of the story is that when I was in the office of the Chief of Naval Operations for the Shore Establishment Maintenance and Development division, the question of maintenance of the house, which was called Tododai, had been raised and it seemed to me, sitting back in Washington, that it was a rather unnecessary expense and that we would be better off giving it back to the Japanese. When I left CNO, of course, I didn't realize - well, let's put it this way. I even took steps to do this and get it returned to the Japanese. So when I arrived, really the deal had been consummated and Walter Price was the last person to live in Tododai. He felt so strongly about it that he wrote a book that gave a pictorial history of the house and all the illustrious people, Japanese and American, who had lived in it. I have a copy around somewhere. Instead of living in what was called the Admiral's quarters, I moved to one of the two houses on the base at Yokosuka that had been built by the Seabees. One was occupied by the Commander, Seventh Fleet, and the other, of course, was originally occupied by the destroyer flotilla commander who was no longer stationed there. As NavFor, Japan, I moved in to that set of quarters.

I thought it was interesting that the old house was turned back, and the Japanese quite properly had great pride in the fact that many of their illustrious officers had lived in it. It was a lovely old house, if you like a Japanese-style house. It, however, was not on the base and as things turned out I was eternally grateful that I had not had to move into it, but moved into a house on the naval base at Yokosuka. I think the basic reason was because during a riot, and there were quite a number of them during my rather short tour there - I was there fifty-one weeks to the day, leaving on practically the same Sunday in July one year later. I would say that there were at least three or four serious demonstrations against the United States, some of them, we felt, Communist-inspired. The police were able to handle the demonstrators at the gates of the base but would not have been able to at Tododai. As a matter of fact, the first time they were rather gentle in their handling of the mobs, suffered themselves from a few busted heads and brickbats, but the second time they knew how to do it and if there were any eggs on heads they occurred on the other side.

It showed how tremendously the Japanese had come along, because immediately after the second riot when the police had been very aggressive and driven off the demonstrators, there were immediate cries throughout all the press of Japan "Police Brutality" breaking up the demonstrators who were as peaceful as they could be.

Well, they weren't peaceful and had staffs, almost like spears, that they put together and used as a battering ram to approach the police.

Q: Were they largely young people?

Adm. C.: They were largely young people. At that time there was the beginning of a party called the Sokagagai, which developed into a political party and it was against nuclear arms in general -

Q: The U.S. occupation?

Adm. C.: U.S. occupation was the focus for that. My tour in Japan I found very interesting. I don't know whether I mentioned earlier that I viewed the whole thing with considerable alarm because of my very deep feelings, bordering on hatred, of the Japanese that you generate during a war, and I wondered how I would react. I found it very easy, Jack. I was surprised. I think General MacArthur had done his job well. Sometimes, I think Japan is a bit too Americanized now, but contrary to my apprehensions I found the Japanese very much to my liking, very much to my liking. I have friends with whom I correspond, not regularly but at least sporadically at Christmas. I found particularly the naval officers straightforward, understanding, honest, and very much to my liking. If I asked for advice, and I did on occasion when the question of the riots came up and whether I should bring the Marines out and have them standing by, I was advised not to and I was told the reasons why, that it would be inflammatory and they felt that the local police could handle the situation. They were right. The local police did handle the situation, even though the Mayor of Yokosuka, with whom I swapped Christmas cards just this last Christmas, is a member of the Communist Party. He's been in office ever since I was there.

I can't speak too highly of the caliber of their naval officers. I didn't know the other services as well, although I went to Tokyo probably anywhere between two and three times a week. As a matter of fact, I think I counted up the times and in fifty-one weeks I went something like 151 times to Tokyo, usually by train to avoid the traffic and home by car, and if it were a morning conference, occasionally by helicopter for a meeting that could have been on the Status of Forces agreements, or a business trip to Tokyo. The social trips, as I said, we went by train and usually had a car come up and drive us home.

I knew most of the CNOs. I had met Admiral Nakayama, who was one of the first, in Norfolk and when I was

ComCruDesFlot Four. He, of course, had retired. Admiral Sugiai, who was then the CNO, was now the equivalent of our Chairman of the Joint Chiefs of Staff during my time there. The CNO was Admiral Nishimura. As I said, we were having dinner -

Q: He had invited you to Yokohama?

Adm. C.: He had invited us to Yokohama to dinner, and my wife was sitting next to him and the conversation was very light. Most of the Japanese are terribly fond of golf, so we were talking about golf, and I think my wife turned to Admiral Nishimura and said, "Do you play golf, Admiral?" He said: "Not very much, Mrs. Chew, I have a bad elbow."

She said: "Is it something like a tennis elbow?" And he said: "No, an American machine gun bullet during the war." But he laughed about it, and one of the others present at the dinner that particular night in the conversation - I think of this because of the openness and frankness with which they talked - we were discussing where he was on the day of Pearl Harbor. I can't think of his name now, but he said: "I was in Honolulu." I said, "What were you doing?" He said: "I was a spy. I was up in the fields of Ewa counting the ships. I knew exactly what ships were there." He was then, I think, a captain in the Japanese Maritime Self-Defense Forces, a very pleasant man, very frank about what he had done.

I think my closest friend in the Japanese Navy was Admiral Ishiguru which, as he laughingly said, meant Blackstone, Ishi being stone and the guru black, or the other way around. His first name was Sumetomo, and he called himself Sam Blackstone. We discussed strategy very frankly, we discussed the development of the Japanese Maritime Self-Defense Force, we discussed our problems quite openly. I had a great deal of respect for him. His wife was charming and I think a not distant, but probably not too close, member of the royal family. She was a delightful person.

Sam also had been wounded at the Battle of Midway and he was I believe the flag secretary on the staff of the admiral commanding the Japanese forces at the Battle of Midway.

Except on extremely rare occasions, most of the entertainment was done in a restaurant or a club. As a matter of fact, Tododai became an entertainment place for the Japanese Navy, and, as I said, they were extremely grateful for its return. We were, on occasion, in Japanese houses, particularly the Ishiguru's, of whom, as I say, I became very fond. In fifty-one weeks with a very busy schedule, and it was extremely busy. I found it difficult to - well, first of all I wanted to learn Japanese, so I started in the second week I was there, taking lessons, and I got as far as "Kore-wa impetsu des" (This is a pencil) and "Sore - wa impetsu des-ka?" (Is that a pencil?) That's about as far as I got and then the rather hectic schedule prevented me from going on. I expected really to stay two years, had I known I was only to stay a year I never would have undertaken it.

I enjoyed our stay there tremendously. I got a completely different view of the Japanese, I think, than had been my preconceived notions of them. They're an aggressive, intelligent nation. I liked their basic honesty. We had very few problems in terms of being cheated, as you would in some other countries, which we're well aware of. There was a certain inate sense of fairness in all of their dealings, I thought. I'm an Anglophile but I'm also a Japanesephile. Both my wife and I have said many, many times after watching some of their operations, particularly the way in which the police handled those crowds, that in any future conflict, which God forbid, I would certainly like them on our side. I have great admiration and great respect and a very genuine sense of warmth and understanding.

Q: Did you have an opportunity to meet any of the retired

senior officers dating from World War II?

Adm. C.: Of course, all of the CNOs and, as they call themselves, the chiefs of the Maritime Self-Defense Force, I knew all of them, starting with Nakayama. They had all been commanders or I think in some cases captains in the Navy -

Q: Middle ranks?

Adm. C.: Yes. I did not meet any of the old senior citizens, no.

Q: Because I understood that their lot was not so good, was it?

Adm. C.: Very probably their lot was not, and of course the tremendous strides that Japan had made economically probably passed them by and put them in a little different category. It was interesting to note that all of these ex-chiefs of the Maritime Defense Force, just as our CNOs, they all had good jobs, generally speaking as consultants or advisors. I think my friend Admiral Ishiguru went with Mitsui, one of them went with Mitsubishi. Admiral Nakayama was with Kawasaki Shipbuilding. There were numerous ex-service people with the Kawasaki aircraft industry, the people down in Kobe that had built the old Kawanishi flying boats and were now busily engaged in trying to develop an ASW seaplane.

Q: I take it they haven't abandoned the seaplane?

Adm. C.: Oh, they developed the seaplane. It had a unique principle. It had a slot in its wings which was supposed to give it additional lift and it had also a very peculiarly designed hull that would get it up off the water quickly. I'm not so sure whether they've abandoned the idea of it as an ASW plane or not, but I think they hoped that if it were not successful in that role it would be successful as a sea-air rescue vehicle, because of its ability to land in a very rough water and take off in very rough water. As I say, whether the ASW role has been abandoned or not I don't know.

When last I was in Japan, which was just at the end of my tour in Taiwan, I went to Kobe and saw the plane, and was greeted by Mr. Kono who was the head of the Kawanishi enterprise. He was hopeful that it would be successful as an ASW vehicle, but he always had in the back of his mind that if it were not, it could be used for sea-air rescue missions. Just what's happened to it now I really don't know.

Q: Tell me about the Maritime Defense Force. How did the Japanese naval officers look upon this? Was it exclusively that, or was it a name that would help placate the anti-militarists and the populace?

Adm. C.: I always had the feeling that it was a name that would not necessarily placate the anti-militarists, but one that would be acceptable to everybody and be compatible with the theory that never again would there be war in Japan. But I think the ships had great pride. Of course, quite a few of them were some of their older designs, one or two I think were our ships, and the gun mounts were ours that we'd given them. They handled them smartly. They had lost none of their skill in changing their name, believe me.

True, they didn't have vessels of any great offensive capability but, after all, remember they did have a submarine or two and I'm sure that they were handled with the same skill that their predecessors were in World War II. I thought it was a very small, efficient force. Whether they had the fierce pride of the old Imperial Japanese Navy or not, I don't think was really significant. They looked to me like a very efficient force, and it's been relied on for escort duties and assistance to us in case we needed them.

Q: What was the function of ComNavFor?

Adm. C.: We had the base of Yokosuka, which was a result of the occupation. It was one of the few parcels of land, with the exception of some air bases, that we have retained. Even at that time, although we had the use of Sasebo and a small base there, these were the two naval bases, the Commander of the Naval Forces, Japan, was the ground commander for the naval establishment existing in Japan at the time, which, as I say, consisted of Yokosuka, which was a fine, modern naval base. Of course, it wasn't anywhere as big as Norfolk, but it had adequate harbors. It's tucked in behind Tokyo Bay. Tokyo Bay runs north and south, and you come up Tokyo Bay, and then turn in behind Yokosuka itself and there are all the dockyards that would take our biggest ships, carriers. It had crane facilities, it had machine-shop facilities, all the shop facilities, and right next door to it was a commercial ship-building firm that had actually built warships during the war. It was called Uraga Dock, and we always felt on the many trips that we made to Tokyo, there were I think seven tunnels between Tokyo and Yokosuka where the road cut through these spurs in the hills as they came down to the bay and in order to straighten out the road they'd tunneled through, and they were great tunnelers as you know. You'd break out from the last tunnel and here you would see this tremendous big overhead crane with "Uraga Dock," and our standard saying was "It may be Uraga Dock to some people, but it's home to us," because we'd turn right into the naval base and be home.

I think you probably know that the base itself at Yokosuka was designed by a Frenchman, a French engineer, in the period of the emergence of the Imperial Japanese Navy, and it was one of their major bases. Their major shipbuilding effort was down in the Sea of Japan at Kure, and the naval academy is down there also. But this was their main operating base on the eastern seaboard. The southern base, of course, was Sasebo, which was quite similar to Yokosuka, smaller, but it also had shipbuilding facilities, and those shipbuilding facilities had been turned back to their civilian ownership. I found it not unlike an American naval base. It had the same facilities and, sure, some of them we had built. For example, the house that we lived in was built by the Seabees at the end of the war, but the houses that the senior staff officers lived in were all Japanese quarters and they were delightful. They were down the hill from us and in cherry blossom time they were just as picturesque as any picture postcard of Japan could ever be. Each with its little garden and little fountain. All my staff lived in them and the captains of some of the ships, the Seventh Fleet flagship lived in one, the captain of one of the big tenders lived in another. As I say, the base itself was very similar to an American base. We had put up facilities such as the exchange and commissary that made it even more American.

We had Japanese liaison officers attached to the base, and actually one was attached to Commander, Naval Forces, Japan's staff, but the function of ComNavFor which is what you basically asked me was to control and guide the shore activities of Japan. There was one other naval establishment, and I use the term "naval" in its proper context, and that was the Marine air base at Atsugi.

Q: That's Tokyo, isn't it?

Adm. C.: Well, all of this is in what you'd call the Tokyo area. Yokosuka is south of Tokyo, on the bay. Atsugi is south and west. There are two bays that come in there - there's Tokyo Bay and then the next one is Segami, and the peninsula that Yokosuka is on is between Tokyo Bay and Segami Wan. The ride to Atsugi in a car in rather moderate traffic would take anywhere from forty-five minutes to an hour, and as a matter of fact I became quite familiar with it because one of the attractions that we had was a golf course at Atsugi. As Commander, Naval Forces, Japan, I was able to give honorary memberships to the senior officers in the Japanese Maritime Self-Defense Force and the Japanese Air Force - what do they call that? The Air Defense Forces and the Ground Defense Forces. All of their senior officers had been given, and used very gratefully, I might add, their honorary memberships at Atsugi.

I played with them quite frequently. They're enthusiastic sportsmen, as you well know, and maybe this is another reason that I found myself getting along well. We played golf not only at Atsugi together but we also played up at their resort area Hakoni. One of the more interesting social aspects of our tour in Japan was the Black Ship Festival which was in celebration of Perry's landing. You go down to the point on which he landed and they have a commemorative service and an exercise and a little celebration, which was very pleasant. It just lasted a day.

As I say, a lot was crowded into a very short period of fifty-one weeks.

Q: What was your relationship with the Commander of the Seventh Fleet?

Adm. C.: I was his next-door neighbor, and friend. Of course, one of my primary functions as the shore commander was to support the Seventh Fleet in terms of providing services, repairs, supplies - all the functions that a shore commander would have in support of the Seventh Fleet. Roy Johnson was the Seventh Fleet commander when I first arrived and before I left my old childhood friend Brick Blackburn became the commander of the Seventh Fleet.

As I say, we lived in similar houses up on top of the hill in Yokosuka. Fascinating, because you had a view to the west and could see Fujiyama, and then the view to the east was Tokyo Bay, and down under Fujiyama was the harbor of Yokosuka with all the ships around back behind Tokyo Bay. It was a very, very impressive view. The house itself was quite simple and we enjoyed it. The Johnsons, as I said, lived next door in a similar house but he was gone much of the time. He was down in the Tonkin Gulf, but occasionally got home for Christmas or something like that. He was at sea most of the time, unless there was some reason or a conference or something that he had to attend, or when the flagship came in for needed upkeep or repairs, or a little period of recreation from the line.

Q: Did you ever have any feedback from the American

labor unions on the work you did for the fleet out there?

Adm. C.: I can't remember any specific accusations or specific complaints because the Japanese completely controlled the activities of the yards. True, the supply officer was at the head of the supply department, an American supply officer, but all of the personnel throughout the entire section were Japanese. Obviously all of the electronics technicians and all of the machine operators were Japanese.

I would say that the major problem came from the fact that their very paternalistic system, in which you look after them from the cradle to the grave, probably caused more trouble than any complaints from the American unions. If you, for example, had a cutback or a reduction in the force it was damned near impossible to lay a man off because it was his livelihood and you'd hired him twenty years ago and you had to take care of him from the cradle to the grave. As I say, I think probably the head of the ships' repair facility basically controlled all of the shops. You had more problems with the Japanese labor under those conditions than you would have had with American unions. They were efficient and they were good. They were very good. One of the carriers came in - I've forgotten which one - that had had a boiler explosion and whatever the carrier's number was it was there so long we called it building 32. There was a big 32 on the side of the stack, or whatever the number was. It was in for almost two months while they did a very expensive boiler repair job, which I was later told could probably not have been done in the United States, it probably would have been too expensive. They were good craftsmen, there was no question about that.

Q: Well, it was that angle that I was thinking about, the fact that the American unions might have complained that they were being deprived of jobs?

Adm. C.: Probably there was some static in that area, but these were operational casualties and consequently you couldn't send a ship all the way back to the United States to have this type of work done. You could, but you would lose its services for so long. So it was cheaper in two respects, not only was it cheaper from the point of view of the actual cost involved, but it was also much cheaper in terms of the loss of the time of the ship on the line. These were arguments that were often heard as to the mobility of the fleet and the self-sufficiency, because we all recognized that having the base in Yokosuka, at least in my view, was a very, very helpful adjunct to the efficient operations of the Seventh Fleet. I think all the Seventh Fleet commanders well recognized it. I know Roy Johnson did and I'm sure Tom Moorer did before him.

Q: You imply that your 150-odd trips to Tokyo involved conferences with Japanese officials on the turning out of the terms of the surrender, were they?

Adm. C.: No. First of all, if I gave the impression that they were mostly for conferences that's wrong. I would say the majority of them were social, involving dinners or receptions, that sort of thing. Those that were official were generally with - the Embassy to consult with the ambassador, Edwin O. Reischauer. I had a great deal of admiration for him and I felt that he listened to his military advisors very carefully. Or problems resulting from the Status of Forces agreement, which was the agreement that had been signed defining the role of the American military forces in Japan. There was a similar agreement that I soon became familiar with when I went to Taiwan. That was a status of forces agreement with the Republic of China. These governed the handling of infractions, criminal cases. Generally speaking, it left jurisdiction of our own people to us, unless it involved something like murder, and then you could waive your jurisdiction and turn the case over to the Japanese authorities. I've forgotten whether there were any Americans in Japanese prisons, but I think there were one or two in which this right had been waived and they'd been tried in Japanese courts.

My official meetings, as I say, had primarily to do with that type of problem. Also, the ambassador met quite frequently to discuss the problems as they related to his particular aspect of life in Japan. He had a very receptive ear to his military advisors.

As you remember, there were quite a few riots in Japan at that time, primarily, we felt, fostered to a certain degree by the Communists. I think Mr. Reischauer agreed with that. There was the then-emerging Zengurkrui, which was a political party that is now a recognized political party with leftist views.

But, predominantly, the trips averaging two to three a week were social or semi-social, but with official overtones.

Q: What was the attitude of the active Japanese naval officers toward these riots?

Adm. C.: I felt that they had very little sympathy for them. They analyzed them pretty objectively. They knew, and told me without any question, that there was a standard fee for hiring a demonstrator. Each demonstrator, as I remember it, got a bottle of saki and so many yen for participating in a parade, and carrying a banner and yelling and chanting and singing. They were well aware of it. They viewed it as a leftist threat, and of course, as you know, the government at that time of Sato was pretty conservative and the opposition was, of course, leftist. So, this was pretty much political opposition to the nuclear weapons aboard our ships. Some of those things we didn't discuss at all, but the fact that American ships may or may not have had atomic weapons aboard them, we were never allowed to discuss. But we all knew they had them.

I think one of the most interesting aspects of my tour in Japan - this is in retorspect, by the way, I did not recognize it at the time, but it was brought to light by an affair called the Pueblo incident, because that ship had been operating similarly during my tenure as Commander, Naval Forces, Japan. I had on two occasions remonstrated with my superiors and said, "Look, you give me operational control of that ship and I don't have force one to do anything about it, and I do not like it." I had a great deal of sympathy for Frank Johnson when he was basically, I feel, censured for his part in the Pueblo affair when it actually took place. As Commander, Naval Forces, Japan, you had command of nothing, except the naval base in Sasebo. You had no operational forces at your beck and call. Of course, as time went on, when the Vietnam conflict grew, there were fewer and fewer forces available there in Japan, anyhow.

Of course, the Air Force had its forces, but these did not come under your command at all. So I was apprehensive when ships of that type made those collection cruises. Fortunately I think there was only one, or possibly two, during my year there that could have been considered as dangerous as the Pueblo.

Q: Why wouldn't a ship like that be put under Commander, Seventh Fleet?

Adm. C.: Well, I think, Jack, that's a good question. It's difficult to answer, probably because the 7th Fleet didn't operate in the Korean area. The ship was under the operational control of NavFor, Japan, which, in my view, was senseless because, as I said, I had no forces whatsoever and basically didn't approve of the way it had been put under my command anyhow.

Q: Does this imply that you had intelligence-gathering as a part of your command?

Adm. C.: This particular mission was supported by ComNavFor, Japan, and, yes, I had an intelligence assistant chief of staff, who performed the normal functions of an intelligence officer on any staff. Just why this particular mission had been assigned to ComNavFor, Japan, I was not quite sure. For example, the other collection platforms, generally speaking, they were submarines, and of course submarines are far less obvious than the Pueblo was.

Q: And they have their own defense.

Adm. C.: They have their own defense, the greatest one of which is their stealth and their ability to be undetected. They were not under the operational control of ComNavFor, Japan, but were under the operational control of the fleet representative, which I found rather peculiar, and that was when I voiced my objections.

Q: Your objections got no response?

Adm. C.: About not being able to respond in case something happened.

Q: Yes, but they got no response when you made them?

Adm. C.: I think the feeling was that that particular vessel was a merchant ship type in international waters and it would be relatively, if not completely, safe. I think this was the prevalent feeling of everybody at the time, and that you were just worrying about something that wasn't going to happen, when in fact it turned out that it did happen. Maybe I was a worry wart. I don't know. But I was apprehensive about it every time there was a mission of that type and voiced my objections.

It's interesting in the aftermath of history, but when this incident occurred I was in Taiwan, on the golf course, and my aide came running after me and his face was white as a sheet, and he said: "The <u>Pueblo</u> has been attacked." And I said, "What do you want me to do about it?" He said, "I just wanted to let you know."

"As you well know," I said, "here in Taiwan, I don't have any forces either and I'm sure the Chinese aren't going to react to this incident, except to be concerned by it. So I guess I might as well finish my last two holes, then I'll come in and read about it." That's exactly what I did. But I thought to myself then, "I wonder what Frank Johnson's been able to do." It turned out that he could do very little in time.

Q: Wasn't it an anomaly in that you had command jurisdiction over a ship like that and yet the intelligence to be gathered was operational, and what could you do with it?

Adm. C.: It was passed on up the line. It was passed on to CinCPacFlt and on to Washington for whatever -

Q: Where it belonged!

Adm. C.: Where it belonged. I had very little use for it except to keep me informed of the situation in that particular area. In fact, those activities were very closely held. Few people were authorized to even know of the collection content. You had to have special clearance to even be told what had happened.

Q: That's why it seems so strange.

Adm. C.: None of which, by the way, did I feel was of such tremendous significance that it warranted all that security, and I think that's been pretty well borne out. But this was the situation that I foresaw and I was frankly quite grateful that I wasn't there at the time of the Pueblo, even though I had remonstrated.

For a family living in Japan for a year, it was

truly a remarkable experience. You could see among other things the tremendous growth of the Japanese economy, just in the fifty-one weeks that we were there. Buildings were going up, freeways were being built all over Tokyo.

Q: This upsurge only began at the beginning of the sixties, didn't it?

Adm. C.: That's right. As I said, I think MacArthur had indoctrinated them well, or somebody had. It was a very interesting little episode. Whether I told you or not, I don't know, but one of the big freeways right in the middle of Tokyo with interchanges going every which direction, and there was a little tiny house not quite the size of this room that had been at the intersection of the streets, it was triangular, and it was sitting right in the middle of all these freeways. The guy refused to move. He just refused to move until finally he couldn't get in the house and really I guess the condemnation proceedings were successful and they finally ousted the guy. I used to like to drive to Tokyo just to see that house, because it was so incongruous in the middle of all this prosperity, here's this funny little triangular Japanese house sitting in the middle of a cloverleaf.

Some of the nights we would spend in Tokyo. There was a service-operated hotel called the Sanno. We contributed some funds to its running from the naval command. You see, there were the U.S. Forces, Japan, commanded by an Air Force lieutenant general, Mo Preston. Then there was an Army command in Japan, so that you had a unified command in Japan, just as you do in Europe. The U.S. Force commander was Air Force, the Navy was ComNavFor, Japan, and the Army force commander was Army Forces, Japan, with headquarters at Camp Zama, which again was right outside of Tokyo.

The Marines had bases at Atsugi and Iwokuni, the Air Force had a field at Tachikawa and a couple of others whose names have escaped me. But generally speaking all the headquarters were centered in the Tokyo area.

We did have contact with the equivalent of the Secretary of Defense. At that particular time, it was interesting that he did not have cabinet position, but was the civilian head of the Self-Defense Forces. I think later on he was elevated to cabinet position. We would discuss, as I mentioned to you, the problems arising from the Status of Forces agreement or from the aid bills. There was a chief of MAAG also in Tokyo - Military Assistance Advisory Group chief, who happened to be a naval officer at the time I was there, an admiral by the name of George Luker. He, of course, concerned himself primarily with the furnishing of equipment and the normal functions of any MAAG.

It was a full fifty-one weeks and I thoroughly enjoyed it. I've been back to Japan, once as AsForPac, Antisubmarine Warfare, Pacific commander, once on my way to Taiwan, and then again on a pleasure trip to see the World Exposition in Osaka. Each time I've renewed acquaintanceships with my old friends and have been able to see them, talk to them, and of course each time I've gone I've been more impressed with the tremendous change in Japan, even to the point now where they have used-car lots and those little waving flags like we do here at home. Except for the signs, I must admit that the average big city in Japan is beginning to look more like an American city every day.

I was home and my very good friend Admiral Colwell was staying with us - he'd made a trip out from the States - when the telephone rang and it was the communications watch officer, and he said, "I have a message here for you, Admiral. I don't think I'd better read it over the phone, but I'd like to bring it up to you." So he brought it up and it said, in essence, you're going to be ordered to Washington as Assistant Chief of Naval Operations for Plans and Policy, which is known as 06B.

I only relate this because, at that particular time,

I had had thirty-five years' service and was coming up for what is called "plucking," and I was interested in knowing what my next job was going to be, or, more bluntly, whether I had any chances of being retained. Mathematically it looked as if they might need people with some special qualifications which would reduce my chances of being retained. So the assignment of Op-06B gave me hope that I would be retained, and it turned out that I had already left Japan and was in Honolulu on my way back when the results of the plucking board came out, and I was retained. I simply relate that to show the importance sometimes of a job. Not that there are any particular jobs in the Navy that automatically ensure retention and or promotion, but there certainly are those that are more significant. Generally speaking, ComNavFor, Japan, had been historically more like a district commandant job, which was not only vulnerable but was almost certain to lead to eventual retirement. And usually it was occupied by those senior enough to be retired.

Q: Wouldn't it be true that your assignment back in the Department was determined by the fact that you weren't going to be plucked?

Adm. C.: I didn't know that when I was ordered to ComNavFor, Japan, quite frankly, and if you want to talk about selection and things like that, which really isn't germane to this type of thing, I was a little apprehensive, based on the pattern of things. Anyone who at that particular stage of his naval career, and remembering that things were changing and there was increased emphasis on youth, I wasn't the youngest guy in the world, I was a bit apprehensive about even being assigned to ComNavFor, Japan. Some of my friends said, "Look out, this is the end of the line." And I said, "Well, the only thing I can do is go and do the best job I can and hope that it doesn't turn out that way.

That's the way I'd looked at it all my life and there wasn't any particular reason to change. I don't think my retention had anything particularly to do with what I did in Japan.

Q: So you came back with a certain amount of elation!

Adm. C.: I came back with considerable elation. I was still feeling that having been assigned that particular job, it would be difficult to understand a plucking at that time. But I really didn't know. I didn't know until I arrived in Honolulu and was met by Admiral Sharp and my first question was, "Admiral, has the plucking board come out yet?" And he said, "What are you worried about?" I said, "I'm worried from simply the practical point of view that there are so many that are obviously going to be plucked, and if there are certain specific requirements which my particular qualifications don't meet, mathematically, I ain't got a very good chance." And he said, "If you're going to 06B that should tell you a great deal." I said, "Well, it gives me encouragement but I'd still like to see it in writing." I think Admiral Sharp thought that I was very foolish to be so concerned. "Hell, Jack, I had that job," was his answer to my query about the results of the board.

While I was there the results came out and I was informed that I had been retained.

I think that about covers my fifty-one weeks in Japan.

Interview #9 with Vice Admiral John L. Chew, U.S. Navy
(Retired)

Place: His residence in Providence, Annapolis, Maryland

Date: Wednesday morning, 21 March 1973

Subject: Biography

By: John T. Mason, Jr.

Q: Well, Sir, now we're returning to Washington and Op-06B. Tell me about the job sheet for work there.

Adm. C.: Op-06B, as we all know, is the Assistant to the Deputy Chief of Naval Operations for Plans and Policy. For once in my entire naval career, I felt that I was going to a job with which I was completely familiar. In fact, it was so obvious that when I walked down into the JCS area, the 06 and 06B are the principle shops concerned with JCS matters, I saw the same faces and problems. Years later I'm sure some of the problems will again creep up.

Q: You mean they never get solved?

Adm. C.: I don't think they ever get solved. As a matter of fact, one of the persons said:

"My goodness, you're back already," having been gone what I considered a very long time. He, poor soul, was still there.

So with that background I felt rather at home in 06B. It was interesting to note that I hired a house in Alexandria by telephone one night, because, after all, we had no place to go, and I was able to get a house in Alexandria through a friend, so we were fortunate in being able to stay temporarily in Wentworth Hall in Fort Myer. They were very generous and loaned their facilities to the Navy when they were not being completely filled by Army personnel. We stayed there for a week or so, and then moved into a house in Alexandria, and I started my job at 06B. My immediate boss was Admiral Andrew Jackson, who was 06. He now lives just a few doors up the street from us. My classmate was the Vice Chief, Admiral Rivero and, of course, Admiral MacDonald was the CNO, all of whom I had known throughout my career in the Navy. So I felt very much at home, as I explained earlier.

As a matter of fact, one day about two weeks after I had been there my wife and I were talking about the future - because I had been retained we were discussing I wonder what happens now, and I told her:

"You know, I think I do know what I'm doing for a change. I feel confident in this particular job. The chances are I will stay on in 06B for two or three years - "

Q: Is that so!

Adm. C.: Yes, I felt very strongly. "I'll stay for at least two or three years and there'll be a younger 06 coming in, and I will provide the continuity, and then I will have a couple of years as district commandant or whatever the twilight job is, and that will sort of end up my naval career at the statutory age of sixty-two." I felt very strongly that that would be the case.

As events turned out, of course, it wasn't quite true, but I felt that in this particular job - let me go back a bit. As we all know, the Joint Chiefs make the final military recommendations to the Secretary of Defense and, through him, to the President. There were what were called the Op-Deps, namely the operational deputies of the various services, and Admiral Jackson was, of course, the Navy representative. They could make recommendations on problems of lesser importance. And then they had what they called the "little Op Deps," who were the Assistant Deputy Chiefs, and they met once a week and they could make recommendations or decisions, as the case may be, on problems of even less importance. Obviously, the question is, well, what kind of a problem is that that the "little Op Deps" can settle. They could settle problems of manning or possible joint determination as to whether a job should be held by Army, Navy, or Air

Force, and if so, how many problems that required a joint recommendation but were not of enough significance to warrant attention by either the Op Deps and certainly not by the Chiefs. So we met once a week, the little Op Deps - sometimes if there were a lot of problems of that nature we could meet twice a week, and I found that the problems of briefing the Chief - that is, the Chief of Naval Operations - keeping abreast of all the problems that he had to face was really a very interesting job.

As I said, I felt familiar in it because a great many of the problems that I had faced when I was in the Joint Chiefs of Staff as the Deputy for Operations were still with us, and I think this will be ever true as long as you have problems that are developed from force requirements and money and prestige. So that I felt under less pressure, while at the same time I felt I was making a contribution.

Q: Could you give me a specific example of the sort of problem you dealt with and unraveled, so to speak?

Adm. C.: I was there such a short time, four months, I really didn't have time to unravel very much.

Q: Well, Sir, you say that it was an assignment of short duration. Was this because Jackson went out and the whole regime changed?

Adm. C.: I left before Admiral Jackson. I remember very distinctly it was Thanksgiving, before the Army-Navy game, and I had been called to the CNO's office and, as was my usual policy, I got my little pad of paper and pencil and started thinking I wonder what the hell I've done now as I went up to Admiral MacDonald's office. It was the day before the Army Navy game.

I walked into the CNO's office and the admiral said: "Sit down, Jack." So I sat down, got out my pencil, and he said:

"Do you own a house in Washington?"

I said, "No, Sir, I do not. I rent."

He said, "Can you get out of the lease?" I said, "Very probably. I rent from a naval officer who understands the problems and exigencies of the service. I guess so."

So he said, "Well, I'm going to send you to AsForPac." I gulped and he said, "It's time we have a surface naval officer with experience in destroyers. The two previous commanders of the Antisubmarine Warfare Forces have been aviators. It's time we now have a surface officer. You're getting along in age. If you don't do this, why, you'll never have three stars."

I gulped again and said, "Yes, Sir," And he said,

"Now, there's one other thing. You may not divulge this to anyone, except your wife. You may not talk about it and you may not mention it."

"Aye, aye, Sir."

"The reason is because there have been, on occasion, some assignments made and before they were cleared by the White House they were leaked and this caused great concern in the White House. If it happens again the possibility always exists that the White House will say 'Had we known he was a bad boy - '"

Q: Especially a White House with that sovereign!

Adm. C.: A White House with that sovereign 'we won't approve his nomination to three stars.'

So I went home that evening treading on air, got my wife and told her, and she said:

"Isn't that strange. I always thought that we'd love to go to Honolulu. When do we leave?"

And I said, "We leave very soon. We leave right after Christmas." She said, "Great! What do we do about the kids?"

I said, "Don't tell them anything. Just make out like we never heard a thing until it has been confirmed by the White House."

She said, "How long will that be?" and I said, "I

don't know - two weeks, maybe a month."

As it turned out, I was called over to the White House and talked to one of the assistants, Mr. Califano. He gave the Good Housekeeping stamp of approval, and then I was allowed to divulge the fact that I was going to Pearl Harbor as commander of the Antisubmarine Warfare Forces, Pacific.

The Army-Navy game party that we had that Saturday was interesting because there were a great many Navy and Army people, and here again I had to be completely silent on what obviously was bursting within me. But I survived, and as you see that was the end of November. We had just the month of December and I was on my way again. Fortunately, I was able to rent the house or make sure it didn't go unrented for my very kind landlord, Phil Gildeson, who later became one of my ASW commanders. Possibly you could have considered it a little conflict of interest if there'd been any trouble!

We departed from Washington in the middle of winter by plane for Honolulu, the whole family very excited.

Q: The children went with you?

Adm. C.: Oh, yes, the children went with us, and during the year and a half that I was there we were able to have our older children visit us, those that were in college and had finished college. Of course, the three younger children who were with us went to school there. The other two both were in college at the time, although they were with us during the summer.

I didn't know much about AsForPac. I'd often wondered why there was such a command, and I think really when I got there my first effort was directed towards really determining why there should be such a command and what it should do. There was a history, almost of contest really, as to the original formation of the command, there being considerable diversity of opinion on CinCPacFlt's staff and command as to whether such a command was, in fact, justified. I think it had come up during Admiral Hopwood's tenure as Commander-in-Chief of the Pacific Fleet, and I think also at that time it was an effort that was made to upgrade the ASW capabilities, but also to upgrade the prestige of the ASW forces in light of the seriously enhanced capabilities of the Russians. I think that was the basic reason behind it. We recognized that the Russian building program was going ahead by leaps and bounds, that their capabilities were increasing fantastically rapidly, and that in order to get the proper emphasis on antisubmarine warfare it was considered necessary to set up specifically a command in the Pacific and a command in the Atlantic, which was done. There was a force called ASW Force, Atlantic, as well as ASW Force, Pacific.

Q: Where were the Russian submarines most visible? In the Pacific.

Adm. C.: No, they were visible both in the Atlantic and the Pacific. During that period they worked farther and farther out from their bases. In the Atlantic, for example, from their home bases in the Baltic, while in the Pacific they came from Vladivostok and worked farther and farther towards our bases.

Q: Your immediate boss was Johnnie Hyland?

Adm. C.: No, my immediate boss was Roy Johnson. In the development of this command, the two schools of thought were that, yes, it was necessary to develop or to set up commands specifically for antisubmarine warfare forces; and no, it wasn't, that it really was a function of the Commander-in-Chief of the Pacific Fleet, and therefore such a command was not necessary.

Later events, that is, the combination of the First Fleet and the Antisubmarine Warfare Forces, Pacific Fleet, into one command, lends credence to the question as to just how the command was to operate. As I said, my first thought was to see really what should we be doing, in light of the increased activity of the Russian submarine fleet - and when I say "increased activity" I mean cruising farther asea and being detected occasionally in areas close to Honolulu or close to our vital interests even near the West Coast. Should we develop a capability of conducting strategic antisubmarine warfare as compared to tactical warfare. Johnnie Hyland, when he was Seventh Fleet, and I used to discuss this because he felt that the protection of his fleet, i.e., the Seventh Fleet, was basically a matter for his concern, with which I agreed because he was the tactical commander on the spot. But the Pacific Ocean is so vast that I felt that there should be a coordinated, centralized command for the conduct of operations against the submarines in their strategic role, i.e. missile submarines as, possibly, opposed to attack submarines. But even then, in regard to protection of shipping on the vast ocean reaches, I felt that it was the function of a command.

We were really not clear in our own minds what the purpose of the command was. At a conference in San Diego shortly after I'd been there Roy Johnson asked me that question. In essence, what do you think you should be doing and what is your role. I said, "It's a little fuzzy in my mind and what I propose is an in-depth study to determine how we should combat the Russian submarine menace, because it is growing by leaps and bounds, everybody knows it. All you've got to do is read the intelligence reports."

And he said, "Okay, I'll approve it."

We had a good staff in AsForPac, competent people, and we were able to get a civilian contractor to come in and analyze our functions, analyze responsibilities as we saw them, and the net result of that study was to develop what is now the antisubmarine command center on Ford Island, which was nonexistent before I got there.

As you can easily see, the strategic antisubmarine warfare was closely connected with the SOSUS system. The SOSUS system is still pretty highly classified. The center of the SOSUS system when I went to AsForPac was on the West Coast, in San Francisco, and I felt that if we were to conduct antisubmarine warfare within the whole confines of the Pacific Ocean it seemed to me the best place for it was in Honolulu, with the backup on the West Coast. Of course, the heart really of strategic antisubmarine warfare is the SOSUS system because unless you know where these guys are there ain't much you can do about them.

We were fortunate in seeing the SOSUS system develop rather effectively. We had very good fortune in tracing sound paths through cold water and through the thermal layers and finding areas where we could detect a submarine at far greater distances, for example, than we could in certain other paths of water. We had a very sophisticated computer program to analyze the waters of the Pacific. With this huge amount of data we were sometimes able to pinpoint the Russians when they sallied forth from their bases, in Vladivostok, or a little farther south.

Q: They were obliging and supplied you with examples!

Adm. C.: They gave us the examples. We were never quite sure whether we were able to detect all of them. In fact, I'm sure we weren't, but it gave us a perfect opportunity to at least have a study in depth of what we were faced with.

Of course, the forces that Commander, Antisubmarine Warfare, Pacific, had to operate were the CVS groups, the support carrier groups, with their ASW aircraft, and the two or three squadrons of destroyers that were specifically earmarked for ASW efforts. They, I think, have been supplanted by the DEs which are considered more effective now for ASW. But those were the forces that we had. Primarily those forces were assigned to the Seventh Fleet or to the First Fleet, and maybe that's the reason why the First Fleet and AsForPac have now been combined and AsForPac has been abolished.

Q: The First Fleet doesn't exist now?

Adm. C.: The First Fleet doesn't exist either. I frankly don't even know what the name of the combined force is.

Q: Isn't it Third Fleet?

Adm. C.: That's right, it's called the Third Fleet, which really is just ducking the problem. ASWForPac doesn't exist either, so it would appear that those forces that were assigned to First Fleet for workup in San Diego were sent to Honolulu for their operational readiness inspections, ORIs. In my day our staff conducted all of the operational readiness inspections on the CVS groups before they went out to the Seventh Fleet to support Admiral Hyland and his operations in the Tonkin Gulf. So maybe that's the tie-in. Maybe in the long run it will be effective as a method of control.

Prior to my leaving, the results of the study - well, the study had been completed but it hadn't been approved, and frankly I would like to have stayed on to try to see, to have the installations completed to determine whether we had really solved the problem and whether this was an effective means of combating the Russian submarine menace. I wasn't given that opportunity, but at least the command center there on Ford Island was actually constructed, and what amounted to another SOSUS read-out station was, I think, finally completed.

Q: Let me ask you what role the Arctic played in your operations?

Adm. C.: Well, the SOSUS stations were located there and, of course, here again this had to do with the temperature of the water and obviously the Arctic stations were very effective because of the temperature gradients, so that they could on occasion, and hopefully on all occasions, as I say we were never quite sure, pick up the people coming out of the Russian bases in Asia.

Q: Were there any special studies made during the summer in the Arctic in your time there, out from San Diego and the submarine labs there? I'm thinking of Waldo Lyon and his work.

Adm. C.: I can't answer that, Jack. I just plain don't remember. We had so much data that was coming in all the time that we were trying desperately to keep up with it and analyze it ourselves, so any additional data that went in through San Diego we would eventually get, yes, in its completely analyzed form, I would expect.

Q: The reason I ask is because I know that during earlier periods, when Lyon was engaged in these studies in the Arctic, he had to work in conjunction with the commander of the antisubmarine forces in the Pacific. As a matter of fact, he had to borrow a submarine from them.

Adm. C.: Well, yes, but here again you see you had a strange division of responsibility. The Commander, Antisubmarine Warfare Forces, didn't operate the submarines. Commander, SubPac, Operated the submarines. Commander, Antisubmarine Warfare Forces, didn't operate the CVS groups except during ORI. First Fleet operated them during their work-up period. We only technically trained them and organized them and gave them their ORI inspection, then sent them out to the Seventh Fleet, where they operated in support of Admiral Hyland.

Q: It seems almost a confusion of commands!

Adm. C.: This is why I tried to preface my remarks with the fact that the initial set-up of the command was fraught with controversy. One school of thought was that there should be simply a deputy for ASW forces, since all the forces belonged to the Pacific Fleet anyhow, that the Commander, Antisubmarine Warfare Force guy should simply be a deputy to CinCPacFlt. Then, of course, you get into the question of how does he stand in relation to the Deputy CinCPacFlt, so in order to eliminate that problem they set up a separate command. I think it's very interesting to note that I went to the CinCPac briefings every day - CinCPacFlt briefings, excuse me. I would always go to his regular briefings to be kept up to date with what was going on within CinCPacFlt forces. We had occasionally a little discussion with the Seventh Fleet commander on the subject that I mentioned previously as to what is strategic warfare and what is tactical warfare. He wanted complete control of his antisubmarine warfare forces within the Seventh Fleet area because of the possibility of a threat, which could easily have developed.

I was inclined to agree with him, but I felt that I should have overriding authority if it was determined, for example, that the threat was not simply localized to the Seventh Fleet but became an oceanwide threat. And this was the confusion that existed in the command, and this conference that I said "I think we ought to have pretty much of an in-depth study and get some real technical know-how because this is a terribly technical problem. It has to do with capabilities that are very elaborate, sensitive, expensive systems, and a lot depends on that system."

Other means of locating submarines by aircraft, by helicopter, with sonar, by surface ships are really for local contacts, once the general area of the submarine has been determined. Then to localize the contact and prosecute the contact you have available those three platforms - ASW aircraft, the ASW helicopter and the surface ship, and each one, of course, has its very distinct advantages.

Chew #9 - 408

Q: Under whose aegis were the antisubmarine exercises performed?

Adm. C.: Generally speaking, they were in the form of an operational readiness inspection and they were performed under the aegis and control of AsForPac. As a matter of fact, one of our more important assistant chiefs of staff was the assistant chief of staff for operational readiness. He was the guy individually responsible for the conduct of inspections, the developments of the problems, and evaluation of the ASW group as it completed its inspection, and whether it was deemed to be ready to meet the requirements for ASW protection of the Seventh Fleet.

Q: Can you tell me about one of these exercises?

Adm. C.: It was pretty much a standard exercise.

Q: Was it a yearly thing?

Adm. C.: It was an exercise in preparation for deployment to the Seventh Fleet whatever their deployment period happened to be. It was always done before they deployed to the Seventh Fleet. There were at that time three ASW groups and let's assume they were deployed about every six months, so you had an ASW exercise between every four and six months. They lasted about two weeks and they could take any one of half a dozen forms, but generally they would be an exercise in the nature of a submarine having been located in a large area of the Pacific, presumably by SOSUS, or possibly by a merchant ship sighting, a random sighting to give you a base from which to operate.

Then it was the development and localization of the contact by the forces made available to the ASW commander. Of course, he had his carrier, he had his carrier air groups, he had his helicopters, and he had his surface-ship screen. Generally the success in localizing first the contact and then developing it - they were pretty good at it. Of course, as I said, it depended initially if it were a strategic type of operation, on the initial establishment of the contact by whatever means, by random sighting, by SOSUS, by a destroyer in transit, but of course that would be a pretty haphazard way of determining the location of a submarine within a given area.

Essentially, that type of operation was conducted and controlled by our staff. I maintained very close liaison with CinCPacFlt. In fact, whether I was called a deputy or not was academic. I felt that I was his principal ASW commander and almost a deputy anyhow.

Q: Where were your offices? In Makalapa?

Adm. C.: No. We were fortunate in having quarters on the end of Ford Island, and all of the ASW staff was on Ford Island. I suppose traditionally those had been NavAirPac staff quarters during the war days. The house in which we lived was built on the old Army fort, which most people don't know existed. The fort, believe it or not, didn't look to seaward. It looked towards Aiea.

Q: Well, it was an Army fort!

Adm. C.: It was an Army fort looking toward Aiea. Remember Army forts were pretty prosaic buildings, they were a hunk of concrete with a casemate at each end and the magazine in between. Our house was built on that hunk of concrete and the casemates at each end formed the two porches at the corner. The house was long, with a living room, dining room and kitchen, and down below in the magazine spaces and the casemate spaces themselves were some stewards' quarters. The bedrooms and baths went the long way of the casemates. And, as I said, the porches were thick concrete. It was a lovely house because it was in the palm trees and it looked out on Aiea.

Of course, the first question is why was it facing

that way.

Q: It was built by the Army!

Adm. C.: Well, but the arcs of the guns were obviously pointed towards the beach, towards the main island of Oahu. Delving into it, I finally determined that the reason it had been built that way was because of World War I and the internment of some German ships at Pearl Harbor, and theoretically this fort was to make sure they stayed there, or to sink them if they started out. But not to fire on the main island of Oahu.

Getting back to why the whole staff was on Fort Island. I wanted it that way. Our offices were down in the old aviation administration building, and later the insides were torn out and the command center was established. I never have seen it, but I've always been interested and hopefully some day when I go back it will still be there and I'll take a look.

Every morning I'd get in the barge, it's one of the few active flag barges in the Navy, because it was used every day, many, many times a day. In the morning I would go over to the morning briefing, come home to my office work. I was fortunate enough to be able to ride a bicycle or to walk, if I so desired, from one end of Ford Island up to the administrative section of the island. I preferred my bicycle. I was extremely fortunate in having a little nine-hole golf course outside my back door, which I dearly loved. Our children obviously enjoyed Honolulu probably more than any other place that they've ever lived.

But, as I said, I found it a job that, having been established under certainly conditions of controversy, was still not clearly defined as to its complete responsibilities. Apparently, later events have borne out what I have said, by this recent combination of AsForPac and the First Fleet under the Third Fleet.

Q: Let me ask, during your time were there any demonstration exercises for the benefit of SEATO?

Adm. C.: Let me answer that question a little differently. I had on my staff an Australian, and this was to provide the link with our Australian allies. I also had a Canadian on my staff.

Q: Because of the Arctic?

Adm. C.: Yes. In fact, we had a little international staff, and from a tactical point of view it was very nice because we were able to have a little wine mess! A plain ordinary American staff would not have been afforded that pleasure. Since we were international, at least to the extent of having an Australian lieutenant commander and also a Canadian lieutenant commander we were truly international and were able to serve beer and wine, if we so desired, in our mess in the administration building.

That was our connection, and I might add that during my time at AsForPac I went - in answer to your question - to Thailand and discussed their ASW problems under the aegis of SEATO. I had planned a trip to Australia but was unable to carry it out because of other commitments, but I felt it very necessary to go and confer with the Seventh Fleet to see how his ASW requirements were being met, because I was responsible for furnishing him with the trained forces to do the job for him. Then, as I said, I went on to Thailand to discuss their problems and had a trip planned for Australia but was never able to carry it out.

Q: It was interested in reading the citation you received for your work with this force and it mentioned the aspect of research. Would you develop that for me?

Adm. C.: I think the research aspect of it concerned our efforts that had to do with sound passage through water. I mentioned it a little earlier. The actual detection of a platform i.e., a submarine, was influenced markedly by ocean currents and by ocean temperatures, so that if we knew, for example, the locations of the currents we could predict the temperatures, or could actually determine the temperatures, we would have a better predication factor of locating a submarine. A great deal of research was done in this area and it bore out what we expected - that under certain conditions we would have a far higher possibility of locating a submarine at any given point under one set of conditions than we would have under another set of conditions.

Now, of course, the thermal layer effect was well known in tactical ASW, but it wasn't known, or at least we had not enough information to determine what type of propagation was possible within any given type of water for these tremendous distances. We're talking about 2,000 or 3,000 miles. So it was really a research effort to determine propagation functions from sound waves within the ocean currents and various levels of temperatures, and so on, in addition to the bottom contours.

Q: Where were all these data collated? On Ford Island?

Adm. C.: Originally the SOSUS data were developed in San Francisco, but the results were studied on Ford Island. I had in addition to my Australian and in addition to my Canadian a computer expert, who was primarily responsible for the storing and analysis of this type of data. And we were able to use the big submarine computer which was right next door, so that most of the study results were developed on Ford Island. It was a tremendous research effort.

There was one officer on my staff who I think later on, after he retired, went to one of the research organizations, Jim Hoblitzell. He was primarily the guiding force in the development of these studies. I, of course, after a year and a half was terribly interested because I thought we were making progress and I was hopeful that I would be allowed to stay for two reasons, to see if our command concept was proper and to see whether after the construction of the command center we would have an effective means of controlling ASW warfare in the Pacific. It's a tremendous problem, Jack, and one that I think everybody was a little apprehensive about. Some we knew we would pick up, and some we picked up unpredictably.

Q: Do we have - or is this classified - any knowledge of what the Russians are doing in antisubmarine warfare? Are they doing anything comparable?

Adm. C.: Yes, I think they do. Maybe not quite as extensively but certainly we were pretty sure that they were able to locate our ships in their tours along the

Asiatic littoral. In fact, they showed positive indications that they had a system maybe not comparable to SOSUS but certainly equivalent to it.

Q: Were you plagued with so-called fishing trawlers in the Pacific at this time?

Adm. C.: Every now and then, as I remember, some of our ASW exercises we had our typical Russian with us, yes. And, of course, as you know, there was always a duty trawler off Guam, which was one of the bases for the Polaris boats - I guess we call them Poseidon boats now. His station was right off the entrance to Apra Harbor, and I remember normally during the briefings at CinCPacFlt it was routine to report that the guy was still there or "he had been relieved by such and such another trawler." Yes, to answer your question, we always felt sure of surveillance. We normally felt sure of surveillance along the West Coast, we often had a trawler to the north of Oahu. We were very careful about monitoring our transmissions and urging everybody to exercise extreme care because we knew that we were being very carefully watched.

I don't know whether they had an effective means of analyzing. Maybe they did - analyzing the data, but I'm sure they had a lot of it and I think probably have quite a lot of data on our ASW exercises, simply from monitoring the traffic. It was inevitable that they would be able to intercept a great deal.

I like a story that Ike Kidd told the other day at the Alumni Meeting about the efficiency of the Russians when he was the commander of the Sixth Fleet. He cited two examples, one of an exercise that the officer in tactical command was conducting. Partway through the exercise the OTC sent over a message and said, "Do you have enough fuel?" to all ships, and the Russian came right up and said, "Absolutely, if you can finish your exercise on time." That was the first one. The second one was that in the usual procedure they sent out an F-4 to intercept one of these "Bears" that always shadows the Sixth Fleet. He made his intercept, said, "Open your bomb bay doors," and the Russian agreed to open his bomb bay doors and they were empty. For some reason or other his Tacan was out, so he picked up his transmitter and requested information on course and distance to the carrier. And the Russian called him over and held up a piece of blackboard "250, 57 miles." So the Russian knew and he didn't!

Those are humorous examples, but I would think that with the effort that they've put into it and the constant surveillance they would have amassed a great deal of data which they're probably able to handle just about as well as we're able to handle and analyze their data.

We always felt it was important to attempt to maintain a strategic plot of the submarines that were operating in the Pacific. We were never quite sure that it was altogether accurate, but certainly it was our job to be able to know precisely where they all were at any given time.

Q: Were they numerous enough to be formidable?

Adm. C.: Yes, I think you could call them formidable, if you can call a Polaris with its eighteen missiles formidable. Some of them didn't have that many, but I would call them so, yes. And, of course, within the last five years, which is what it's been since I was commander, Antisubmarine Warfare Forces, their capabilities obviously have increased immeasurably.

Q: There's another aspect of ASW that you had cognizance of?

Adm. C.: Yes. There was a range that was developed on the island of Kauai for precise calibration, precise location of submarines, torpedo runs, and fine data of that nature. In other words, it was a triangulation range operated from the shore that could pinpoint a ship, a weapon, and a platform, and give you a better analysis of the conduct of an attack. You would think that we would have had that somewhere. In some forms we do. For example, I think there's one for the use of the submarines in Puget Sound, but this was a coordinated ASW range strictly for ASW use. It, too, was being developed and improved and completed as I left, so I don't know how much it's been used.

Q: Was this done at your instigation?

Adm. C.: Well, it had been there, but we tried to improve it and make it more effective and more accurate. We'd gotten some money from our shore establishment people to put up some proper calibration type centers, the equipment necessary to carry out the work. I'd say, yes, it was at my instigation to develop it to its present state and, as I say, whether it's used extensively or not now I really don't know. It was certainly a part of the tactical ASW.

As the Commander of the Antisubmarine Warfare Forces, Pacific, I felt, as I said earlier, that my main concern was with strategic warfare, but after all, you can't conduct strategic warfare unless you know how to conduct the actual localization and development of the contact. So it spilled over into the tactical aspects, and after all an ORI, or operational readiness inspection, was simply a tactical exercise after the contact had been localized.

I might add that during our morning briefings at CinCPacFlt we would always give the location of all the submarines in the Pacific, at least that we were able to detect. We would, for example, if a "possible" developed into a "probable" either because of intensification of a sonar contact, if it looked to be threatening, forces could be requested and assigned to develop and hopefully localize the contact. This provided us a built-in means for conducting an exercise where the target forces were being provided by the other guy. I always liked that, but we weren't able to conduct too many, particularly if the intruder were located within the Hawaiian area where we did have some forces that were, as I said, specifically trained in ASW capabilities. It was always good fun to send out destroyers, or VS aircraft to try to localize the contact, and, of course, it was always more fun, and I think Admiral Burke was one of the guys who said if you can surface one of these fellows I'll give you either a bottle of whiskey or a cigar - I've forgotten which! But it was a great feather if you could locate a Russian submarine and surface him, then take a picture of him. This was the game, and I think they played it pretty well, trying to determine our capabilities. We were very careful not to divulge too much, even it we were able to surface, not to talk too much. One of my constant admonitions to all forces was to try to keep their damned mouths shut.

Q: Did Admiral Sharp show an active interest in this whole operation?

Adm. C.: Yes, he was concerned with the strategic aspect of it, but during that time he was obviously concerned with the Vietnam War, although I didn't have the close liaison with Admiral Sharp that I did with Admiral Johnson. I would go over occasionally, but not the daily contact that I maintained with CinCPacFlt. Yes, he was interested obviously. I, of course, was a great admirer of Admiral Sharp, as I was of Admiral Johnson, too. We were very close. We had one other meeting place that afforded us an opportunity to discuss occasional problems uninterrupted by other people, and that was on the golf course because we played fairly frequently, maybe once or twice a month.

Q: No microphones!

Adm. C.: No microphones, but unfortunately the little ever-present radio that could call him back to reality in case of a crisis. But generally speaking, we could get in a round uninterrupted.

Chew #10 - 423

Interview #10 with Vice Admiral John L. Chew, U.S. Navy
(Retired)

Place: His residence in Providence, Annapolis, Maryland

Date: Wednesday morning, 5 December 1973

Subject: Biography

By: John T. Mason, Jr.

Q: Well, after all these months it's certainly great to have you back on tape again, Jack, and to resume this very interesting story. I think you want to begin by telling me about your last assignment, that of July 1967, when you became Commander of the U.S. Taiwan Defense Command.

Adm. C.: Thank you, Jack. I hope my long absence hasn't addled my brain. I wouldn't be a bit surprised!

My assignment to the Taiwan Defense Command came as quite a shock, at least to me, and was the forerunner of a policy with which I concur. But having been the Commander of ASW Forces for just about a year and a half, I was called, I think it was in either February or March by the Chief of the Bureau and was informed that I was to be assigned Commander of the Taiwan Defense Command. I remonstrated to the best of my ability over the telephone and said that I had these ongoing programs which I mentioned previously, the development of the strategic ASW control center, the studies on propagation that had been primarily initiated by me, and that I thought I would be given the opportunity to see them to some sort of a conclusion.

I was told that if I didn't like the assignment I would revert to two stars and be assigned to an appropriate district.

Q: That was a kind of Navy blackmail, wasn't it?

Adm. C.: It was a kind of Navy blackmail, and the policy that eventuated and was finally published when I was actually in Taiwan was that, once having served in a three-star billet for a reasonable length of time - whatever that might be, a year or two years, probably two years, there would be no reversion. With that policy I fully concur. However, it forced a great many people to a little earlier retirement, including me.

I was able to go back to Washington and make my remonstrances personally, but, as I said, I didn't get anywhere and we started making preparations to move to Taiwan.

Q: Who was Chief of the Bureau then? Duncan?

Adm. C.: Who was Chief before Duncan?

Q: Smedberg.

Adm. C.: I think Duncan had just taken over as Chief.

Our arrival in Taiwan was quite an event. I'd been told that the proper way to get there was to fly commericially to Okinawa and then the Taiwan Defense Command plane would come up and pick us up in Okinawa so that we could arrive on the button at a given point in time, to coin a phrase -

Q: Because of ceremonies?

Adm. C.: Because of the relieving ceremonies. We arrived I think it was eleven o'clock on the appointed day, having circled the airport in Taipei for about twenty minutes, or at least long enough in the rather turbulent air to have our youngest son pea green and seasick as he could possibly be - airsick, I suppose, is a better word. We finally touched down and all of the assembled joint forces were there to meet me. We had the normal review of the forces which I participated in many times as visiting dignitaries appeared and were given the same treatment, with Stanley in the background not knowing whether he was going to be violently ill or not - it was a rather harrowing experience, with Mrs. Chew in white gloves, Stanley in a white face. But we finally got through with it.

Q: You were relieving whom?

Adm. C.: I was relieving Bill Gentner. The actual relieving ceremony was not until a couple of days later, on his departure.

That evening, the Vice President, C. K. Yen, gave a welcoming dinner, again one of the many that I attended while accompanying various dignitaries who visited Taiwan during my three years.

Q: By this time you were a veteran in terms of oriental ceremony, were you not?

Adm. C.: Not exactly, because the ceremonies in Taiwan were a little different from those in Japan. Of course, I had been in Taiwan, as I mentioned previously, to view the Double Ten festivities when I was the Commander of Naval Forces, Japan, so I was familiar and I did know by name and personally a few of the top-ranking people.

The Taiwan Defense Command, of which I was to be the commander, was an unusual command in one sense. It was simply a planning command and the mission was to plan for the defense of Taiwan and to conduct operations if they became necessary. And contrary to most public utterances, there were not very many people, Americans, on Taiwan defending it per se, as it was often intimated in the press.

Q: The reliance was on the Chinese forces?

Adm. C.: The reliance was on the Chinese forces, and the development of the command was rather interesting. The first commander of the Taiwan Defense Command was Admiral Pride, who was also the commander of the Seventh Fleet. It was only the second commander, Artie Doyle, who moved ashore, and the Seventh Fleet command was separated from the Taiwan Defense Command. Doyle, of course, was followed by Roland Smoot and then by Charlie Melson, and then by Bill Gentner, whom I relieved.

I think it's interesting to note that the Taiwan Defense Command itself it not a very large organization. It was the standard joint staff with pretty much a standard joint staff organization. There was an administrative section, quite small - a J-2, which was by far the largest section because of the intelligence aspects of association with the Chinese, a small planning section, a fairly small logistics section, which as time went on became more and more important because of its dealings with the Status of Forces Agreement and its responsibilities in the real estate field.

Q: What do you mean by that?

Adm. C.: Well, our forces in Taiwan operated under a status of forces agreement and the chief of staff of the Taiwan Defense Command was the U.S. representative at the status of forces meetings, which administered the agreements. For example, if there were infractions of civil regulations the question of how best to handle them was usually brought up and discussed in the status of forces agreement meetings.

Real estate arrangements, turning back property that had been used by the United States to the Chinese were discussed by the status of forces agreement - or rather committee, excuse me. This took on a more significant aspect from the earlier days when it was being developed and the status of forces agreements were being negotiated. They had pretty well been negotiated and this was simply how best to administer them.

The planning section was concerned primarily with the development of a joint plan to protect the island of Taiwan.

Q: Did you have Chinese on this staff?

Adm. C.: We planned concurrently with the Chinese. So far as Chinese on the Taiwan Defense Command staff, there was only one, and he was my Chinese aide. It was strictly a U.S. joint staff. There were a couple of Chinese nationals I think in the logistics section, but they were concerned with administrative details.

The staff, as I said, functioned pretty much as a joint staff. We were not large and, contrary to many of the press statements of the forces that were defending Taiwan, they were essentially exaggerated because the forces - and I might go back. I think the reason for the fact that the Taiwan Defense Commander was a naval officer was that the primary forces available in case of an attack on Taiwan would be, of course, the Seventh Fleet, and, as I said, the original commander had been the Seventh Fleet commander.

Q: Well, you make this point that there were no large American forces available to you. Would you want to hazard some sort of a prognosis then as to the ability of the Taiwanese to defend themselves?

Adm. C.: Well, I think this of course was my primary job and I'd like to go from the discussion of the Taiwan Defense Command staff, go one step further to point out that in case of hostilities the three component commands that would have become the U.S. forces in support of the Taiwanese Commander, Patrol Force, would have become the Navy component commander, the commander of the Air Force, Taiwan, who would have become the Air Force component commander, and the chief of the MAAG, who was an Army officer, would have become the Army component commander.

The plans, of course, envisaged basically the use of the Seventh Fleet, augmented by Air Force units, and a fairly significant logistics support effort by the Army. But the basic plan for the defense of Taiwan did not envisage the use of United States ground forces unless urgently needed. I think it's significant to note that.

It's also significant to note that during the early stages the MAAG, or the Military Assistance Advisory Group, was by far the largest and I say without bitterness the most influential command on the island. This was true primarily because it was the command responsible for the furnishing of equipment to the Chinese forces, and although the commander of the Taiwan Defense Command by fiat was the senior military commander on the island, I think the Chinese deferred to the chief of the MAAG because, after all, he was the person from whom all good things would come!

Q: He held the purse strings!

Adm. C.: He held the purse strings.

When I had gotten to Taiwan I had been warned by my

predecessor, Bill Gentner, of considerable problems with the MAAG. Earlier problems, I think, had been generated from personalities. Such was not the case with me because the Chief of the MAAG and I were very good friends and did our best to resolve a situation that was, in my view, not in the best military order. For example, by directive, I was responsible for coordinating the military assistance program, but the MAAG had the large staff that developed the program, and two or three days before it was due it would come to us too late to do anything about it, particularly with our rather limited staff personnel. Yet I still, by dictate, was responsible.

This had been discussed pretty thoroughly with Commander-in-Chief, Pacific, and with the ambassador because apparently it had developed over the years, the tension between MAAG and TDC, and as I said, in some cases it had been augmented by personality clashes, which I repeat was not the case between General Ciccolellea and me.

Q: He was of Italian extraction?

Adm. C.: Yes. He was later Deputy First Army Commander at Fort Meade, after I came back and retired.

Q: Who was the U.S. ambassador, by the way?

Adm. C.: Walter McConnaughy. He was an Old China Hand. He had, I think, been responsible for the basic recommendation to get out of China in 1949. He had been the consul general in Taipei, when it was Formosa and under Japanese rule. So he was truly an experienced Asian diplomat, and I might add a delightful man and a very good friend.

Q: Did the ambassador have a real understanding of military needs?

Adm. C.: Yes. I think probably the ambassador had the most comprehensive understanding of military needs, and I was going to go one step further. In our discussions of what I considered the very - but not untenable position between MAAG and TDC - it was finally brought to the ambassador's attention along with recommendations from CinCPac, and it was decided to streamline the organization so that the MAAG was actually under TDC. Because of a situation that arose - I can't quite remember how it came about - oh, I know. The Generalissimo was disturbed about the MAAG cutbacks. It was when Congress was more interested in saving money than in supplying the Chinese forces. From the Chinese point of view this was a very unfavorable situation and rather than compound the felony and reduce the status of the MAAG at that particular point it was considered to be politically infeasible, and consequently the plan to streamline it and put it in what I considered its proper context, was chucked for political reasons.

And I understood the ambassador's point of view. His feeling was that if we downgraded the MAAG at that particular point, having downgraded the military assistance programs, it was almost as if we were saying, "We're about to abandon you," in spite of all our repeated denials to the contrary.

Q: As you observed it, did the Chinese seem to have a policy in which they asked only for what they thought they needed, rather than asking for a surplus of things?

Adm. C.: I think they asked pretty much for what they thought they needed, but sometimes what they thought they needed and what we thought they needed were quite different. For example, there was a period when it became known to the Chinese that we had some surplus older submarines available and they immediately wanted two submarines. Here again, the MAAG supported this. I was a little apprehensive because I wondered (1) what they were going to do with them, and (2) more importantly, the question of their ability to operate them, which would have required a tremendous training effort. It would have required additional funds, and it would have required additional support activities to maintain them. Consequently, I was less enthusiastic, although I was of the opinion, for example, that anything that you can give to your ally in support of his armed forces would be a plus. But looking at it from the colder side of life, I was a little apprehensive and was not as vehement in my support of the submarines as was the chief of the MAAG.

Q: When you focus on a Chinese request of that sort, the thought comes to mind - was their economy strong enough to finance things of this nature on a long-term basis?

Adm. C.: My thought was that it most decidedly was not. Other incidents arose, and one was purely a political incident and perhaps you may remember it. Mr. Sikes made a trip to Taiwan as a member of the esteemed Armed Forces Committee. As a matter of fact, I think he was chairman of the Sub-committee of the Military - I know it was military construction, whether it was military assistance or not, I've forgotten. But he mentioned that he thought it would be a good idea to update the Chinese Air Force which, of course, did not have F-4s, and suggested that they begin on F-4s. This, of course, set the Gimo right on his ear, because he wanted F-4s, and it was a very difficult situation because really we had no intention of getting them F-4s at that particular time, and did not. But, having whetted his appetite and having recommended it, caused quite a flap. The ambassador was caught in the middle of this one because he had the rather difficult job of placating the Gimo, who had had his appetite whetted by the statement of Mr. Sikes that F-4s were available and should be given to them.

Q: I've often wondered what excuse we give for not providing our very best in terms of equipment. This is an illustration.

Adm. C.: I think the original thought was that the planes that we had given them, which were a cut below the F-4, were adequate for the job of the air defense of Taiwan. Of course, as the Chinese Communists got the MIG-21, then they felt, and probably properly so, that their air defenses had been degraded and that they should be updated with a more modern aircraft. And for that reason, I could support the F-4s from the military point of view as a military commander again saying, "Boy, if I had a better air defense, I'd have a much easier job of defending Taiwan in case of an invasion." So, I, from the military point of view supported the F-4s and thought their economy could have handled it. The submarines I was a little less enthusiastic about.

As I said, the ambassador would have to go to see the Gimo after these sorts of minor confrontations. And it was amazing, Jack. People would come to Taiwan. One of the show places, of course, would be Kinmen. Quemoy is what we call it and Kinmen is what they call it. "Kinmen," I think means gold.

Q: There's no gold there!

Adm. C.: No. Anyhow, one of the things that they were most anxious to do would be to take visiting dignitaries to Kinmen. It was a show place. It was beautifully defended. The troops were the very best. The island was immaculate, just immaculate. Everything had been put in order. They took you very proudly to the old ladies' home, the old gentlemens' home, showing that there were still civilians on the island, and most people when they came back were rather enthusiastic about it. Of course, the question came up often - was the stationing of the troops there necessary for the defense of Taiwan?

Their answer, with which I generally concurred, was that it gave them an early warning location that could detect a buildup of any sort.

Q: The island being - what, 100 miles away?

Adm. C.: The islands being right across at the mouth, the harbor, of Amoy. You could sit on Kinmen with your binoculars and look in the windows of the girls' dormitory at the College of Amoy. The closest point of the island to another adjacent island in Communist hands was less than two miles.

Q: And the distance from Taiwan was 100?

Adm. C.: Between 80 and 100.

What I started to say was that people would go to Quemoy, Kinmen, come back enthusiastic about the troops there, their degree of readiness, their moral, the way the Chinese Nationalists had kept the place, and would make rather rash statements about returning to the mainland.

I think I'd better mention "returning to the mainland" because when we first arrived in Taiwan there were tremendous signs, usually in blue and white, along a great many of the highways or wherever you had a prominent place similar to a billboard in our country, speaking of returning to the mainland. In the three years that I was there those signs had diminished to the point that they were practically non-existent.

Q: For what reason?

Adm. C.: The reason for it was perfectly simple. The United States had told them - first of all, they knew that they could never return to the mainland without assistance - and the United States had told them that we weren't about to provide assistance for a return to the mainland, that we honored our treaty responsibilities, which was the defense of Taiwan but did not include a return to the mainland. And they were smart enough to realize that, without assistance from somewhere else, such a return was absolutely impossible.

Q: Now, this returning to the mainland philosophy was intended largely for the people who had been on the mainland and came back to the island, rather than the Taiwanese themselves?

Adm. C.: This, of course, applied primarily to the ruling class of the island of Taiwan. There were approximately two million Chinese and about eleven million Taiwanese. I think total population now is about fourteen million.

Q: Were the Taiwanese themselves enthusiastic about this idea ever?

Adm. C.: No, I don't think so, but the government of Taiwan was wholly Chinese. I think it's important to note that only within recent years in the Army was there ever a Taiwanese, i.e. native Taiwanese, general. All the generals, all the admirals were Chinese. All the soldiers were Taiwanese.

Q: Was there any friction was a result of this seeming policy?

Adm. C.: If there was, I didn't notice it in the armed forces. There was, of course, a very strong Taiwanese independence movement that was frowned upon by the Chinese, and in light of recent events I wonder in my own mind what's going to happen. Our rapprochement, if that's what you want to call it, with the mainland of China, our statement that the Taiwanese problem is a Chinese problem, and it's not really our business. The final outcome would be hard for me to predict. My personal feeling is that there could be two solutions. One, the one I mentioned, Taiwanese independence, which, of course, would be favored by eleven million people; or some sort of an arrangement made by the Chinese Nationalists with the Communists, give them what might be likened to a dominion status and save face on both sides, so that the problem of Taiwan is amicably settled. Whether this could be done or not, I don't know, but those appear to me to be the only two basic solutions because as the Chinese die off, and of course the key figure who eventually will die off is Chiang Kai-shek, he's taking less and less part in the government affairs right now. He is seen only infrequently. When I was there, the first year was almost six years ago, he was active as he could be. He was seen at all public affairs, at the Double Ten celebration, the Army maneuvers, the naval maneuvers, but in the two or three years he has been seen less and less frequently.

So my guess is - and I don't have any idea what the State Department has in mind - that the only possible solution is an independent Taiwan, which we have washed our hands of. As you know, of course, this business of an independent Taiwan has caused a certain amount of friction because people have escaped from Taiwan and come to the United States and supported the independent Taiwanese movement. Whether there can be an agreement between Chiang Ching-kuo, who really has to all intents and purposes, I think, succeeded Chiang kai-Shek as the virtual leader of Taiwan -

Q: This is his son, is it?

Adm. C.: This is the son. There are two sons, Chiang

Ching-kuo and one who is in the Army and was trained in Germany - his name is Chiang Wei-kuo.

Q: He is the son of Madame, isn't he?

Adm. C.: No. Nor is Chiang Ching-kuo.

Q: Well, the Taiwanese way of life is more or less a capitalistic way of life, is it not?

Adm. C.: I'd have to think about the answer to that because really it is a capitalistic way of life, but in actuality it is more of a benign dictatorship.

Q: With a communal kind of existence?

Adm. C.: No, it isn't a communal kind of existence because all the land has been given back to the peasants and they farm it individually. But the governmental system still is in tight control. A humorous example was noticed in the American daily paper. It said the Governor of Taiwan and the Mayor of Teipei have decreed that there will be no more long-haired hippies and no more miniskirts, and they will be delighted to take any young man with his hair an unacceptable length down to the barbershop and get him a haircut. This appeared right in the paper. And they did. I don't think it was completely effective, but at the same time it gives you an idea of how quickly things can be done to quell something that might not be in keeping with the ruling thought.

The old man himself - as I said, the first two years I was there was simply marvelous. He ran the annual military review, which was an over-all assessment that was made each year of the ability of the Chinese forces to defend Taiwan and to analyze the training, the condition of readiness, the general acceptability of the armed forces. And this annual review, which one year was called a training review, was presided over by the Generalissimo in a benign way that reminded me of my days before Chairman Vinson of the Armed Services Committee. He was in complete control, literally sharp as a tack, and I must admit I couldn't help but admire his tenacity and his complete dedication to his view of how China should be run, which of course is not precisely the way all the millions on the mainland feel.

I think it's interesting to note that during my time there my relations with the Chinese were at a fairly high level. I dealt with the President's son when he was Minister of National Defense, which he was the first year I was there, and then he moved to Vice Premier, and now the Premier, or with the Chief of the General Staff, who when I first arrived was General Kao, and in my opinion one of the finest military officers I have ever known. I was devoted to him. He was straight, honest, and competent as any military person I've ever seen.

Q: Where had he been trained?

Adm. C.: He'd been trained in China at their military academy, which was founded by Chiang Kai-shek. Most of the top people, with the possible exception of a few naval officers who had gone to school in England, with the possible exception of a few Army officers who had been trained by the Germans, were primarily trained at their military academy - Whampoa.

What I started to say was that my association with the Chief of the General Staff, with the Minister of National Defense, whom I saw quite frequently, the various chiefs of the services, the commander-in-chief of the Army, the Navy, the Air Force, and the Chinese had a unique fourth service which was called the Combined Service Force, and it was not unlike, I suppose, the proposed Service of Supply that we had rejected. In addition to the Chief of the General Staff, who was General Kao at first, and General Lai, who was the Air Force commander-in-chief when I first arrived, the commander-in-chief of the Army and the commander-in-chief of the Combined Service Force. So there were four commanders-in-chief.

In our advisory capacity General Ciccolellea and I had often recommended that we streamline their armed forces because the organization was quite topheavy. There were more generals and admirals in their armed services than there were in the United States, I think, at the time of World War II. There was no place for them to go. Once they retired they either became a governor of a province or an ambassador, and then rotated back.

A good example is when I was in Japan the commander-in-chief of the Navy was Admiral Ni Yue-si. He, after being commander-in-chief of the Navy was Chief of the General Staff. This again was before I arrived in Taiwan. When I arrived in Taiwan he was the personal military chief of staff to the Gimo and held that position for a number of years, while General Kao was Chief of the General Staff. When General Lai relieved General Kao as Chief of the General Staff, General Kao moved to Admiral Ni's position as chief of staff to the President, Admiral Ni became the ambassador to Turkey.

Q: Kind of musical chairs!

Adm. C.: The musical chairs aren't over. I just learned from a letter from my ex American aide, who's out of the Navy now, that Admiral Ni has returned from Turkey and is again the personal chief of staff to the President, General Kao has moved to National Defense. So you can see how tight the little circle of musical chairs really is.

The commander-in-chief of the Navy who was incumbent during my time there, most of it, moved to a job like the General Planning Board. I was never quite sure what they did, and from that he moved, I think, to an ambassadorship. The Deputy Minister of National Defense was commander-in-chief of the Navy, then Deputy Minister of National Defense, and then to an ambassadorship. So the game of musical chairs continues and will continue basically, I suppose, until they all die out, and they're all getting along in years.

As I said, my relationship with them was ideal. I could speak frankly to most of them, not that I really had to. Our closest association in the military came when we had our annual war games to basically test the defense plan of Taiwan. The forces were put on alert and went through all the procedures that normal war games entail. But the scenario of the war games was always a bit of a problem because no matter what you called it, the mythical kingdom of Tap or the mythical kingdom of

Yap, it was thought to be a return to the mainland and it got to be a political question, so that we had to rewrite the scenario very carefully so that it could not be construed under any circumstances as an exercise in return to the mainland. Our ambassador could see no reason how it could even be suggested that we were planning for the return to the mainland, because, as I said, it was our policy that we were not going to support the return to the mainland.

Q: Are you planning to talk about the intelligence setup in its relationship to your command?

Adm. C.: Yes, I could talk a little about it. As I said, our largest staff section in TDC was the intelligence section, and we had very fine relations with the Chinese and their intelligence setup. With the possible exception of Hong Kong, I would say that Taiwan through electronic means and through other means had as good a reading of what went on in mainland China as any other source in the world. The CIA agency was a little different there. It was called the Army Technical Group, which was the cover name, and it was a separate little agency, obviously operating under the ambassador. We had very close relations with them. There was a rather extensive radio installation - this was actually run by the Air Force - for the collection of intelligence. There were numerous radar stations that we were given the output from, from which we could monitor flights, particularly high flights, on the mainland.

As you know, we still at that time allowed the Chinese to run what were the equivalents of U-2 flights and that could be easily justified to determine the buildup, in case such were eventuating.

Q: Did they have any disasters with those planes?

Adm. C.: Any shootdowns?

Q: Yes.

Adm. C.: I think they did, but it didn't assume the proportions of the Russian shootdowns at all. I think one of them had been shot down, but it was just an airplane that was shot down, period. You see, strange as it may seem, Taiwan considered itself in a state of war against Mainland China and behaved as such. So the fact that a plane on an observation mission was lost, it was simply lost on an operational flight and nothing was said about it, nor did it carry the political implications with the rest of the world, because, again I repeat, Taiwan and Mainland China were in a state of war, and as far as I know they still are.

I think it brings up, the observation aspects of it that I was just mentioning, the Pearl River estuary raids. Possibly you might remember them. My last year there there was a statement in the Chinese Nationalist press that a boat had made an intrusion and that there'd been a little engagement and they'd come off very well against the Chinese Communists. They had been making those incursions periodically, but this one was given rather extensive play in their press and was picked up in the world press. Reporters came to me as the Commander of the Taiwan Defense Command and said, hey, what's going on, what's all this business about the shooting of the Chinese mainland by a boat. And I said, "Well, this has been going on for a great many years. It's an intelligence-collection activity. The Chinese conduct it. I do not necessarily know, nor should I know, when they're going to take place because they're such minor incursions, and I think it's been blown up out of all proportion." Those were my words.

I got a message the next day after that had appeared in the press from the Secretary of State that said:

"From the Secretary of State to Vice Admiral Chew. You leave the policy statements to us back here and keep your mouth shut."

Well, I can understand the Secretary's point of view

but when a reporter comes to me as the Commander of the Taiwan Defense Command and says what's going on, I can't sit there and say jibberish. It's just ridiculous, so I said the things that I thought were appropriate, that it was blown up out of proportion, that there had been previous incursions, many of which had never been detected, and this was a form of intelligence-collecting by nations who considered themselves at war.

After that, it got into the political arena and we were given assurance from Chiang Ching-kuo that in the future any raid of that magnitude, even though it might be very small, would be cleared with the American command before it was undertaken. So I think we made considerable progress in our effort to be more low key.

In this connection, I think it's interesting to note that the defenses of the Chinese mainland were amazingly efficient, and the ability of the Chinese Nationalists to conduct raids successfully was very, very limited. There were plans, of course, as you must recognize, for putting a man ashore for determining where the fortifications were, what the capabilities were, what the troop buildups were, but most of these were completely unsuccessful because the counterespionage on the mainland was so efficient that even though these people spoke the same dialect as the mainland provinces that they were landed in they rarely succeeded in their mission. There were one or two that did, but there were a great many that did not.

Q: What happened to them when they did not?

Adm. C.: They didn't return, so that was the end of them as far as we knew, and it probably was literally the end. I don't think it was ever verified exactly what happened to them, but the chances were they were executed.

The other aspects of intelligence-gathering centered, as I say, mainly on electronic means, the equivalent U-2 flights. The general surveillance in the Taiwan Straits by fishing boats, which would give you a pretty good indication of the possibility of mounting an attack.

While we're talking about the Taiwan Straits, there was one problem that came up. From the early days of Admiral Pride there were two destroyers that were assigned to the Taiwan Straits patrol -

Q: U.S. destroyers?

Adm. C.: Yes. It was called the Taiwan Patrol Force. Then, as we tried to reduce the tensions during my tenure, it was decided to take the destroyers, which had been on a permanently assigned basis from the Seventh Fleet for a given period, and put them on a random assignment.

This again elicited a great hue and cry from the Chinese. They thought this was another indication of our lack of support. Here we were reducing our forces in the area, pulling out our two permanently assigned destroyers, because the two permanently assigned destroyers meant absolutely nothing. It was purely a figment of the imagination that we were there in strength - two destroyers alone, but we at least were there.

It was decided that the patrols would be made by random passages of ships, which was not difficult because there would be ships going into the Vietnam area which could go in between Taiwan and the mainland and conduct a radar search, as they went, and these would be reported to the Chinese so that they would have the feeling that at least ships were there. Every time one went through it was reported religiously to the Chinese to show that our patrol was being maintained even on a random basis.

This type of thing became quite a problem, as you can easily see, because whenever there was a reduction in the military assistance program, whenever there was a reduction in the number of ships that could conduct a patrol, or a withdrawal of an aircraft, it was taken immediately as a lack of resolve on our part to support the mutual defense treaty.

Q: There was a sensitivity!

Adm. C.: Yes, and the ambassador quickly had to run to the Gimo and say everything's going to be all right, Generalissimo, don't worry about it, we're going to support you to the hilt. He had to reassure him, without fail, every time a little incident occurred.

Q: Did Chiang Ching-kuo share that point of view?

Adm. C.: I think initially he did, but I think as time went on he was not so concerned about it. As I've stated I think somewhere else before, in my view Chiang Ching-kuo is a vastly underrated man. For some reason or other, he's been painted as a shy, diffident soul in the American press. To the contrary, he is a very able politician, he is extremely pleasant, charming, and ruthless as need be. As I said, I think he's been vastly underrated in the American press. I think he'll be a fine ruler and I think he's the one person who possibly could effect what I've previously suggested - some sort of a dominion status. He's the only person who could do it.

Q: Tell me about your relationship, as head of the Taiwan Defense Command, with the commander of the Seventh Fleet.

Adm. C.: Well, the commander of the Seventh Fleet was

obviously the repository for all the forces that I might eventually have in support of the mutual defense treaty, and each commander normally made a visit a year and we talked over our mutual problems, which were not of course, very many because he was engaged in a war in Vietnam. Although we had very close and pleasant associations, there was really nothing except the change from the permanent to the random patrol, that caused any need for particularly close association. But we had it. We were always very good friends and each new commander of the Seventh Fleet came and made a visit to Teipei and was royally entertained, as you would expect. He called on the Gimo, called on Chiang Ching-kuo, and all the commanders-in-chief, the Chief of the General Staff, and relations were, of course, very, very cordial. And he was always welcomed with open arms because I think the Chinese also recognized the Chinese also recognized the importance of the Seventh Fleet to the defense of Taiwan.

Q: What was your relationship, if any, with the Royal Navy people in Hong Kong?

Adm. C.: Pleasant but distant. I made frequent trips to Hong Kong. The first time, I called on the governor general and the senior military personnel there, but it was more a courtesy call than it was one for any particular business. Most of my trips to Hong Kong were primarily in the area of recreation from Taiwan. I enjoyed it thoroughly and, as I said, maintained excellent relations with the British in Hong Kong.

Q: You might talk a little about the social life, as you knew it in Taiwan.

Adm. C.: Well, I was going to isolate the social life a little bit. Really, it was a part of the job. Everyone who came through, and they varied in stature from the Vice President - ex-Vice President - who made a visit to Taiwan. The commander-in-chief, Pacific, normally made one every six months, each of the commanders-in-chief of the Pacific forces, i.e., the Pacific Air Force, the Pacific Army Command, and CinCPacFlt generally made a trip through Taiwan and were always entertained. The Vice President, of course, was normally entertained at a dinner by the President. The various chiefs of staff, General Westmoreland came through, Admiral Zumwalt came through just before he was to become CNO, Admiral Moorer had been there. Each time anyone came, there were rounds of meeting ceremonies, usually a dinner party by the appropriate level, either the Minister of National Defense or the Vice President, depending on the particular rank of the visitor.

I had a standard policy that any military commander - joint commander, specifically - who called on the President, I wanted to be there, and it had been arranged that whenever - for example, General Westmoreland as chief of staff of the Army, he was a member of the Joint Chiefs of Staff, I was permitted to go when he called on the President. The same would have been true of the Chairman of the Joint Chiefs of Staff, or the chief of staff of the Air Force in his capacity. If it were simply an Air Force commander, who was not a joint commander per se, then the Air Force commander on the island usually accompanied him. Similarly, if it were an Army commander without a joint hat, then the chief of the MAAG usually accompanied him on his call on the President, if such a call was made.

The last year I was there he was seen less and less, and this partially was a result of - at least, to the best of our knowledge - an automobile accident that occurred on the way up Yang Ming shan, which stands for Grass Mountain and it's where his summer house was and, incidentally, where our quarters were. On the way up there were some sharp curves and apparently his car hit or was hit by either part of his entourage who had to stop suddenly and he suffered a very severe shiplash, and so did Madame. Whether it was more serious on a man of his age or not, I don't know, but from then on he was increasingly less available and, as I understand now, is practically never seen.

I think, as an aside, there's one very interesting political aspect to Taiwan that I never was completely able to live with, but I wasn't able to do much about it. It entailed the commissary privileges for foreign diplomats. This shouldn't be included but there was a list that I had compiled of the limitations that were placed on each foreign diplomat.

Q: They had access to our commissary?

Adm. C.: They had access to our commissary and our exchange, and the rationale behind it was that it made it more attractive for their missions and their embassies to be able to use our commissary and exchange privileges. Consequently, it was desirable for them to recognize Nationalist China on Taiwan.

Q: Building up the status of Nationalist China?

Adm. C.: Building up the status of Nationalist China.

Q: A curious implement for that!

Adm. C.: Curious, but the part that annoyed me - I could go along with the fact that it was obviously an incentive to establish a mission if you could be told before the mission was established, yes, you'll have commissary and exchange privileges at the American exchange and commissary. But what I couldn't live with was the black market, and there were numbers of these gentlemen who bought the strangest things in the strangest amounts and volumes. There was one gentleman, for example, who bought literally pounds and pounds and pounds of coffee. There was another who bought fourteen sets of golf clubs and golf bags. There were those who bought excess amounts of - I think one bought black pepper. I knew about it, and I would go to the ambassador and we would discuss it, and I guess it was decided that discretion was the better part of valor, and rather than bring it up we just lived with it.

Q: So they were getting rich on the side!

Adm. C.: They were getting rich on the side and, of course, this again was the incentive to have them recognize Nationalist China instead of Communist China.

Q: Those figures on the right-hand side, were these limitations on the amount they could purchase in a given month?

Adm. C.: Yes, so you can see that in a year it added up to quite a bit.

Q: Was this unique with Taiwan in your experience?

Adm. C.: As far as I know, it's unique with Taiwan. I don't know of any other place in the world where it's done. Maybe I'm wrong. I don't know for sure, but I was under the impression in discussing it with the ambassador that this was the only place, but he considered it necessary.

Q: Well, it's a violation of the terms by which a commissary is run, isn't it?

Adm. C.: Absolutely. There was another thing that used to further irritate me. Because of the Status of Forces Agreement, retired Army, Navy, and Air Force officers who came through Taiwan did not have commissary and exchange privileges, and here were all these foreign diplomats buying golf clubs and coffee, and a person who came through on a perfectly legitimate trip and wanted to buy a toothbrush couldn't do it. After a great deal of negotiation I finally got that changed, and eventually those who were bona fide members of the armed forces, retired, were entitled to commissary and exchange privileges. I felt that it was quite a feather in my cap. There were quite a few retired people who lived in Taiwan and they were jubilant, obviously.

Q: From your list, recognition of Nationalist China was fairly widespread around the world?

Adm. C.: Yes, and I have been told that a number of these missions have closed.

The British had a unique system. They had a consul general, even though they did not recognize Nationalist China.

Q: That was because of their position in Hong Kong?

Adm. C.: They had an ambassador in Communist China, but because of their position in Hong Kong they had a consul general who lived down at the little port town of Tomsai, which was at the mouth of the river that Taipei is on, and where incidentally, the golf course was. He was in a peculiar situation because here he was representative of a country that was not recognized Nationalist China, nor was he recognized, but he was there purely for I suppose, commercial reasons.

Q: Did this pertain to the French also? They had an

ambassador in Peking.

Adm. C.: I don't think the French were in Taipei at all. There was no French representation whatsoever. There was Spanish.

In closing I might say, Jack, that it was interesting that my departure from Taiwan was somewhat in the same manner as my orders to Taiwan. At the end of two years, I had been informed that my tour was up and that I would be expected to submit a letter requesting retirement. At that time, President Eisenhower died and Chiang Ching-kuo went to the funeral as the representative of Nationalist China, and before he went he said to me, "Jack, I want you to stay on another year. I'm sure the ambassador is willing and I'm sure CinCPac is willing." But there was a great reluctance in Washington to allow continuation for another year. At that time the emphasis was on youth and getting the older people out, and I was getting a little older -

Q: You mean Zumwalt was CNO?

Adm. C.: No, Zumwalt was not then CNO, but the policy had already been enunciated - and this had been put out in writing - that once you had served in a three-star billet you would not revert to two stars and you would be requested to retire and expected to retire. That was the policy I mentioned earlier in which I fully concur.

So Vice Premier Chiang Ching-kuo went back and I think saw Admiral Moorer and requested that I be retained another year. I was informed that a letter of request for retirement was not necessary, that I was being retained for another year. That appeared to me to be perfectly fine. I was prepared and expected to leave at the end of the third year when Admiral Zumwalt came through on his trip prior to his assignment as CNO and asked me if I would stay on until December, my three years being up in July. I said no, that I would not, that I was going home to retire, that I had kids in school, and that it was more than I thought that he should ask, because it always involved a detailing foul-up. There was nothing that involved the national interest and I didn't see any reason to go back in the middle of winter with kids in college and all that sort of thing, so I said no, that I'd prefer not to. He said, "Well, if you will stay another year, would that be satisfactory?"

I said, "If you think it's in the best interests of the service and the country, why, naturally I'll stay. But I think you'll go back and find that I'm on record also as suggesting that people not stay here more than three years. However, if you want me to do it and you think it's in the best interests of the country, naturally I'll do it."

"Well," he said, "I'll get in touch with the Secretary and I'll let you know right away."

So he sent me a message from Singapore and said, sorry, things are too far down the road. You will retire in July or August. Actually, it was the 1st of October when I finally retired.

So we were going to stay, we were going to go, we were not going to go, we were not going to stay, and by that time we were wrecks. Finally, the word came that we would leave in July, after three years in Taiwan.

I came back and had two or three months - two or three weeks of temporary duty in the CNO's office, where I straightened out my papers, finished fitness reports, and had my retirement physical, and ended my naval career on the 1st of October 1970.

Q: What a delightful assignment, though, to conclude it with!

Adm. C.: Wasn't it a delightful one, and it was an interesting assignment, one that I felt that I was fairly well qualified to carry out. I've often laughed about my name, and the Chinese insisted that somewhere along the line I must have been a Chinese because "Chew" is a very good Chinese name, and when you go to Kinmen, for example, you hear of the bravery and the lesson of Chew, who was at one time a national hero.

Q: Spelled differently, however?

Adm. C.: Well, I think the spelling is academic. It's the sound "Chew" because you can spell it Chew, Chu, you could spell it Chow, although that's more of a chow sound. Recognizing the various ways of pronouncing a character, the spelling is academic.

That, I think, concludes, what to me has been a very full life. I've often been asked, Jack - in fact, I was just asked the other day, if I had it to do over again would I rather have been a doctor or a lawyer or a merchant chief, and I can say, unequivocally, no. I've had a marvelous career, I'm proud of it, and I might add that I feel it's most appropriate that younger people be running the Navy now.

Q: Jack, in retirement, have you done anything in the civilian world? Have you been involved with industry in any way?

Adm. C.: No. I was tentatively offered a job as a consultant, but I could see that it was the type of thing that wanted me to capitalize on my contacts in Taiwan and I'd seen enough of that. I didn't want it, so my activities have been relegated to being a member of the board of Historic Annapolis, a member of the board of the Providence Association, and activities with no remuneration of any sort.

Q: Your attitude puts you in good company because this was certainly the attitude of Fleet Admiral Nimitz!

Adm. C.: I've been asked sometimes with a snide look "What are you doing now?" and I use Johnny Davidson's answer to that, "I'm doing a lot of the things that somebody used to do for me and I find that it takes all my time just to go through the everyday business of living."

Q: Well, I do thank you very much for this fascinating series.

Adm. C.: I hope it's significant in some respects. I feel that I didn't prepare well enough for it, but suddenly me memory just wouldn't come back.

Q: You did well enough, Sir.

Index

Interviews with

Vice Admiral John L. (Jack) Chew
U. S. Navy (Retired)

ANDERSON, Admiral George: responsible for development of centralized control of commands in Europe, p. 172; p. 311; p. 315-6; confrontation with McNamara in Missile Crisis, p.332;

AS WARFARE FORCES, PACIFIC: Chew named as Commander Jan. 12, 1966, p. 393-4; background to need for this command, p. 394-5; Chew undertakes study of Russian SS menace, p. 397; result of study - establishment of AS Command Center on Ford Island, p. 397; value of SOSUS system, p. 397-8; ASW forces available, p. 398; Chew discusses division of responsibility as it pertains to ASW Forces, 7th Fleet, etc., p. 401-2; Chew attends daily briefings of CincPacFlt, p. 402; ASW exercises, p. 403; headquarters on Ford Island, p. 405-6; ASW Force command and international relations (SEATO), p. 407-8; research efforts conducted under Chew, p. 408-9; the Triangulation range on Kauai Island, p. 412-3;

ATSUGI: U. S. Marine Air Base, p. 371-2;

BEAKLEY Admiral Wallace: his condemnation of the ROANOKE for shore conduct in Hong Kong, p. 218; reassures Chew on the rescue operation for Scott Carpenter, p. 296;

BLUE, RADM Victor: relieves McCollum as skipper of HELENA, p. 132;

BURKE, Admiral A. A.: Asks Chew to join him in Op-60 - Strategic Plans Division, p. 176; Chew joins staff as head of Psychological Warfare, p. 189-192; p. 227;

CAPE ESPERANCE: Battle of - U. S. ships engaged, p. 54; p. 58-9;

CARNEY, Admiral Robert B.: as CincNelm Chew serves on his staff in London, p. 169-170; becomes CincSouth and moves headquarters to Naples, p. 171-4; p. 176; p. 192; p. 195;

CARPENTER, Lt. Comdr. M. Scott, USN (Ret.): p. 294; Air Force criticizes the Navy for slight delay in his rescue, p. 295-6; MacNamara summons Chew for story of the rescue operation - as aftermath JCS makes Air Force General at Patrick Field DOD coordination for all recovery operations, p. 296-7; p. 299;

CASTRO, Fidel: cuts off water supply to U. S. Naval Base at Guantanamo, p. 320ff;

CHEW, VADM John L. (Jack): personal background, p. 1-4; his wife's illness in London, p. 174-76; his wife dies - he continues to run household in Annapolis, p. 196-7; his selection (1958) to flag rank, p. 234-5; household arrangements as ComNavForces Japan, p. 360-1; the family takes up residence in Honolulu, p. 393-4; his house on Ford Island, p. 405; his retirement (Oct. 1, 1970) p. 452;

1

CHIANG Kai-shek: p. 431; p. 434; p. 442; p. 445-6;

CHINA: comments of Chew about China before the communist takeover, p. 132 ff; p. 143-4; p. 154-5;

CLAY, Gen. Lucius; p. 340; p. 344;

COMNAVFOR Japan: Chew named to the command, p. 357-8; headquarters at Yokosuka, p. 360; Chew's original apprehensions about the Japanese, p. 363-5; duties of ComNavFor, p. 369-71; the Black Ship Festival, p. 372-3; duties and trips to Tokyo, p. 376-7;

COAST WATCHERS: p. 108-9; p. 116;

COLWELL, VADM J. B.: p. 112;

CONTINGENCY PLANS: Chew comments on Plans and revisions of plans, etc., p. 184-7;

CUBAN MISSILE CRISIS: Chew describes activities in JCS, p. 308-320;

DAVIS, Lt. Gen. Lee: Commanding General at Cape Canaveral, p. 288; some friction develops with Navy because of faulty landing of the 2nd sub-orbital flight capsule with Virgil Grissom, p. 288;

DENNISON, Admiral Robert L: succeeds Burke as Op.-60, p. 192-3; p. 196; p. 311; p. 317-8;

DESTROYER FLOTILLA FOUR: p. 281 ff; involved in MERCURY recovery program, p. 282-3; Canaveral became a secondary base for Chew, p. 286-7; p. 287; spread of ships in Task Force for rescue efforts, p. 288; emergency ships in Indian Ocean - communications, p. 291-3; Chew's impressions of the MERCURY astronauts, p. 300-2;

DIEM, Ngo-dinh: President of South Vietnam, p. 344-5;

DOMINICAN REPUBLIC CRISIS: p. 354-6;

DUKE, VADM Irving T.: gunnery officer on HELENA, p. 40; p. 42-3; p. 53;

EISENHOWER, The Hon. Dwight L.: p. 11;

ELLENDER, Senator Alan: p. 254;

ESPIRITU SANTO: base of HELENA during her operations around Guadalcanal, p. 52 ff; facilities of the base, p. 66-68;

FELT, Adm. C.D.: CincPac, p. 346-7;

FENNO, RADM F. W. (Mike): p. 220-1;

GLENN, Lt. Col. John, USMC (Ret.): made the first MERCURY space flight (Feb. 20, 1962) (after ENOS, the rhesus monkey), p. 286; p. 288-9; p. 290-1;

GRISSOM, Virgil: in the second sub-orbital MERCURY flight the capsule was lost upon landing, p. 284; p. 287-8;

GUADALCANAL: the mission of the HELENA - to protect the marine garrison on the island, p. 52 ff; Battle of Guadalcanal (Nov. 13, 1942), p. 57-60;

GUANTANAMO: Castro cuts off water to naval base, p. 320 ff; President Johnson sends delegation to Guantanamo for report - Gen. Taylor designates Chew as senior member and representative of JCS, p. 321; the report of the delegation, p. 326;

GULF OF PO HAI: p. 144-5;

USS HELENA: Chew becomes Assistant Gunnery officer (1939), p. 40 ff; the ship's armament, p. 42; she becomes unit of Pacific Fleet, p. 44; the attack on Pearl Harbor, p. 45-7; repairs at Mare Island, p. 51; off to Guadalcanal, p. 52 ff; her performance in first Battle of Cape Esperance, p. 53-6; Battle of Guadalcanal (Nov. 13, 1942), p. 57 ff; repairs in Sydney, p. 68; makes first combat tests on VT fuse, p. 69-70; shell bombardments of Japanese shore positions, p. 69; in Kula Gulf, p. 71; the story of the sinking of the HELENA in The Slot, p. 73 ff;

USS HELENA (CA): Chew assigned to new (1945) HELENA, building in Boston, p. 121; p. 125 ff; after shakedown cruise she goes to U. K. and the Mediterranean - finally to China, p. 130-1; her five-month stay in Shanghai, o, 132-7; Chew relieved as Exec in March, 1947; p. 140;

HILL, Admiral Harry W.: p. 163-4; the new honor system, p. 164; p. 166-8;

HONG KONG: p. 139; Chew relieved in Hong Kong of command of STICKELL p. 147;

HOOVER, Captain Gilbert: p. 59; relieved of his command of HELENA and severely criticized for not searching for survivors from JUNEAU, p. 62-4;

HYLAND, Admiral John: p. 396; p. 399;

ISHIGURU, Adm. Sumetomo (Sam Blackstone): Japanese friend of the Chews, p. 365; p. 367;

JACKSON, VADM Andrew M.: p. 389; p. 391;

JAMES, RADM Ralph L.: p. 220-1;

JAPAN: post WW II, p. 214-7;

JAPANESE PEOPLE: Chew's reactions during his command of NavFor Japan, p. 363 ff; p. 376;

JCS (Joint Chiefs of Staff): p. 195-6; p. 198; they devise command structure for NASA recovery flights, p. 296;

JOHNSON, President Lyndon: sends delegation to Guantanamo in crisis over water, p. 321, p. 327; p. 337-8;

JOHNSON, Admiral Roy: Commander, 7th Fleet, p. 373; p. 375; Commander Pacific Fleet, p. 396-7; p. 415;

JCS (Joint Chiefs of Staff): Chew assigned to staff, p. 306-7; VADM Riley demands he report immediately, p. 307; the Cuban Missile Crisis, p. 308 ff; problem of centralized authority, p. 317-8; concerns of JCS at time of Kennedy assassination, p. 336-8; disagreement over appointment of Adm. Sharp to succeed Adm. Felt, p. 347; JCS desire to avoid split decisions on military matters, p. 348; the National Military Command Center as evolved from the Cuban Missile Crisis, p. 351-2; an exercise - air lifting a complete army division to Europe, p. 353-4; the Dominican Republic crisis, p. 354-6; Vietnam and Laos, p. 356-7;

USS JUNEAU: p. 57-9; her final torpedoing and sinking, p. 61;

KENNEDY, President John F.: his assassination, p. 321; p. 336; p. 352;

KHYBER PASS: Visit to the Pass, p. 180-1;

KOLUMBANGARA: Island in the SLOT - objective for survivors from the HELENA, p. 80;

LAOS: p. 340;

HMNZS LEANDER: p. 70;

LeMAY, General Curtis: p. 341; p. 349-50;

LONG BEACH, California: the disastrous landing at the dock, (ROANOKE - CL), p. 219-23;

MacNAMARA, Robert S.: SecDef: hears Chew's account of rescue of Scott Carpenter (MERCURY space flight), p. 296-7; p. 315; Zumwalt presents report to SecDef on fact finding committee on water supply at Guantanamo, p. 328; Chew believes the decisions had been made even before the fact-finding trip, p. 328-330; confrontation between CNO Anderson and Secretary MacNamara, p. 332-3; his policies in Vietnam, p. 341;

MARITIME SELF-DEFENSE FORCE - Japan: p. 365; p. 367;

USS MARYLAND: p. 16; Chew's first tour of duty after graduation, p. 18; the Presidential review in the Hudson, p. 23;

McCOLLUM, RADM Arthur H.: skipper of new heavy cruiser HELENA (1945) p. 129; called to Washington for Pearl Harbor hearings - turns over ship to Executive - Chew - who was also temporary gunnery officer, p. 129-30;

McCOUNAUGHY, The Hon. Walter: U. S. Ambassador to Taiwan, p. 424;

McDONALD, Admiral David: as CNO gives Chew job as ASW Force, Pacific, p. 391-2;

MERCURY SPACE PROGRAM: see entries under: DESTROYER FLOTILLA FOUR; NASA; SHEPARD; GRISSOM; JOHN GLENN; SCOTT CARPENTER; MacNAMARA;

USS MONAGHAN: p. 27; Chew present for the pre-commissioning, p. 28; p. 34;

MOUNTBATTEN, Admiral Lord Louis: comments on the RAF and the RN, p. 177-8; p. 181-2;

MSTS: Chew becomes (Apr. 1950) Deputy Commander MSRS, p. 257-81; VADM Roy A. Gano was Commander, p. 258-9; scope of MSTS responsibilities, p. 259-60; negotiations with labor unions, p. 263; p. 266-7; p. 269; relations with the Navy, p. 279;

NASA: in the days of the MERCURY program NASA was located at Langley Field, Virginia - p. 285; p. 292; p. 294;

U. S. NAVAL ACADEMY: Chew's early interest, p. 4; an appointment from Carl Vinson, p. 5-6; Academy days, p. 6 ff; summer cruises, aviation summer, p. 12-17; after his rescue from Vella LaVella Chew assigned as Ordnance Instructor, p. 113 ff; introduces innovations in Ordnance, p. 114-7; the Academy in wartime, p. 121-5; Chew returns to Academy and the Executive Department (1948) - becomes head of Leadership Department, p. 159; summer course at Johns Hopkins, p. 160; implements the honor system, p. 163-5;

USS NECHES - AO: Chew has a tour of duty in her, p. 35-6; p. 201; p. 205;

NIMITZ, Fl. Adm. Chester W.: reviews case of Captain Gilbert Hoover - his decision completely vindicated Hoover - but two late to save his career, p. 64;

NISHIMURA, Adm. (Japanese) CNO - his dinner party for Adm. Chew, p. 264-5;

NITZE, The Hon. Paul: p. 347;

NMCC (National Military Command Center): the evolvement of the Center as result of experience with Cuban Missile Crisis, p. 351-3;

NOUMEA: destination of men rescued from HELENA, p. 110;

Op-06B: PLANS AND POLICY: Chew returns from Japan to become Assistant CNO for Plans and Policy, p. Op-06B, p. 384-5; p. 389-93;

OP-60: p. 176; p. 189-191; Chew becomes head of Joint Plans Section, p. 191-2; nature of work in Plans, p. 194-5; liaison with State Department, p. 198-9;

USS OVERTON - DD: Chew goes to four-piper - training Reserve Crews, p. 24-25;

PARSONS, RADM W. S. (Deke): present on HELENA for first tests with VT fuse - p. 69-70;

USS PAWCATUCK: (AO-108); Chew takes command, p. 197 ff; her main duty to replenish other ships, p. 201; comments on refueling at sea, p. 204-5; p. 209;

PEARL HARBOR: The Japanese attack, p. 45-50;

PIRIE, VADM Robert: p. 163;

USS PITTSBURGH: carried Adm. Wright (Cinc Nelm) and party on tour of Far East, p. 182 ff;

POST GRADUATE SCHOOL: p. 38-9;

PSYCHOLOGICAL WARFARE DIVISION of Op. 60: Chew becomes head of division under Adm. Burke (1953), p. 189;

USS PUEBLO: p. 378-82;

RAMAGE, VADM Lawson P. (Red): p. 267; p. 278;

REISCHAUER, Edwin O.: U. S. Ambassador to Japan, p. 376;

RESPONSIBILITY - AS A POLICY: p. 219-224;

RILEY, VADM Herbert: p. 307; p. 314; p. 320;

USS ROANOKE: Chew takes command, p. 207-8; p. 210-12; p. 218-9; the disastrous landing at dock in Long Beach, p. 219-223; patrol off Indonesia during crisis, p. 225; preparation for shore leave, p. 226;

RUSSIAN SUBMARINES: see entries under: AS WARFARE FORCES PACIFIC. Russian trawlers on surveillance, p. 410-12;

SASEBO: p. 369; p. 371;

SCOTT, RADM Norman: p. 53; p. 59;

U. S. SEVENTH FLEET: p. 373; p. 375; p. 379; p. 403-4; Commander 7th
            Fleet periodic visits to Taiwan, p. 443-4;
            see also: AS WARFARE FORCES.

SHANGHAI: The HELENA anchored for five months in Shanghai, p. 132-7;

SHARP, Adm. U. S. Grant: split decision on the JCS on the appointment
            of Adm. Sharp to succeed Adm. Felt as CincPac, p. 347; p.
            415;

SHEPARD, RADM Alan B. Jr.: made the first sub-orbital MERCURY space
            flight, p. 282; p. 300;

SHEPHERD, The Hon. Harry: Chairman of House Appropriations Committee,
            p. 252-3;

SHIP'S CHARACTERISTICS BOARD: Chew becomes director of the staff (in
            Op. 04), p. 228; functions of the Board, p. 228-31; p. 234;

SHORE ESTABLISHMENT AND MAINTENANCE DIVISION: p. 236; Chew, as RADM, be-
            comes Director, p. 236 a get-acquainted inspection trip,
            p. 237; requirements for Congressional appearances,
            p. 238-9; procedures followed in getting appropriations,
            p. 240-4; explanation of duel system in Congress of
            authorization first and appropriation later for a spe-
            cific project, p. 249; illustrations of projects, p.
            251-2; p. 257-8;

SIKES, The Hon. Robert: p. 251; p. 255-6;

SOSUS: see entries under: AS WARFARE FORCES, PACIFIC.

STENNIS, Senator John: p. 250; p. 254-5;

USS STICKELL: Chew becomes skipper (1947), p. 140; to Honolulu for ASM
            training, p. 141; division ordered to China, p. 142 ff;
            serves as SAR ship in Okinawa, p. 148; handling problem
            of venereal disease, p. 148-50;

SYDNEY, Australia: p. 68;

TAIWAN DEFENSE COMMAND: After protesting to BuPers Chew takes command
            in Taipei, p. 418; Mission of this command, p. 419-20
            the staff, p. 420-2; the MAAG problem, p. 423-5;
            Taiwanese rearmament, p. 426 ff; Quemoy (Kinmen),
            p. 428; the Intelligence Section of TDC, p. 437-8;
            continuing state of war with mainland, p. 438-9;
            Taiwan Patrol Force, p. 441; official visits, p. 444-5;
            foreign diplomatic missions shop at U. S. Commissary,

p. 446-8; Chew serves two years - Chiang Ching-kuo gets permission for him to stay a third year, p. 450-1; Zumwalt asks Chew to stay on for extended term - but proves impossible, p. 451;

TAYLOR, General Maxwell: Chairman of the JCS, p. 313-4; p. 321; p. 333-5; p. 342-3; p. 350; p. 354;

TODODAI: Japanese Admiralty House, p. 360-1; p. 365;

TSINGTAO: p. 132;

UNGER, Lt. Gen. Ferdinand T. (Fin): High Commissioner of the Ryukus, p. 357-8;

URAGA DOCK: p. 370;

VELLA LAVELLA: the final objective of the HELENA survivors, p. 82 ff; rescue and return to Noumea, p. 108-10;

VIETNAM: p. 340; p. 356-7;

VINSON, The Hon. Carl: gives Chew appointment to Naval Academy after he establishes residence in Georgia, p. 5-6;

WARD, Adm. A. G.: p. 318-9;

USS WASP: her sinking, p. 65-66;

WHEELER, General Earl: Chairman of JCS, p. 342-3;

WRIGHT, Admiral Jerauld: becomes Cinc Nelm (1952), p. 174; an inspection trip to the Far East, p. 177-180;

YOKOSUKA: p. 369; facilities of the naval base, p. 370 ff;

ZUMWALT, Admiral Elmo: as Captain was representative of SecNav to look at Cuban water supply (Guantanamo), p. 324; p. 327; p. 329;

www.ingramcontent.com/pod-product-compliance
Lightning Source LLC
Chambersburg PA
CBHW080625170426
43209CB00007B/1517